McCall's Best Recipes

1989

Oxmoor House®

Library of Congress Catalog Number: 88-043142
ISBN: 0-8487-0776-1

Manufactured in the United States of America
First printing 1989

Published by arrangement with Oxmoor House, Inc.
Book Division of Southern Progress Corporation
P.O. Box 2463, Birmingham, AL 35201

McCall's
    Editor in Chief: A. Elizabeth Sloan
    Managing Editor: Lisel Eisenheimer
    Food Editor: Marianne Langan
    Senior Associate Food Editor: Mary B. Johnson
    Test Kitchen Supervisor: Holly Sheppard
    Associate Food Editors: Janet Andreas,
        Donna Meadow, Karen Sethre White
    Assistant Food Editors: Carmen McLeod,
        Mennie Nelson
    Executive-Dining Room Chef: Melva Victorino
    Photographer: Victor Scocozza

Oxmoor House, Inc.
    Executive Editor: Ann H. Harvey
    Production Manager: Jerry Higdon
    Associate Production Manager: Rick Litton
    Art Director: Bob Nance

McCall's Best Recipes 1989
    Editor: Olivia Kindig Wells
    Copy Editor: Melinda E. West
    Editorial Assistant: Leigh Anne Roberts
    Senior Designer: Cynthia R. Cooper
    Production Assistant: Theresa Beste
    Artists: Melissa Jones, Melinda Goode

Cover: *Three-Fruit Cream Tart, page 128.*

Back cover: *(Clockwise from top right) Almond Chiffon Bundt Cake, page 82; Chicken Yakitori, Sweet-and-Sour Rice, pages 102 and 103; Steamed Ginger Pudding, page 19; Steaks With Béarnaise Butter and Sweet-Potato Chips, page 30.*

To subscribe to *McCall's* magazine, write to *McCall's*, Box 56093, Boulder, CO 80322.

Contents

McCall's
Annual Collection

McCall's *food staff includes (left to right) Holly Sheppard, Test Kitchen Supervisor; Karen Sethre White, Associate Food Editor; Carmen McLeod, Assistant Food Editor; Melva Victorino, Executive-Dining Room Chef; Marianne Langan, Food Editor; Mennie Nelson, Assistant Food Editor; Janet Andreas, Associate Food Editor; Mary B. Johnson, Senior Associate Food Editor.*

It has given our staff a great sense of pride to put together this, our first, collection of recipes for the year from the food pages of *McCall's.*

We know that our readers enjoy our recipes, based on the number of wonderful letters we receive throughout the year. We like to think our pages offer something for everyone, using products that are readily available and giving explicit and clear directions that help you to recreate the beautiful recipes as we have photographed them.

The presentation of food is important. I have always believed we are a nation that eats with our eyes and that even mistakes in flavoring or less than perfect cooking techniques will often be overlooked when the dish presented is pretty. That's one of the reasons we are so particular in showing as many innovative garnishes as possible.

Our staff is responsible for the development of every recipe on our pages. Each month we select appropriate recipe ideas, and each member of the staff picks the recipes she would like to develop. Next, she researches these recipes, looking for new and unusual flavor combinations as well as easy methods for preparations. She then moves into the kitchen and starts cooking. An average day means tasting between 20 and 25 dishes and giving an objective and critical review of each. (And some of us actually go home and cook for our families.) Each recipe is tested over four times before it is published. And each recipe is rechecked by someone on the staff who did not do the initial development.

Once we have selected the recipes we like best and have made them taste and look the way we think they should, they are all presented to our management for photography selection. Often this is a difficult decision because each recipe is worthy of a photograph.

The recipes are prepared once again for the photograph—and yes, it is the real food and yours should look just as attractive—if you follow our directions.

As you can tell from our pictures, we like beautiful food placed in appropriate and appetizing environments. Food to me is beautiful, and it deserves careful attention. As a result, each photograph contains ideas for you to apply to your own food presentation.

At *McCall's* we are in touch with the latest trends and procedures in cooking and eating. We know you, our readers, love desserts as well as casseroles but you are also looking for lighter foods, along with easy-to-prepare dishes. That's why our pages include these timely topics.

We hope you will enjoy owning this fine collection and will reach for it many times throughout the year.

Marianne Langan, Food Editor

January

Take the chill out of winter
with a steaming hot casserole
or a pot of savory stew.
All the delicious recipes pictured
and listed below, plus more one-dish
meals, promise warmth and flavor along
with ease of preparation.

Veal Stew in Noodle Ring

Cheesy-Wild-Rice-and-Ham Bake

Veal-and-Kidney Pie

Creamy Chicken-and-Vegetable Casserole

Dilled Salmon Casserole

Beef Short Ribs With Vegetables

Sweet-Potato Shepherd's Pie

Creamy Chicken-Filled Gougère

Stew and Casserole Cookbook

Presenting our most delicious all-in-one meals ever! The casseroles are easy-to-make classics—each with a surprising twist. And the stews range from robust beef short ribs to spicy chicken tucked inside puff pastry.

Cheesy-Wild-Rice-and-Ham Bake

(pictured, page 7)

2 packages (6 ounces each) white-and-wild-rice mix
3 tablespoons butter or margarine
3 tablespoons all-purpose flour
¾ teaspoon dry mustard
Dash ground red pepper
½ teaspoon salt
2 cups milk
1½ cups (6 ounces) shredded sharp Cheddar cheese
2 pounds broccoli
2 cups boiling water
1 can (2.8 ounces) French-fried onions
8 slices (⅛-inch thick) Virginia ham

Page 7: (From top) Veal Stew in Noodle Ring, Cheesy-Wild-Rice-and-Ham Bake.

Pages 8 and 9: (Clockwise from top right) Veal-and-Kidney Pie, Creamy Chicken-and-Vegetable Casserole, Dilled Salmon Casserole.

Pages 10 and 11: (Clockwise from top left) Beef Short Ribs With Vegetables, Sweet-Potato Shepherd's Pie, Creamy Chicken-Filled Gougère.

1. Prepare rice mix as package label directs.

2. Meanwhile, in medium saucepan, over medium heat, melt butter; remove from heat. Stir in flour, mustard, pepper and salt until smooth. Gradually add milk; return pan to heat. Bring to boiling, stirring constantly, until mixture is thickened. Reduce heat; stir in cheese until melted; set aside.

3. Preheat oven to 350°F. Pare and split broccoli stalks lengthwise; cut in 2-inch pieces. In large skillet, cook broccoli in boiling water 5 minutes, or until just tender; drain. Toss half of broccoli with 1 cup cheese sauce; spoon lengthwise in center of shallow 2½-quart baking dish. Stir ¾ cup French-fried onions into rice mixture. Spoon one-third of rice mixture on each side of broccoli. Cut ham slices crosswise in half, and roll each half. Arrange 4 ham rolls on each section of rice mixture in baking dish.

4. Spoon remaining rice over broccoli in baking dish. Arrange remaining broccoli on sides of casserole, over ham rolls. Place remaining ham rolls, seam side down, over rice. Cover with aluminum foil. Bake 25 minutes. Spoon remaining cheese sauce over broccoli and ham; sprinkle with remaining French-fried onions. Bake, uncovered, 5 minutes longer.

Makes 6 to 8 servings.

Veal Stew in Noodle Ring

(pictured, page 7)

2 to 4 tablespoons salad oil
2 pounds boneless veal shoulder or leg, cut in ⅛-inch-thick strips
6 ounces mushrooms, halved
3 medium cloves garlic, crushed
1 can (about 14 ounces) beef broth
½ cup sweet vermouth
1 teaspoon dried thyme leaves
½ teaspoon salt
¼ teaspoon pepper
Noodle Ring (recipe follows)
1 package (9 ounces) frozen cut green beans, thawed
1 medium yellow squash, cut in ¼-inch slices
1 medium tomato, cut in 8 wedges
½ cup water
¼ cup unsifted all-purpose flour

1. In 5-quart saucepan, heat 2 tablespoons salad oil. Brown veal, several pieces at a time, on both sides. Remove pieces to bowl as they brown. Add 1 to 2 tablespoons oil as necessary. Add mushrooms and garlic; sauté 3 minutes. Return veal to saucepan. Add beef broth, vermouth, thyme, salt and pepper. Bring to boiling and reduce heat; simmer, covered, 30 minutes.

2. Meanwhile, make Noodle Ring.

3. Add beans, squash and tomato to veal mixture; cook 10 minutes longer. In small bowl, blend water with flour until smooth. Add to stew; simmer, stirring, 2 minutes, or until gravy slightly thickens. Spoon into center of Noodle Ring.

Makes 8 servings.

Noodle Ring

¾ cup heavy cream
3 large eggs
3 tablespoons butter or
  margarine, melted
4 cups cooked wide egg
  noodles (about 12 ounces
  uncooked)
1½ cups (6 ounces) shredded
  Parmesan cheese

1. Preheat oven to 375°F. Generously grease 6½-cup ring mold.

2. In large bowl, beat cream, eggs and butter. Stir in noodles and cheese; mix well. Evenly spoon into prepared mold. Place mold in roasting pan; fill pan halfway with warm water. Bake 35 minutes, or until top is golden and mixture is firm.

3. With small knife, loosen edges of mold; invert onto serving plate.

Makes 8 servings.

■ Never discard stale bread; process several slices at a time in the blender or food processor to crumbs. Store in a jar with a tight-fitting lid up to 2 weeks in the refrigerator.

Creamy Chicken-and-Vegetable Casserole
(pictured, pages 8 and 9)

¼ cup (½ stick) butter or
  margarine
½ pound mushrooms, sliced
1 medium red pepper, cut in
  ½-inch strips
1 medium green pepper, cut in
  ½-inch strips
1 medium onion, chopped
1 package (10 ounces) frozen
  spinach, thawed and
  squeezed dry
1 can (10¾ ounces) condensed
  creamy chicken mushroom
  soup
1 cup sour cream
1 teaspoon paprika
⅛ teaspoon pepper
12 slices bacon
3 whole chicken breasts,
  boned, skinned and split
  (about 2 pounds)

1. In large skillet, over medium heat, melt butter. Sauté mushrooms, red and green peppers and onion 3 minutes. Stir in spinach; cook 2 minutes longer. Remove from heat; add soup, sour cream, paprika and pepper; mix well. Spoon into bottom of a shallow 2-quart casserole.

2. Preheat oven to 350°F. Wrap 2 pieces bacon around each chicken breast half; arrange on top of vegetables. Bake 35 minutes, or until chicken is tender and lightly golden.

Makes 6 servings.

■ To extract the most juice from citrus fruits, squeeze them at room temperature. Place refrigerated fruit to be juiced in the microwave for 30 seconds to 1 minute at 50% power.

Dilled Salmon Casserole
(pictured, page 8)

1 package (5.5 ounces) au
  gratin potatoes
2⅓ cups water
3 cups milk
4 teaspoons Dijon-style
  mustard
1 can (15½ ounces) red
  salmon, drained and flaked
1 cup cornflake crumbs
¼ cup tartar sauce
¼ cup finely chopped fresh
  dill
1 large egg
3 tablespoons lemon juice
1 package (1¾ ounces)
  white-sauce mix
2 tablespoons capers
1 bag (16 ounces) frozen
  broccoli, cauliflower and
  carrot combination, thawed

1. In medium bowl, combine potatoes, water, ⅔ cup milk and 3 teaspoons mustard; mix well, and set mixture aside.

2. In large bowl, combine salmon, cornflake crumbs, tartar sauce, 2 tablespoons dill, the egg and 1 tablespoon lemon juice; mix well. Divide mixture in four equal parts; shape each into a 1-inch-thick oval patty.

3. Preheat oven to 400°F. In medium saucepan, combine white-sauce mix and remaining 2⅓ cups milk. Bring to boiling, whisking, until thickened. Remove from heat; stir in remaining mustard, dill, remaining lemon juice and the capers.

4. Toss thawed vegetables with 1 cup dill sauce; spoon into bottom of 2-quart casserole. Top with potato mixture. Arrange salmon patties on top of potatoes. Bake, uncovered, 35 minutes, or until hot and bubbly.

Makes 4 servings.

Stew and Casserole Cookbook

Veal-and-Kidney Pie

(pictured, page 9)

1 veal kidney (about ¾
    pound), cut in 1-inch pieces
1¾ pounds boneless veal, cut
    in 1-inch pieces
1¾ cups unsifted all-purpose
    flour
3 tablespoons salad oil
1 can (12 ounces) beer
1 tablespoon prepared mustard
2 teaspoons Worcestershire
    sauce
1¼ teaspoons salt
¼ teaspoon ground red pepper
1 pint (10 ounces) pearl
    onions, peeled
3 medium carrots, pared and
    cut in 1½-inch diagonal
    pieces
1 package (10 ounces) frozen
    peas
2 tablespoons chopped fresh
    chives
⅓ cup shortening
6 to 7 tablespoons cold water
1 large egg yolk

1. On sheet of waxed paper, lightly coat kidney and veal with ¼ cup flour. In 5-quart saucepan, heat oil. Brown kidney and veal, several pieces at a time, on all sides. Remove to bowl as they brown.

2. Add beer, mustard, Worcestershire, 1 teaspoon salt and the red pepper. Return meats to pan. Bring to boiling; reduce heat and simmer, covered, 45 minutes. Add onions, carrots and peas; simmer, covered, 15 minutes longer, or until vegetables are tender.

3. Make pastry: In medium bowl, combine remaining 1½ cups flour, the chives and ¼ teaspoon salt. With pastry blender or two knives, cut in shortening until mixture resembles coarse crumbs. With fork, stir in 5 to 6 tablespoons cold water until dough holds together.

4. Preheat oven to 400°F. Spoon veal mixture into 10- or 11-inch quiche dish. On lightly floured surface, roll pastry in a 12-inch round;

place over veal mixture. Fold edge under; crimp decoratively. With cookie cutter, cut out round in center to allow steam to escape. In small cup, beat yolk with 1 tablespoon water; brush over pastry. Bake 35 minutes, or until pastry is golden.

Makes 6 to 8 servings.

Beef Short Ribs With Vegetables

(pictured, page 10)

½ pound bacon, coarsely
    chopped
4 pounds beef short ribs, cut
    in serving-size portions
⅓ cup unsifted all purpose
    flour
2 large onions, chopped
1 can (about 14 ounces) beef
    broth
1 cup water
1 bay leaf
½ teaspoon dried rosemary
    leaves
1 teaspoon salt
¼ teaspoon pepper
1 pound potatoes, pared and
    quartered
4 large carrots, cut in 1½-inch
    pieces
1 small head (1 pound) green
    cabbage, cut in 1-inch
    wedges
⅓ cup tomato paste
¼ cup chopped parsley

1. In 5-quart saucepan, over medium heat, cook bacon until crisp. With slotted spoon, remove bacon to plate. Drain off all but 3 tablespoons drippings. Coat short ribs with flour. In drippings, brown ribs, several pieces at a time, on all sides. Remove to bowl as they brown.

2. Add onion to drippings; sauté 3 minutes. Return bacon and ribs to pan. Add broth, water, bay leaf, rosemary, salt and pepper. Bring to boiling. Reduce heat; simmer, covered,

45 minutes. Add potatoes and carrots; cook 15 minutes. Place cabbage on top; cook 10 minutes, or until vegetables are tender.

3. Remove and discard bay leaf. With slotted spoon, remove meat and vegetables to serving platter. Skim fat from cooking liquid. Add tomato paste and parsley. Simmer, stirring constantly, 3 minutes, or until gravy thickens slightly. Return ribs and vegetables to pan; cook until heated through.

Makes 6 servings.

Creamy Chicken-Filled Gougère

(pictured, pages 10 and 11)

1 cup water
⅓ cup butter or margarine
1 teaspoon salt
1⅓ cups unsifted all-purpose
    flour
4 large eggs
1 cup (4 ounces) shredded
    Cheddar cheese
2 tablespoons salad oil
1 pound boneless, skinless
    chicken breasts, cut in
    1-inch pieces
1 large onion, thinly sliced
2 medium cloves garlic,
    crushed
1 can (about 14 ounces)
    chicken broth
1 cup half-and-half
1 package (10 ounces) frozen
    peas
1 package (9 ounces) frozen
    artichoke hearts
1 package (10 ounces) frozen
    whole baby carrots
1 medium red pepper, cut in
    ½-inch strips
¼ teaspoon crushed
    saffron
¼ teaspoon pepper

1. Preheat oven to 425°F. In heavy, medium saucepan, bring water, butter and ½ teaspoon salt just to boiling; remove from heat.

With wooden spoon, beat in 1 cup flour all at once until smooth. Return to low heat, and continue beating until dough leaves side of pan and forms a ball—about 1 minute. Remove from heat. Add eggs, one at a time, beating until smooth after each addition; stir in cheese.

2. Spread one-third of the dough over bottom of ungreased, shallow 2-quart baking dish. Spoon remaining dough into pastry bag fitted with ½-inch star tip; pipe around sides of baking dish on top of dough. Bake 30 minutes, or until gougère is golden-brown.

3. Meanwhile, in 5-quart saucepan, heat salad oil. Brown chicken, several pieces at at time, on all sides. Remove pieces to bowl as they brown. In drippings, sauté onion and garlic 3 minutes. Add chicken and any juices, 1 cup broth, the half-and-half, peas, artichoke hearts, carrots, red pepper, saffron, ½ teaspoon salt and the pepper. Bring to boiling. Reduce heat; simmer, covered, 10 minutes, or until chicken and vegetables are tender.

4. In small bowl, blend remaining broth and remaining ⅓ cup flour until smooth. Add to chicken mixture; simmer, stirring, 2 minutes, or until thickened. Immediately spoon into hot gougère.

Makes 6 servings.

■ Garlic is a favorite ingredient for adding flavor to stews and casseroles. To aid in preparation, keep in mind that garlic peel will slip off easily if you use this method: Place the clove on your cutting board, and press down on it hard with the flat edge of a wide blade knife, such as a French knife. The garlic skin will fall off almost by itself. (Remember, though, that garlic doesn't need peeling if you're putting it through a garlic press.)

Sweet-Potato Shepherd's Pie
(pictured, page 11)

2½ pounds ground lamb
½ cup (1 stick) butter or margarine
1 medium onion, finely chopped
2 medium cloves garlic, crushed
¼ cup unsifted all-purpose flour
1 cup beef broth
2 large eggs, beaten
1 teaspoon dried rosemary leaves
¾ teaspoon salt
¼ teaspoon pepper
4 hard-cooked large eggs
2 packages (10 ounces each) frozen chopped spinach, thawed and squeezed dry
1 can (2 pounds, 8 ounces) sweet potatoes or yams
½ teaspoon ground nutmeg

1. In large skillet, over medium-high heat, brown lamb. Remove with slotted spoon; drain; place lamb in large bowl. In medium saucepan, over medium-high heat, melt ¼ cup butter; sauté onion and garlic 3 minutes. Remove from heat; stir in flour. Gradually add broth; return to heat. Bring to boiling, stirring, until thickened. Remove from heat, and cool slightly; gradually stir in two eggs.

2. Add sauce, rosemary, ½ teaspoon salt and ⅛ teaspoon pepper to lamb; mix well. Spoon half of meat mixture into an 8-inch springform pan. Arrange hard cooked eggs, end to end, in a circle in center of pan; cover with remaining meat mixture.

3. Preheat oven to 375°F. Spread spinach over meat. Drain and discard syrup from sweet potatoes. In food processor, puree sweet potatoes with remaining butter, the nutmeg, ¼ teaspoon salt and ⅛ teaspoon pepper. Spread 1 cup sweet-potato puree evenly over spinach. Place remaining puree in

pastry bag fitted with ½-inch star tip; pipe in decorative pattern over all. Place springform pan on jelly-roll pan to catch any drippings. Bake 35 minutes, or until heated through.

Makes 8 to 10 servings.

Macaroni-and-Sausage Casserole

4 cups hot cooked elbow macaroni
1 pound sweet or hot Italian sausage, casings removed
¼ pound ham, diced
2 tablespoons finely chopped red pepper
2 tablespoons finely chopped green pepper
2 green onions, chopped
1 jar (26 ounces) spaghetti sauce
2 large eggs
2 cups half-and-half
¼ cup grated Parmesan cheese
1 cup (4 ounces) shredded Monterey Jack cheese

1. Preheat oven to 350°F. In bottom of shallow 2-quart casserole, place macaroni. In medium saucepan, over medium heat, brown sausage 5 minutes, breaking up into small pieces with spoon. Add ham, red and green pepper and green onions; cook 3 minutes longer. Add spaghetti sauce; mix well. Spoon sauce over macaroni.

2. In medium bowl, beat eggs with half-and-half and Parmesan cheese. Pour over meat sauce; sprinkle with Monterey Jack cheese. Bake 30 minutes, or until set and lightly golden.

Makes 8 to 10 servings.

■ For a complete meal, serve a quick salad with a hot casserole. Just slice ½ cucumber and ¼ red onion; mix with greens and low-calorie dressing.

Stew and Casserole Cookbook

Curried Pork Stew With Rice Balls

2 tablespoons salad oil
2 pounds boneless pork loin or shoulder, cut in 1-inch pieces
3 medium cloves garlic, crushed
1 tablespoon grated ginger root
1 tablespoon curry powder
1 can (about 14 ounces) chicken broth
¾ cup water
½ teaspoon salt
¼ teaspoon pepper
1 medium green pepper, cut in ½-inch strips
2 medium celery stalks, cut in 1-inch pieces
1 medium red onion, cut in ½-inch wedges
3 cups cooked rice, not converted (about 1 cup raw)
7 tablespoons all-purpose flour
2 large eggs
¼ cup minced cilantro
½ cup chopped toasted cashews

1. In a 5-quart saucepan, heat oil. Brown pork, several pieces at a time, on all sides; remove to bowl as they brown. Sauté garlic and ginger in drippings 2 minutes. Add curry; cook, stirring, 30 seconds. Add pork, broth, ½ cup water, the salt and pepper. Bring to boiling; reduce heat. Simmer, covered, 45 minutes.

2. Add green pepper, celery and onion; cook 5 minutes. In bowl, combine rice, 4 tablespoons flour, the eggs and cilantro; mix well. Shape by rounded tablespoonfuls into balls; place on top of stew. Cook 12 minutes, or until rice balls are firm and vegetables are tender.

3. With slotted spoon, carefully remove rice balls to platter. In small bowl, blend remaining ¼ cup water with 3 tablespoons flour until smooth. Stir into stew; simmer, stirring, 2 minutes, or until slightly thickened. Stir in cashews; serve with rice balls.
Makes 6 servings.

Ham-and-Pea Stew

1 ham bone
½ pound green split peas
4 cups water
2 cups cubed Virginia ham
1 small onion, quartered
¼ cup loosely-packed parsley leaves
½ cup fine dry bread crumbs
2 large eggs
2 tablespoons salad oil
2 cups firmly-packed 1-inch pieces escarole
1 package (10 ounces) frozen whole baby carrots
1 teaspoon salt
⅛ teaspoon pepper

1. In 5-quart saucepan, bring ham bone, peas and 4 cups water to boiling. Reduce heat; simmer, covered, 45 minutes.

2. In food processor, finely chop ham, onion and parsley. In medium bowl, combine ham, onion, parsley, bread crumbs and eggs; mix well. Shape rounded tablespoonfuls of ham mixture into balls. In nonstick skillet, heat oil. Brown ham balls, a few at a time, on all sides. Set aside.

3. Remove and discard bone from peas. Add escarole, carrots, ham balls, salt and pepper. Bring to boiling. Reduce heat; simmer, covered, 5 minutes, or until tender. If stew is too thick, add ½ cup water.
Makes 4 servings.

Vegetarian Casserole

½ pound dried black beans
½ pound dried lentils
1 jar (26 ounces) spaghetti sauce
2 tablespoons salad oil
4 large red or green peppers, cut in ¼-inch strips
2 large cloves garlic, crushed
1 cup grated Parmesan cheese
1½ cups (6 ounces) shredded smoked Gruyère cheese

1. Day before: Wash and sort black beans. In 5-quart saucepan, place beans and enough water to cover by 2 inches; cover. Refrigerate at least 6 hours or overnight.

2. Bring beans and their soaking liquid to boiling. Reduce heat; simmer, covered, 1½ hours. Wash and sort lentils. In 3-quart saucepan, place lentils and enough water to cover by 2 inches. Bring to boiling; reduce heat. Simmer, covered, 1 hour; drain.

3. Preheat oven to 350°F. In food processor, puree lentils with spaghetti sauce; set aside.

4. In large skillet, heat oil. Add peppers and garlic; sauté 5 minutes, or until tender. Drain beans.

5. Combine lentil and pepper mixtures, beans and ½ cup Parmesan; mix well. Place in shallow 2½-quart baking dish. Sprinkle with Gruyère and remaining Parmesan. Bake 35 minutes, or until bubbling.
Makes 8 to 10 servings.

Beef-Paprika Stew With Biscuits

2 tablespoons salad oil
2 pounds boneless chuck, cut in 1½-inch pieces
4 medium onions, cut in 1-inch wedges
1 large clove garlic, crushed
1 tablespoon paprika
1 can (16 ounces) whole tomatoes
1 can (16 ounces) tomato paste
¾ cup water
1 teaspoon salt
¼ teaspoon pepper
4 medium carrots, cut in 1½-inch pieces
4 medium celery stalks, cut in 1½-inch pieces
2 cups buttermilk baking mix
1 cup sour cream
½ cup shredded zucchini
⅓ cup butter or margarine, melted

1. In oven-safe 12-inch skillet, heat oil. Brown beef, several pieces at a time, on all sides. Remove pieces to bowl as they brown. Drain off all but 2 tablespoons drippings from skillet.

2. Add onions and garlic; sauté 3 minutes. Add paprika; cook 1 minute longer. Stir in tomatoes and their juice, tomato paste, water, salt and pepper. Bring to boiling; add meat and any juices. Reduce heat; simmer, covered, 1 hour. Add carrots; cook 20 minutes longer. Add celery; cook 10 minutes longer, or until vegetables are tender.

3. Preheat oven to 450°F. In medium bowl, combine baking mix, sour cream, zucchini and butter. With wooden spoon, stir just until soft dough forms. Drop by tablespoonfuls onto hot stew. Bake, uncovered, 10 minutes, or until biscuits are golden.

Makes 6 servings.

Veal à la King in Phyllo Baskets

1 pound boneless veal, cut in ½-inch pieces
1 can (about 14 ounces) chicken broth
Phyllo Baskets (recipe follows)
¼ cup (½ stick) butter or margarine
¼ cup diced green pepper
1 small onion, finely chopped
¼ cup unsifted all-purpose flour
1 can (10½ ounces) condensed cream-of-mushroom soup
⅛ teaspoon ground white pepper
¼ cup slivered pimiento
2 tablespoons sherry

1. In medium saucepan, over medium-high heat, bring veal and broth to boiling. Reduce heat; simmer, covered, 30 minutes. Drain veal; reserve broth.

2. Meanwhile, make Phyllo Baskets. In medium saucepan, over medium heat, melt butter. Sauté green pepper and onion 3 minutes, or until tender. Remove from heat; stir in flour until smooth. Gradually add 1½ cups reserved chicken broth. Bring to boiling. Reduce heat; simmer, stirring constantly, until thickened. Add veal, soup and white pepper. Return to boiling. Remove from heat; stir in pimiento and sherry. Spoon into Phyllo Baskets.

Makes 4 servings.

Phyllo Baskets

8 sheets phyllo dough
½ cup (1 stick) butter or margarine, melted

1. Preheat oven to 375°F. Cut four 6-inch squares of aluminum foil; set aside. Brush one sheet of phyllo with butter. Fold in half lengthwise. Then fold in thirds to make a 6-inch square; place on one foil square. Repeat with another phyllo square and butter.

2. Place second phyllo square over first, alternating corners. With thumb and forefinger, pinch sides so that foil and dough form a basket, with foil as support for sides. Place on baking sheet. Repeat with remaining phyllo, butter and foil squares. Bake 12 minutes, or until golden brown.

Makes 4 baskets.

■ Phyllo leaves must be kept moist. Once the package is opened, cover with dampened cloth and plastic wrap. Rewrap unused phyllo tightly in plastic wrap.

■ When using fresh herbs instead of dried, use three times the recommended amount. And, by the way, to allow herb flavor to fully develop, be sure to simmer the food for at least 30 minutes.

Stuffed Braised Flank Steak

¼ cup (½ stick) butter or margarine
1 medium onion, chopped
¾ cup chopped mushrooms
1 medium clove garlic, crushed
2 cups (¼-inch) French-bread cubes
1 large egg
1 jar (1 ounce) pine nuts (¼ cup)
¼ cup chopped parsley
½ teaspoon dried basil leaves
¼ teaspoon dried oregano leaves
½ teaspoon salt
2 pounds flank steak, butterflied (see *Note*)
2 tablespoons salad oil
1 can (10¾ ounces) condensed golden mushroom soup
2 tablespoons brandy
½ cup water
1 package (16 ounces) frozen broccoli, green beans, pearl onions and red-pepper mixture

1. In 8-quart Dutch oven, over medium heat, melt butter. Sauté onion, mushrooms and garlic 3 minutes. Remove from heat; add next 7 ingredients; mix well. Spread over steak, leaving a 1-inch border. Roll steak from long side, jelly-roll fashion; secure with string.

2. Wipe pan clean. In same pan, heat oil. Brown stuffed steak on all sides. Add soup, brandy and water. Bring to boiling. Reduce heat; simmer, covered, stirring occasionally, 1 hour, or until meat is fork-tender.

3. Add frozen vegetables to pan; simmer 10 minutes longer, or until heated through. Remove and discard strings from meat. Slice meat, and serve with vegetable sauce.

Makes 6 servings.

Note: To butterfly steak, cut lengthwise about four-fifths through. Open; flatten slightly by gently pounding with mallet or rolling pin.

Micro-Way: Great-Tasting Gifts

Piquant Cheese Spread

1 tablespoon butter or
  margarine
1 small onion, chopped
1 small clove garlic, crushed
2 packages (10 ounces each)
  sharp Cheddar cheese,
  shredded (5 cups)
1 package (8 ounces) cream
  cheese, cubed
¼ pound blue cheese,
  crumbled
¼ cup sherry
1 teaspoon Worcestershire
  sauce
1 teaspoon dry mustard
¼ cup chopped parsley or 1½
  teaspoons paprika
Chopped nuts or toasted
  sesame seeds

1. In large glass bowl, cook butter on HIGH 30 seconds. Add onion and garlic; cook on HIGH 1 minute. Add cheeses; cook on MEDIUM 1 to 3 minutes, or until softened.

2. With electric mixer at low speed, beat in sherry, Worcestershire and mustard until fluffy.

3. To make logs, on large sheet of waxed paper, spread one-third (about 1¼ cups) cheese mixture in a 9-by-6-inch rectangle. Sprinkle with parsley or paprika. Starting from short side, roll jelly-roll fashion; twist ends of paper to seal. Repeat with remaining mixture. Or shape mixture into three balls. Refrigerate until slightly firm. Coat with nuts or sesame seeds. Rewrap in plastic wrap; refrigerate.

Makes 3 logs or 3 balls.

Note: Recipes were tested in 600- to 700-watt microwave ovens.

Spice Cran-Apple Liqueur

4 medium Granny Smith
  apples (1½ pounds)
2 cups white wine
2 cinnamon sticks
1 teaspoon whole cloves
2 cups sugar
1 package (12 ounces)
  cranberries, coarsely chopped
1 teaspoon grated orange peel
2 cups brandy

1. Pare and core apples; cut in eighths. In large glass bowl, combine apples, ½ cup wine, the cinnamon and cloves. Cook on HIGH 8 minutes, or until boiling, stirring occasionally. Add sugar; cook on HIGH 4 minutes, or until sugar dissolves, stirring once.

2. Add cranberries, orange peel, brandy and the remaining wine; mix well. Pour into 2-quart glass container; cover tightly. Store in cool, dark place three weeks, shaking occasionally.

3. Strain through double thickness of cheesecloth; repeat until liquid is clear. Pour liqueur into 1-quart bottle or decanter; cover tightly. Store in cool, dark place for two weeks before serving or gift-giving. Reserve soaked apples and cranberries to serve over ice cream or pound cake.

Makes 1 quart liqueur.

■ A substitution for 1 cup milk: 1 cup skim milk plus 2 tablespoons butter or margarine.

Steamed Ginger Pudding

1 cup (2 sticks) unsalted butter
   or margarine
½ cup granulated sugar
2 large eggs
2½ cups unsifted all-purpose
   flour
1 tablespoon baking powder
½ teaspoon ground ginger
1 cup milk
¼ cup B&B liqueur
1½ cups golden raisins
½ cup chopped crystallized
   ginger
Orange Hard Sauce (recipe
   follows)
¼ cup apple jelly

1. Lightly grease a deep 6-cup glass bowl; line bottom and sides with plastic wrap. In large bowl, cream butter and the granulated sugar until fluffy; beat in eggs, one at a time. On waxed paper, combine flour, baking powder and ginger; mix well. On low speed, beat flour mixture, milk and liqueur into butter mixture until smooth. Stir in raisins and ginger.

2. Spoon into prepared bowl. Cover with plastic wrap, turning back one corner to vent. Cook on MEDIUM, turning bowl every 2 minutes, until cake tester inserted in center comes out clean—about 12 minutes. Let stand 10 minutes.

3. Make Orange Hard Sauce.

4. Turn pudding onto serving plate. In glass cup, cook jelly on HIGH 2 minutes, or until melted; brush over pudding. Serve pudding with Orange Hard Sauce.

Makes 6 to 8 servings.

Orange Hard Sauce

1 cup (2 sticks) unsalted butter
   or margarine
1½ cups confectioners' sugar
¼ cup orange juice
¼ cup Grand Marnier
1 tablespoon grated orange
   peel

In small bowl, beat butter, confectioners' sugar, juice, Grand Marnier and orange peel until fluffy.

Makes 2 cups.

Sugar-and-Spice Cashews

3 cups cashews
¼ cup (½ stick) butter or
   margarine
1 cup sugar
¼ cup light corn syrup
1 teaspoon vanilla extract
½ teaspoon ground cinnamon
¼ teaspoon ground cloves

1. Place nuts in a microwave-safe 13-by-9-by-2-inch baking dish. In large glass bowl, cook butter on HIGH 1 minute or until melted. Add sugar and corn syrup. Cook on HIGH 2 minutes; stir. Cook on HIGH 3 minutes more; do not stir. Add vanilla, cinnamon and cloves; stir once to mix.

2. Immediately pour sugar mixture over nuts; toss to coat completely. Cook nuts on HIGH 3 minutes, stirring occasionally. Spread nuts on waxed paper; let cool completely. Break up any large clusters. Store in airtight container.

Makes 1 quart.

February

Tantalizing beef dishes and
accompaniments abound! Try our
tempting brisket—its mouth-watering
stuffing is studded with vegetables.
That's just one of many delicious
beef ideas in this chapter. The recipes
listed below are pictured on
the following pages.

Vegetable Stuffed Brisket

Crunchy Cauliflower and Broccoli

Ground-Beef-and-Vegetable Timbale

Beef Medallions Italiano

Oven-Barbecued Beef Ribs
With Rainbow Slaw

Flank Steak With Fresh-Fruit Salsa

Creole Rib Steaks With Southern Fried Grits

Sesame Steak Stir-Fry

Spanakopita

Chilied Beef in Cornmeal Cups

Syrian Meatballs

Steaks With Béarnaise Butter
and Sweet-Potato Chips

Beef Cookbook

For a hint of foreign flavor, sample our chilied beef in delicate cornmeal cups or our flaky phyllo pastry filled with ground beef, feta cheese and spinach.

Vegetable Stuffed Brisket
(pictured, page 21)

2 medium onions
¼ cup (½ stick) butter or margarine
1 small green pepper, chopped
1 small red pepper, chopped
1 small carrot, chopped
½ pound ground pork
½ pound ground veal
2 large eggs
1 teaspoon dried thyme leaves
1½ teaspoons salt
½ teaspoon pepper
3 pounds thin-cut beef brisket
2 tablespoons salad oil
1 cup beef broth
1 bay leaf
¼ cup water
2 tablespoons all-purpose flour
¼ cup sour cream
Crunchy Cauliflower and Broccoli (recipe follows)

1. Chop 1 onion. In medium skillet, melt butter. Add chopped onion, peppers and carrot; sauté 3 minutes. In medium bowl, combine vegetables, pork, veal, eggs, ½ teaspoon thyme, 1 teaspoon salt and ¼ teaspoon pepper; mix well.

2. With thin, sharp knife, cut brisket horizontally along one long side to within ½ inch of the sides to create a large pocket. Fill with vegetable-meat mixture. Secure open side with wooden skewers.

3. Quarter remaining onion. In large Dutch oven, heat oil. Brown stuffed brisket on all sides. Add broth, quartered onion, bay leaf, remaining ½ teaspoon thyme, ½ teaspoon salt and ¼ teaspoon pepper. Bring to boiling; reduce heat, and simmer, covered, 1 hour.

4. Remove brisket to serving platter; cover and keep warm. Strain broth; return broth to pan. In small bowl, blend water with flour until smooth. Stir into broth. Bring to boiling, stirring constantly; simmer 1 minute, until thickened. Remove from heat; whisk in sour cream. Serve brisket with Crunchy Cauliflower and Broccoli.
Makes 8 servings.

Crunchy Cauliflower and Broccoli
(pictured, page 21)

1 cup (4 ounces) shredded extra sharp Cheddar cheese
½ cup fine dry bread crumbs
¼ cup (½ stick) butter or margarine, melted
1 medium head cauliflower, cut in flowerets
1 medium bunch broccoli, cut in flowerets

1. In small bowl, combine cheese, bread crumbs and melted butter; mix well.

2. In large saucepan, bring 1 inch salted water to boiling. Add cauliflower and broccoli; cook, covered, 3 minutes, or until just tender. Drain vegetables.

3. Preheat broiler. Place vegetables on jelly-roll pan; sprinkle with cheese mixture. Broil, 4 inches from heat, 5 minutes, or until topping is golden.
Makes 6 to 8 servings.

Page 21: Vegetable Stuffed Brisket, Crunchy Cauliflower and Broccoli.

Pages 22 and 23: (Clockwise from top left) Ground-Beef-and-Vegetable Timbale, Flank Steak With Fresh-Fruit Salsa, Beef Medallions Italiano; (Inset, above right) Oven-Barbecued Beef Ribs With Rainbow Slaw; (Inset, below right) Creole Rib Steaks With Southern Fried Grits.

Pages 24 and 25: (Clockwise from top right) Chilied Beef in Cornmeal Cups, Spanakopita, Sesame Steak Stir-Fry; (Inset, above right) Steaks With Béarnaise Butter and Sweet-Potato Chips; (Inset, below right) Syrian Meatballs.

Ground-Beef-and-Vegetable Timbale

(pictured, page 22)

2¼ cups water
1 teaspoon salt
1 cup uncooked long-grain
  white rice
¼ cup (½ stick) butter or
  margarine, softened
¾ cup grated Parmesan cheese
3 large eggs
1 pound ground beef
1 medium onion, chopped
1 package (1 pound) frozen
  broccoli, carrot, water-
  chestnut and red-pepper
  combination, thawed and
  chopped
1½ cups fresh-bread crumbs
¼ cup tomato sauce
1 teaspoon fennel seed
Additional grated Parmesan
  cheese

1. In medium saucepan, bring water and ½ teaspoon salt to boiling. Add rice; reduce heat and simmer, covered, 15 minutes. Drain; place in medium bowl. Add butter, ¾ cup cheese and 1 egg; mix well.

2. In large skillet, over medium-high heat, brown beef. Add onion; cook 3 minutes longer. Remove from heat; stir in 2 eggs, vegetables, 1 cup bread crumbs, the tomato sauce, fennel seed and ½ teaspoon salt; mix well.

3. Preheat oven to 350°F. Butter a 2-quart soufflé dish or casserole. Line with heavy-duty aluminum foil; butter foil generously. Sprinkle remaining bread crumbs over inside of prepared dish. With back of wooden spoon, press rice mixture evenly to line bottom and side of dish. Fill center of rice with meat mixture. Bake 1 hour.

4. Invert serving plate over soufflé dish. Holding both plate and dish, invert. Carefully remove dish and foil. Sprinkle additional grated cheese on top; garnish with carrot flowers and parsley, if desired.
  Makes 12 servings.

Flank Steak With Fresh-Fruit Salsa

(pictured, page 23)

¼ cup orange juice
2 tablespoons chili sauce
2 tablespoons soy sauce
2 tablespoons salad oil
2 medium cloves garlic,
  crushed
1 teaspoon grated orange peel
1 teaspoon sugar
½ teaspoon salt
⅛ teaspoon hot-red-pepper
  sauce
1½ pounds flank steak
Fresh-Fruit Salsa (recipe
  follows)

1. In 12-by-9-by-2-inch baking dish, combine first 9 ingredients; mix well. Add steak to marinade; turn to coat. Cover; marinate in refrigerator, turning occasionally, 3 hours or overnight.

2. Make Fresh-Fruit Salsa.

3. Preheat broiler. Place steak on rack in broiler pan. Broil, 6 inches from heat, 6 minutes on each side for medium-rare. Thinly slice steak; serve with Fresh-Fruit Salsa.
  Makes 6 servings.

Fresh-Fruit Salsa

(pictured, page 23)

1 small pineapple
1 medium papaya
1 large Granny Smith
  apple
1 small green pepper,
  chopped
1 small red pepper,
  chopped
¼ cup rice vinegar or
  white-wine vinegar
2 tablespoons sugar
1 tablespoon minced cilantro
½ teaspoon crushed
  red-pepper flakes

1. Halve the pineapple lengthwise, through leaves. Set aside one-half for garnish. Remove and discard peel, leaves and core from remaining half; cut pineapple in ½-inch cubes. Halve papaya lengthwise. Remove and discard seeds; set aside one-half for garnish. Pare remaining half; cut in ½-inch cubes. Halve apple; set aside one-half for garnish. Remove and discard core and peel; cut in ½-inch cubes.

2. In medium bowl, combine pineapple, papaya and apple cubes with green and red peppers, vinegar, sugar, cilantro and red-pepper flakes; mix well. Cover and refrigerate salsa mixture.

3. Cut reserved pineapple, papaya and apple halves in lengthwise slices; arrange fruit slices on serving platter with steak. Serve salsa with flank steak.
  Makes 6 servings.

■ Defrost frozen beef in the refrigerator in its wrapping. Allow four to seven hours per pound for a large (two pounds or more) roast, three to five hours per pound for a small (under two pounds) roast and 12 to 14 hours for a 1-inch-thick steak.

Oven-Barbecued Beef Ribs With Rainbow Slaw

(pictured, page 23, inset)

Rainbow Slaw (recipe follows)
6 pounds beef ribs (about 2
  racks, 14 ribs)
1 cup hoisin sauce (see *Note*)
1 cup ginger ale
½ cup minced green onion
¼ cup prepared mustard
1 to 2 tablespoons grated
  ginger root
2 medium cloves garlic,
  crushed

1. Make Rainbow Slaw. Cover; refrigerate several hours.

2. Preheat oven to 375°F. Place
ribs in large roasting pan. In medium
bowl, combine hoisin sauce, ginger
ale, green onion, mustard, ginger
and garlic. Generously baste both
sides of ribs with sauce.

3. Bake ribs 1 hour, or until meat
is cooked and ribs are well-glazed.
Cut ribs into individual serving portions; arrange on platter. Garnish
with green-onion curls, if desired.
Skim and discard fat from sauce in
pan; serve sauce with ribs. Serve ribs
with Rainbow Slaw.

Makes 6 to 8 servings.

Note: Hoisin sauce is available in
Oriental markets.

Rainbow Slaw

(pictured, page 23, inset)

½ cup peanut oil
¼ cup rice vinegar
2 tablespoons peanut butter
1 tablespoon soy sauce
1 tablespoon grated ginger root
1 tablespoon brown sugar
½ pound red cabbage,
  shredded
½ pound green cabbage,
  shredded
2 carrots, julienned
1 red or yellow pepper, cut in
  thin strips
¼ pound snow pea pods, cut
  in thin strips

In large bowl, whisk first 6 ingredients until blended. Add vegetables
to bowl; toss well to coat evenly.
Cover and refrigerate several hours.
Serve with ribs.

Makes 6 to 8 servings (about 6
cups).

Beef Medallions Italiano

(pictured, page 22)

4 slices bacon
4 beef-tenderloin filets, about
  1½ inches thick (5 to 6
  ounces each)
¼ cup pine nuts
1 medium onion, chopped
2 large cloves garlic, crushed
¼ cup beef broth
¼ cup Madeira wine
1½ pounds fresh spinach,
  stems removed
1 jar (7 ounces) roasted red
  peppers, drained and
  quartered
1 jar (7 ounces) marinated
  artichoke hearts, drained
Cooked orzo

1. In large skillet, over low heat,
cook bacon 5 minutes. Wrap one
slice bacon around each beef filet;
secure with wooden picks. In hot
bacon drippings, cook filets 5 minutes on each side for medium-rare.
Remove beef to a serving plate;
cover and keep warm.

2. In drippings, sauté pine nuts
just until golden; with slotted spoon,
remove to custard cup. In same
drippings, sauté onion and garlic 3
minutes. Add broth and Madeira,
stirring to loosen brown bits. Bring
to boiling; add spinach, peppers and
artichoke hearts. Cover; cook 3 minutes, stirring once, or until spinach
is just wilted. Place filets on top of
spinach; add any juices from meat.
Cook, covered, until heated
through. Garnish with sautéed pine
nuts. Serve with orzo.

Makes 4 servings.

Chilied Beef in Cornmeal Cups

(pictured, page 25)

2 tablespoons salad oil
1 pound boneless chuck, cut in
  ½-inch cubes
½ pound chorizo sausage, cut
  in ¼-inch diagonal slices
1 large onion, chopped
1 can (15 ounces) pinto beans
  in chili sauce
1 jar (12 ounces) chunky salsa
1 tablespoon Worcestershire
  sauce
½ cup water
Cornmeal Cups (recipe follows)
1 cup (4 ounces) shredded
  Cheddar cheese

1. In 5-quart saucepan, heat oil
over medium-high heat. Brown beef
cubes and sausage slices on all sides;
remove to medium bowl. In drippings, sauté onion 3 minutes. Add
beans with sauce, salsa, Worcestershire sauce and water.

2. Add beef, sausage and any
juices to bean mixture. Bring to
boiling; reduce heat, and simmer,
covered, 1 hour, or until tender.

3. Meanwhile, make Cornmeal
Cups. Spoon beef mixture into
Cornmeal Cups; top with shredded
cheese. Serve with chopped tomato
and shredded lettuce, if desired.

Makes 6 servings.

Cornmeal Cups

(pictured, page 25)

3½ cups water
2 teaspoons granulated beef
  bouillon or 2 beef-flavored
  bouillon cubes
¼ cup (½ stick) butter or
  margarine
1 teaspoon salt
2 cups yellow cornmeal
½ cup grated Parmesan cheese
1 large egg

1. Lightly grease six 8-ounce
soufflé dishes or custard cups. Line
with heavy-duty aluminum foil; generously grease foil.

2. In large saucepan, bring water, bouillon, butter and salt to boiling. Gradually stir in cornmeal. Reduce heat; simmer, uncovered, stirring occasionally, 5 minutes. Remove saucepan from heat; stir in Parmesan cheese and egg.

3. Preheat oven to 375°F. Press about ¾ cup cornmeal mixture to line bottom and side of foil liner in each prepared dish. Crimp edges of mixture, if desired. Bake 25 minutes, or until edges are light golden.

Makes 6 cups.

Creole Rib Steaks With Southern Fried Grits

(pictured, page 23, inset)

4 strips bacon, coarsely
    chopped
1 medium green pepper,
    coarsely chopped
1 medium onion, thinly sliced
2 stalks celery, cut in ½-inch
    pieces
2 medium cloves garlic,
    crushed
1 can (28 ounces) whole
    tomatoes in puree
1 bay leaf
½ teaspoon dried thyme leaves
¼ teaspoon hot-red-pepper
    sauce
½ teaspoon salt
4 boneless rib steaks, 1 inch
    thick (about 8 ounces each)
Salt and pepper
Southern Fried Grits (recipe
    follows)

1. In large skillet, cook bacon until crisp. Remove bacon; set aside. Discard all but 2 tablespoons drippings; in drippings, sauté pepper, onion, celery and garlic 3 minutes. Add tomatoes and puree, bay leaf, thyme, pepper sauce, ½ teaspoon salt and reserved bacon. Simmer, uncovered, 10 minutes, or until slightly thickened. Remove and discard bay leaf; cover Creole sauce to keep warm.

2. Sprinkle both sides of steaks with salt and pepper. Place on rack over broiler pan. Broil, 5 inches from heat, about 6 minutes per side for medium-rare. Spoon Creole sauce over steaks; serve with Southern Fried Grits.

Makes 4 servings.

Southern Fried Grits

(pictured, page 23, inset)

1 quart plus 2 tablespoons
    water
1 teaspoon salt
1 cup regular (not quick-
    cooking) white hominy grits
1 cup (4 ounces) shredded
    Monterey Jack cheese
¼ cup minced parsley
2 large eggs
1 cup fine dry bread crumbs
2 to 4 tablespoons salad oil

1. In 3-quart saucepan, bring 1 quart water and the salt to boiling; gradually stir in grits. Simmer, uncovered and stirring occasionally, 25 minutes, until mixture is very thick. Stir in cheese and parsley. Spread mixture in a 13-by-9-by-2-inch baking pan; cover pan with plastic wrap. Freeze several hours, or until firm.

2. Using a 2-inch round cutter, cut grits into 15 rounds. In pie plate, beat eggs with 2 tablespoons water. Place bread crumbs on waxed paper. Dip rounds in egg mixture; then coat with crumbs.

3. In large skillet, heat oil over medium-high heat; fry grits 5 minutes on each side, or until golden-brown. (Add more oil as needed.) Drain on paper towels.

Makes 6 servings.

■ Be sure to cool cooked beef in the refrigerator for several hours before freezing.

Spanakopita

(pictured, page 24)

1½ pounds ground beef
1 large onion, chopped
1 package (10 ounces) frozen
    chopped spinach, thawed
    and squeezed dry
½ cup chopped parsley
⅓ cup chopped fresh dill or 1
    teaspoon dried dillweed
1 large clove garlic, crushed
1 teaspoon grated lemon peel
¼ teaspoon salt
¼ teaspoon pepper
1 medium-size red pepper,
    chopped
½ pound feta cheese,
    crumbled
1 cup coarsely chopped
    pistachio nuts
2 large eggs
¾ cup (1½ sticks) butter or
    margarine, melted
16 sheets phyllo dough

1. In large skillet, brown beef over medium-high heat. Add onion, spinach, parsley, dill, garlic, lemon peel, salt and pepper; cook, stirring, 3 minutes longer. Remove from heat, and stir in red pepper, cheese, nuts and eggs; mix well.

2. Preheat oven to 375°F. Brush 13-by-9-by-2-inch or shallow 2½-quart baking dish with some of the melted butter. Place 1 sheet phyllo on bottom and up sides of prepared dish. Brush with melted butter. Repeat with seven more sheets phyllo, brushing each with butter.

3. Spoon beef mixture into phyllo-lined dish. Cover with remaining 8 sheets phyllo, brushing each with melted butter. With spatula, tuck down any overhanging phyllo into sides of dish. Brush top with remaining melted butter. With sharp knife or small scissors, cut top layer of phyllo to make 2-inch diamond-shape pieces. Bake 40 minutes, or until golden-brown. Sprinkle with additional pistachios, if desired.

Makes 12 servings.

Sesame Steak Stir-Fry
(pictured, page 24)

8 tablespoons salad oil
3 tablespoons sesame seeds
2 large onions, thinly sliced
½ cup ginger-flavored soy
sauce
¼ cup red-wine vinegar
3 large cloves garlic, crushed
1 tablespoon Oriental bean
sauce (see *Note*)
1 tablespoon slivered ginger
root
2½ to 3 pounds boneless
top-round steak, 1½ inches
thick
1¼ cups beef broth
2 tablespoons cornstarch
½ pound mushrooms
½ pound snow pea pods,
trimmed
1 can (15 ounces) baby corn
ears, drained
½ pound bean sprouts
1 large red pepper, thinly
sliced

1. In large skillet, heat 2 table-spoons salad oil; sauté sesame seeds 3 minutes, or until golden-brown, stirring often. Place in shallow glass baking dish; add onions, soy sauce, vinegar, garlic, bean sauce and ginger. Stir to combine. Add steak; turn to coat. Cover; refrigerate 4 hours or overnight, turning occasionally.

2. Drain steak, reserving mari-nade. In large skillet, heat 2 table-spoons salad oil and 2 tablespoons marinade. Over medium-high heat, brown steak 10 minutes on each side. Place on platter; keep warm.

3. In medium saucepan, combine remaining marinade, the broth and cornstarch; blend until smooth. Heat to boiling, stirring constantly. Simmer 1 minute, until thickened and smooth; keep mixture warm.

4. In skillet used for steak, heat 2 tablespoons salad oil. Over high heat, sauté mushrooms, stirring con-stantly, 3 minutes, or until golden-brown. Place on serving platter with steak; keep warm. In same skillet, in

1 tablespoon salad oil, stir-fry snow pea pods and corn 2 minutes, or until pea pods are tender-crisp. Re-move to serving platter with steak; keep warm. In 1 tablespoon salad oil in same skillet, stir-fry bean sprouts and red pepper 2 minutes, or until pepper is tender-crisp. Arrange on platter with steak.

5. Garnish platter with preserved kumquats and parsley, if desired. Spoon part of sauce over steak; serve remaining sauce with steak.
Makes 6 servings.
Note: Oriental bean sauce is avail-able in Oriental markets.

Steaks With Béarnaise Butter and Sweet-Potato Chips
(pictured, page 25, inset)

¾ cup (1½ sticks) butter or
margarine
3 medium shallots
½ cup parsley leaves, washed
2 tablespoons tarragon vinegar
½ teaspoon dried tarragon
leaves
½ teaspoon freshly ground
pepper
Salad oil
2 pounds sweet potatoes, pared
and very thinly sliced
crosswise
4 shell or New York strip
steaks, 1 inch thick (10
ounces each)

1. In food processor, blend but-ter, shallots, parsley, vinegar, tarra-gon and pepper until smooth. Reserve 3 tablespoons butter mix-ture; place remainder in pastry bag fitted with ½-inch star tip. Pipe in four swirls onto sheet of waxed paper; refrigerate.

2. In large skillet, heat ½ inch oil to 375°F. Fry potato slices on both sides, one-fourth at a time, until crisp. Remove with slotted spoon to paper-towel-lined tray. Keep warm

in oven while cooking steaks.

3. In clean, large skillet, melt re-served butter mixture in 2 table-spoons oil. Sauté steaks about 5 minutes on each side, or until de-sired degree of doneness. Transfer steaks to heated serving platter; place a swirl of butter mixture on each steak. Garnish platter with tar-ragon leaves, if desired. Serve steaks with sweet-potato chips.
Makes 4 servings.

Syrian Meatballs
(pictured, page 25, inset)

1 pound ground beef
2 slices white bread, crumbled
½ cup milk
1 large egg
¼ cup coarsely chopped
blanched almonds
1½ teaspoons chopped mint
1 teaspoon salt
¼ teaspoon pepper
5 tablespoons salad oil
1 pound eggplant, cut in
½-inch cubes
1 medium onion, chopped
3 medium cloves garlic, crushed
1 can (28 ounces) whole
tomatoes
¼ cup pitted green olives,
slivered
2 teaspoons ground cumin
¼ teaspoon ground cinnamon
Pita bread
Lettuce leaves, shredded
Sour cream
Sliced almonds

1. In large bowl, combine beef, bread, milk, egg, chopped almonds, mint, salt and ⅛ teaspoon pepper; mix well. Shape mixture into 1-inch balls. In large skillet, heat 2 table-spoons oil; cook meatballs, half at a time, about 5 minutes, or until evenly browned. Remove from skil-let; set aside.

2. In same skillet, heat 3 table-spoons oil; cook eggplant, onion and garlic 5 minutes, or until onion is

tender. Add tomatoes and their juice, olives, cumin, cinnamon and ⅛ teaspoon pepper. Simmer, uncovered and stirring occasionally, 15 minutes, or until sauce thickens slightly. Return meatballs to sauce. Cook 5 minutes longer, or until heated through.

3. Spoon meatball mixture into pocket in pita bread. Serve with shredded lettuce, sour cream and sliced almonds.

Makes 6 servings.

Spicy Oriental Steak

¼ cup salad oil
½ cup teriyaki sauce
¼ cup toasted sesame seeds
2 tablespoons cider vinegar
4 green onions, thinly sliced
1 tablespoon shredded ginger root
1 large clove garlic, crushed
⅛ teaspoon ground red pepper
2 pounds top-round London broil
2 teaspoons cornstarch

1. In 12-by-8-inch shallow baking dish, combine oil, teriyaki sauce, sesame seeds, vinegar, onions, ginger, garlic and pepper; mix well. Add meat; turn to coat. Cover; refrigerate 4 hours or overnight.

2. Place meat on rack in broiling pan. Place marinade in small saucepan. Broil steak, 6 inches from heat, 6 minutes on each side for rare. Meanwhile, stir cornstarch into marinade. Bring to boiling, stirring; cook 1 minute, or until thickened. Thinly slice steak; serve with sauce.

Makes 6 to 8 servings.

■ Keep beef in its unopened package in the refrigerator, and use within four days (within two days for ground beef). Wrap cooked beef in aluminum foil, and use within five days.

Beef Croquettes With Red-Pepper Sauce

¼ cup (½ stick) butter or margarine
1 small onion, finely chopped
½ cup unsifted all-purpose flour
1 teaspoon salt
⅛ teaspoon pepper
1 cup milk
2½ cups cooked ground beef
2 tablespoons chopped parsley
2 teaspoons Worcestershire sauce
½ teaspoon hot-red-pepper sauce
1 large egg
2 tablespoons water
½ cup fine dry bread crumbs
Red-Pepper Sauce (recipe follows)
Salad oil

1. In medium saucepan, melt butter over medium-high heat. Sauté onion 3 minutes; stir in ¼ cup flour, salt and pepper. Gradually stir in milk; cook, stirring, until mixture is very thick. Transfer to large bowl; add beef, parsley, Worcestershire sauce and pepper sauce. Cover; refrigerate until beef is well chilled— about 4 hours.

2. Shape chilled beef mixture into 8 cone-shaped croquettes. In small bowl, beat egg with water. On separate sheets of waxed paper, place remaining ¼ cup flour and the bread crumbs. Coat each croquette first in flour, then in egg, then in crumbs.

3. Make Red-Pepper Sauce.

4. Meanwhile, in deep-fat fryer or 5-quart saucepan, heat 1½ inches oil to 375°F. Fry croquettes, a few at a time, turning frequently with slotted spoon, about 3 minutes, or until browned on both sides. Remove croquettes; drain on paper towels. Serve with Red-Pepper Sauce.

Makes 4 servings.

Red-Pepper Sauce

1 jar (7 ounces) roasted red peppers
½ cup beef broth
1½ teaspoons sugar
⅛ teaspoon seasoned pepper

In food processor or blender, puree peppers with beef broth, sugar and pepper. In small saucepan, heat sauce gently.

Makes ¾ cup.

Filet Steaks With Sherried Mushroom Sauce

4 beef-tenderloin filets, 1 inch thick (8 ounces each)
Salt
Pepper
1 tablespoon butter or margarine
1 tablespoon olive oil
½ pound mushrooms, thinly sliced
2 tablespoons minced shallots
½ cup prepared brown gravy
¼ cup dry sherry
¼ cup water

1. Sprinkle both sides of steaks with salt and pepper. In large skillet, melt butter in oil. Over medium heat, cook steaks 6 minutes on each side for medium rare. Remove to a platter; keep warm.

2. In drippings, sauté mushrooms and shallots 3 minutes. Add gravy, sherry, water and ¼ teaspoon salt; simmer 3 minutes. Pour any juices that collect from steak into skillet. Spoon sauce over steaks.

Makes 4 servings.

■ When freezing uncooked beef, wrap individual portions in aluminum foil, plastic freezer wrap or freezer paper.

Sauerbraten

5-pound rump roast
2 cups dry red wine
2 cups red-wine vinegar
2 leeks, washed and thinly
  sliced
2 carrots, sliced
2 celery stalks, coarsely
  chopped
12 whole peppercorns
12 whole juniper berries
6 whole cloves
2 bay leaves
1 teaspoon salt
½ pound bacon, chopped
¼ cup unsifted all-purpose
  flour
½ cup water
Gussie's Spaetzles (recipe
  follows)
½ cup gingersnap crumbs
¼ cup brown sugar

1. Place meat in large bowl. Add next 10 ingredients. Turn meat to coat with marinade. Cover; refrigerate two days, turning occasionally.

2. Preheat oven to 350°F. Remove meat from marinade; pat dry. In 5-quart Dutch oven, cook bacon until crisp. With slotted spoon, remove; set aside. Pour off all but 2 tablespoons drippings. Add meat and brown on all sides; remove to a platter. Remove all but 2 tablespoons drippings from pan; blend in flour. Gradually stir in marinade, vegetables and water. Add meat; bring to boiling. Cover. Simmer in oven 2½ hours, or until tender.

3. Make Gussie's Spaetzles.

4. Remove meat to a platter; keep warm. Pour cooking liquid through strainer into large glass measure; skim off any fat. Discard bay leaves. Return 3 cups liquid to pan. Add reserved bacon, gingersnap crumbs and brown sugar. Simmer, stirring constantly, until gravy thickens. Slice meat and spoon part of gravy over it; serve remaining gravy with meat. Serve with spaetzles and, if desired, sour cream.

Makes 8 to 10 servings.

Gussie's Spaetzles

3 cups unsifted all-purpose
  flour
¾ teaspoon salt
¼ teaspoon ground nutmeg
¼ teaspoon paprika
1 cup water
3 large eggs
½ cup (1 stick) butter or
  margarine, melted

1. In large bowl, combine flour, salt, nutmeg and paprika. Add water and eggs. Beat at low speed until smooth (batter will be thick).

2. In 5-quart saucepan, bring 2 inches salted water to boiling. Place about ¼ cup batter near one edge of a wet, small wooden cutting board or metal pancake turner. Over saucepan, with pastry scraper, wet surface of batter with cooking water. Flatten batter slightly with scraper. With a cutting and scraping motion, shave off long threads of batter about ⅛-inch thick into boiling water. Continue with remaining batter on board.

3. Cook spaetzles about 1 minute, or until they float to surface of water. Remove with slotted spoon to a large bowl; keep warm. Continue with remaining batter, using ¼ cup at a time. Toss spaetzles with melted butter.

Makes 8 to 10 servings.

Mexican Mini Loaves With Rice and Beans

1½ pounds ground beef
1 cup crushed corn chips
1 cup chunky salsa
1 large egg
½ teaspoon chili powder
½ teaspoon ground cumin
½ teaspoon salt
½ teaspoon pepper
Rice and Beans (recipe follows)

1. Preheat oven to 350°F. In large bowl, combine beef, corn chips, ¾ cup salsa, the egg, chili powder, cumin, salt and pepper.

2. Shape into four oval loaves; place in 13-by-9-by-2-inch baking pan. Top each loaf with 1 tablespoon salsa. Bake 45 minutes.

3. Make Rice and Beans; serve with meat loaves.

Makes 4 servings.

Rice and Beans

2 tablespoons salad oil
1 medium onion, chopped
1 can (4 ounces) chopped
  green chiles, drained
¾ cup uncooked long-grain
  white rice
2 cups water
1 beef-flavored bouillon cube
1 cup canned pinto beans,
  drained
½ cup (2 ounces) shredded
  Monterey Jack cheese

In medium saucepan, heat oil over medium-high heat; add onion and chilies and sauté 3 minutes. Add rice, water and bouillon cube. Bring to boiling. Reduce heat; simmer, covered, 20 minutes, or until rice is tender. Stir in beans and cheese.

Makes 4 servings.

■ Select bright red beef—it's the freshest. Vacuum-packaged beef and the interior of packaged ground beef will be more purplish-red, since it hasn't come into contact with the air.

■ To determine the number of servings you'll get per pound of meat, keep these approximations in mind: Boneless cuts yield three to four servings per pound; cuts with bone yield two to three servings per pound; cuts with a lot of bone (like back ribs or short ribs) yield one to one and a half servings per pound.

Carbonnade

¼ pound bacon, coarsely
  chopped
1½ pounds boneless chuck, cut
  in 1½-inch pieces
1½ pounds boneless pork
  shoulder, cut in 1½-inch
  pieces
2 large Spanish onions, thinly
  sliced
1 can (35 ounces) plum
  tomatoes
1 bottle (12 ounces) dark beer
1 can (about 14 ounces) beef
  broth
2 tablespoons sugar
1 tablespoon dried thyme
  leaves
1 bay leaf
1 teaspoon salt
½ teaspoon pepper
1 pound new potatoes, unpared
  and quartered
3 large carrots, pared and cut
  in 1½-inch pieces
3 large celery stalks, cut in
  ½-inch pieces
½ pound medium mushrooms,
  quartered
½ cup unsifted all-purpose
  flour

1. In 6-quart saucepan, over medium heat, sauté bacon until crisp.
With slotted spoon, remove to plate,
and set aside. In bacon drippings,
brown beef and pork, several pieces
at a time, removing to bowl as they
brown.

2. In drippings sauté onions 5
minutes, or until tender. Drain tomatoes, reserving liquid; set tomatoes aside. Add beer, 1 cup broth,
the tomato liquid, sugar, thyme, bay
leaf, salt and pepper to onions. Return meat and any liquid to pan.
Bring to boiling. Reduce heat; simmer, covered, 45 minutes.

3. Add potatoes and carrots; simmer, covered, 15 minutes longer.
Add celery, mushrooms and tomatoes; simmer, covered, 7 minutes, or
until vegetables are tender.

4. In small bowl, stir remaining

broth with flour until smooth. Add
to stew; simmer, stirring, 2 minutes,
or until thickened. Remove and discard bay leaf. Sprinkle carbonnade
with sautéed bacon.

Makes 8 to 10 servings.

Continental-Style Poached Tenderloin

2 tablespoons salad oil
2-pound beef tenderloin
  (trimmed weight)
8 small white onions, peeled
1 can (about 14 ounces) beef
  broth
¼ cup dry red wine
1 bay leaf
½ teaspoon cracked pepper
1 large bunch parsley
4 medium parsnips, pared and
  halved lengthwise
2 medium yellow squash
  (1 pound), halved crosswise
  and quartered lengthwise
2 medium zucchini (1 pound),
  halved crosswise and
  quartered lengthwise
1 tablespoon butter or
  margarine
2 tablespoons all-purpose flour

1. In 5-quart Dutch oven, heat oil
over medium-high heat; add tenderloin and brown. Remove to platter;
cover. In drippings, sauté onions 3
minutes; add meat, broth and next 5
ingredients. Bring to boiling; reduce
heat; simmer, covered, 30 minutes,
or until meat thermometer registers
135°F for medium rare.

2. With slotted spoon, remove
meat and parsnips to platter; cover.
Add squash and zucchini to broth.
Simmer, covered, 5 minutes, or until
tender. With slotted spoon, place
squash and zucchini with meat.
Strain cooking liquid. In same pan,
melt butter; stir in flour. Gradually
stir in strained liquid. Bring to boiling, stirring; simmer 3 minutes.
Spoon over meat and vegetables.

Makes 8 servings.

Steak With Peppercorns

2 tablespoons black
  peppercorns
2 tablespoons green or pink
  peppercorns
2 medium cloves garlic,
  crushed
½ teaspoon dried thyme leaves
4 shell or rib eye steaks, 1 inch
  thick (about 12 ounces each)

Red Butter Sauce
½ cup B&B liqueur
3 tablespoons red-wine
  vinegar
2 large shallots, finely
  chopped (about ¼ cup)
¼ teaspoon salt
⅛ teaspoon pepper
½ cup (1 stick) unsalted
  butter or margarine,
  well chilled

1. In a spice grinder or blender,
crush peppercorns until coarsely
ground; on a sheet of waxed paper,
mix with garlic and thyme. Rub into
both sides of steaks.

2. Prepare outdoor grill for barbecuing, or preheat broiler. Grill
steaks, 6 inches from heat, turning
once with tongs, for rare. Place on
warm tempered serving dish; cover
loosely to keep warm.

3. Make Red Butter Sauce: In
large saucepan, combine ¼ cup
B&B, the vinegar, shallots, salt and
pepper; over high heat, reduce to
about 1 tablespoon. Cut butter into
8 pieces. Remove pan from heat to
cool slightly; with a whisk, quickly
beat in 2 pieces of butter until mixture is creamy. Return pan to low
heat; beat in remaining butter, one
piece at a time, until sauce is consistency of heavy cream. Pour sauce
into sauce boat.

4. In a small saucepan, warm remaining ¼ cup B&B. Pour over
steaks; stand back and, with a long
match, ignite. Serve steaks immediately with sauce.

Makes 4 servings.

Lite Eating: Elegant Oriental Dinner

MANDARIN CHICKEN CRÊPES
HONEY-MARINATED BEET SALAD
MERINGUE-TOPPED PEARS
MINT TEA

Mandarin Chicken Crêpes

½ cup unsifted all-purpose
  flour
½ cup skim milk
2 large eggs, beaten
1 tablespoon chopped fresh or
  1 teaspoon dried thyme
  leaves
Nonstick cooking spray
¾ pound chicken cutlets
3 tablespoons soy sauce
1 tablespoon lemon juice
2 teaspoons minced ginger root
¾ cup chicken broth
2 teaspoons cornstarch
1 teaspoon honey
1 can (15 ounces) straw
  mushrooms, drained

1. In blender, combine flour with milk, eggs and thyme. Blend until smooth; let stand 2 hours. Lightly coat bottom of 8-inch crêpe pan or skillet with nonstick cooking spray; place over medium-high heat. Pour 2 tablespoons batter in center of pan; swirl pan to coat bottom. Cook 1 minute, or until firm; with spatula, turn over, and cook 30 seconds. Turn out on aluminum foil; make 7 more crêpes with remaining batter. Keep warm while making filling.

2. Cut chicken crosswise in ¼-inch strips. Place in bowl; toss with 2 tablespoons soy sauce, the lemon juice and 1 teaspoon ginger. Marinate 15 minutes.

3. In small saucepan, blend remaining 1 tablespoon soy sauce and ginger with broth, cornstarch and honey; stir until cornstarch is dissolved. Bring to boiling, stirring; simmer 1 minute.

4. Coat skillet with cooking spray; sauté chicken until just firm—3 minutes. Stir in mushrooms and ¼ cup sauce; bring to boiling.

5. Fill each crêpe with one-eighth of chicken mixture. Place crêpes on a serving platter, and top with remaining sauce.

Makes 4 servings; 250 calories each serving.

Honey-Marinated Beet Salad

2 tablespoons raspberry vinegar
1 teaspoon honey
½ teaspoon coarse Dijon-style
  mustard
1 can (16 ounces) whole beets,
  drained and quartered
1 small head Boston lettuce,
  leaves rinsed and patted dry
2 small Belgian endive, leaves
  separated

1. In medium bowl, combine first 3 ingredients. Add beets; toss.

2. Arrange lettuce leaves and endive on serving platter; top with beets. Drizzle top of salad with remaining dressing.

Makes 4 servings; 50 calories each serving.

Meringue-Topped Pears

2 large egg whites
2 teaspoons sugar
2 tea cookies, crumbled
Nonstick cooking spray
2 pears, halved and cored

1. Preheat oven to 250°F. In small bowl, with electric mixer at high speed, beat egg whites until frothy. Sprinkle sugar over whites; beat until stiff. Fold in half of cookie crumbs.

2. Coat small baking dish with nonstick cooking spray. With spatula, spread one-fourth of egg-white mixture over cut side of each pear half. Sprinkle with remaining crumbs. Place in prepared dish; bake 40 minutes. Serve warm.

Makes 4 servings; 120 calories each serving.

■ Take the mess out of measuring honey or molasses. Warm the measuring cup or spoon by rinsing it with hot water before adding the honey or molasses. The liquid won't stick, so that your measurement will be more accurate, and cleanup will be easier.

Quick & Easy: Tortellini—Pronto!

TORTELLINI WITH SHRIMP
SALAD WITH ROASTED-PEPPER
DRESSING
CRUSTY ITALIAN BREAD
WHITE-WINE SPRITZERS
CAKE AND ICE CREAM
WITH MOCHA SAUCE

Tortellini With Shrimp

1 package (8 ounces)
   spinach-cheese tortellini
1 package (8 ounces) cheese
   tortellini
¾ cup (1½ sticks) butter or
   margarine
1 small onion, sliced
1 medium clove garlic, crushed
1 pound deveined shelled
   shrimp
½ pound plum tomatoes, cut
   in wedges
¼ pound boiled ham, cut in
   ¼-inch strips
1 cup frozen peas
½ cup grated Parmesan cheese
Additional Parmesan cheese,
   shredded
Freshly ground pepper

1. Cook tortellini as package labels direct. Drain and keep warm. In large skillet, melt butter. Add onion and garlic and sauté 3 minutes. Add shrimp; sauté 3 minutes. Add tomatoes, ham, peas and ½ cup grated cheese; cook 1 minute.

2. Toss with tortellini; sprinkle with additional shredded cheese. If desired, garnish with fresh basil; sprinkle with freshly ground pepper.
   Makes 4 servings.

Salad With Roasted-Pepper Dressing

2 jars (7 ounces each)
   marinated artichoke hearts
1 can (14 ounces) hearts of
   palm
½ head escarole
½ head green leaf lettuce
½ head Boston lettuce
½ cup pitted black olives
¼ cup chopped roasted red
   pepper
2 tablespoons red-wine vinegar

1. Drain marinated artichoke hearts, reserving liquid. Drain hearts of palm; rinse.

2. In salad bowl, arrange escarole, green leaf and Boston lettuce leaves. Top with artichoke hearts, hearts of palm and olives.

3. In blender, puree red pepper with reserved marinade and red-wine vinegar; spoon over salad.
   Makes 4 servings.

Cake and Ice Cream With Mocha Sauce

1 package (11¾ ounces) frozen
   chocolate-swirl pound cake,
   thawed
1 package (6 ounces)
   semisweet-chocolate pieces
½ cup marshmallow creme
⅓ cup water
¼ cup confectioners' sugar
2 tablespoons almond-flavored
   liqueur
1 tablespoon instant espresso
   coffee powder
1 pint vanilla ice cream

1. Cut cake in eight ½-inch-thick slices.

2. In saucepan, cook chocolate, marshmallow creme, water and the sugar until smooth; boil 1 minute. Stir in liqueur and coffee powder.

3. Place two slices cake on each plate; top with one scoop ice cream and the warm sauce.
   Makes 4 servings.

■ To dress up Italian bread, try Prosciutto Parmesan Pull-Apart Loaf: In a small bowl, combine ¾ cup butter, ⅓ cup Parmesan cheese, ½ cup (2 ounces) prosciutto, ¼ cup fresh chopped basil (or ¼ cup fresh chopped parsley and 1 tablespoon dried basil leaves), and 1 teaspoon freshly cracked pepper; blend well. With serrated knife, slice 1 loaf (1 pound) Italian bread diagonally almost all the way through 12 times, at 1½-inch intervals; spread 1 rounded tablespoon prosciutto butter between sections, using half of butter mixture. Turn loaf around; slice loaf diagonally almost all the way through 12 times, making diamond patterns of 1½-inch sections; spread with remaining butter. Heat in 450° oven 10 minutes, or until crust is crisp and loaf is heated through. Makes 12 servings.

Micro-Way: Liven Up Your Leftovers

Ham-and-Rice Pie

4 large eggs
2 cups hot cooked rice
1½ cups (6 ounces) shredded
   Cheddar cheese
2 tablespoons butter or
   margarine
½ cup chopped green onions
½ cup chopped red pepper
¼ pound mushrooms, sliced
½ teaspoon dried tarragon
   leaves, crushed
½ teaspoon salt
⅛ teaspoon pepper
½ pound cooked ham, cut in
   2-by-¼-inch strips
1 cup cooked chopped broccoli
¼ cup unsifted all-purpose
   flour
¼ cup sour cream

1. Grease 9-inch glass pie plate. In small bowl, beat 1 egg; stir in hot rice and 1 cup cheese until cheese melts. Spread over bottom and up side of prepared pie plate.

2. In large glass bowl, melt butter on HIGH 1 minute. Add next 6 ingredients. Cook on HIGH 4 minutes, stirring occasionally. Add ham and broccoli.

3. In small bowl, beat remaining eggs, flour and sour cream until blended. Add with remaining cheese to vegetable mixture; mix well. Pour into prepared plate; cook uncovered, on HIGH 3 minutes, and then on MEDIUM 20 minutes, rotating dish a quarter turn every 5 minutes, or until center is just set. Let stand, covered, 5 minutes.

Makes 8 servings.

Chicken Enchiladas

2 tablespoons salad oil
1 large onion, chopped
1 large green pepper, cut in
   ¼-inch strips
1 medium clove garlic, crushed
1 can (4 ounces) chopped
   green chiles
1 to 2 pickled jalapeño
   peppers, minced
3 tablespoons lime juice
2 tablespoons chopped cilantro
1 pound cooked chicken, cut
   in ¼-inch strips
1 cup (4 ounces) shredded
   Monterey Jack cheese
8 flour tortillas
½ cup (2 ounces) shredded
   Cheddar cheese
Sour cream

1. In large glass bowl, in oil, cook the onion, green pepper and garlic on HIGH 3 minutes. Add green chiles, jalapeños, lime juice and cilantro. Cover mixture with plastic wrap; turn back one corner to vent.

Note: Recipes were tested in 600- to 700-watt microwave ovens.

Cook on HIGH 3 minutes. Add chicken and ½ cup Monterey Jack cheese; mix well.

2. Wrap half of the tortillas in dampened, microwave-safe paper towels. Heat on HIGH 30 seconds to 1 minute, or until warm to the touch. Work with one tortilla at a time, keeping remainder covered. Place ½ cup chicken mixture in a line across center of a tortilla; roll tortilla around filling. Place, seam side down, on microwave-safe serving platter. Repeat with remaining tortillas and filling. Sprinkle Cheddar cheese and remaining Monterey Jack cheese over all. Cook on HIGH 4 minutes, or until cheese is melted and enchiladas are heated through. Serve with sour cream.

Makes 8 enchiladas; 4 servings.

■ Want an easy way to get thin, perfectly cut slices of meat? Freeze meat for 30 minutes prior to carving with a sharp knife.

Turkey Curry

¼ cup (½ stick) butter or margarine
1 large onion, cut in wedges
1 tart apple, unpared, cored and chopped
2 large carrots, pared and sliced
2 large celery stalks, sliced
1 large clove garlic, crushed
1 tablespoon curry powder
¼ cup unsifted all-purpose flour
⅛ teaspoon crushed red-pepper flakes
1½ cups chicken broth
1 cup frozen peas
2 teaspoons grated lime peel
3 cups cubed, cooked turkey
½ cup raisins
½ cup heavy cream
Cooked white rice

1. In large glass bowl, melt butter on HIGH 1 minute. Add onion, apple, carrots, celery, garlic and curry powder. Cook on HIGH 5 minutes, stirring once. Stir in flour and pepper flakes until smooth.

2. Gradually stir in broth; add peas and lime peel. Cook on HIGH 5 minutes, or until boiling, stirring once. Add turkey, raisins and cream; cook on MEDIUM 5 minutes, or until heated through. Serve over cooked rice.

Makes 4 servings.

Pastitsio

1 package (8 ounces) elbow macaroni
1 tablespoon salad oil
1 large onion, chopped
1 large clove garlic, crushed
1 can (16 ounces) whole tomatoes
1 can (6 ounces) tomato paste
¼ cup water
½ teaspoon ground cinnamon
½ teaspoon salt
¼ teaspoon dried oregano
3 cups chopped cooked beef
1 package (10 ounces) frozen chopped spinach, thawed and squeezed dry
¼ pound feta cheese, crumbled
2 tablespoons butter or margarine
2 tablespoons all-purpose flour
1½ cups milk
2 large eggs
½ cup grated Parmesan cheese
Chopped parsley

1. In saucepan, undercook macaroni on range; drain.

2. In large glass bowl, in oil, cook onion and garlic on HIGH 3 minutes. Add tomatoes, their liquid and next 5 ingredients. Cook on HIGH 4 minutes; stir in beef.

3. In 2½-quart casserole, spread half of macaroni. Top with spinach, feta cheese and half of meat sauce. Spoon remaining macaroni and then meat sauce on top; set aside.

4. In glass bowl, melt butter on HIGH; stir in flour. Add milk; cook on HIGH 5 minutes; stir once. Beat eggs and ¼ cup cheese; beat into milk mixture. Pour over meat sauce; sprinkle with remaining cheese. Cook on HIGH 5 minutes, then on MEDIUM 20 minutes, rotating a quarter turn every 5 minutes. Sprinkle with parsley.

Makes 8 servings.

March

These are our most spectacular,
most scrumptious desserts ever!
One to splurge on is the
Sherry-Pecan Torte, with rich layers
of cake and whipped cream, all
adorned with strawberry fans.

Sherry-Pecan Torte

Grape Cream Tart

Mrs. Sethre's Candy Pudding

Neapolitan Chocolate Box

Very Coconut Custard Tart

Chocolate-Ribbon Cheesecake

Apple Tatin With Custard Sauce

Raspberry Black-Bottom Pie

Macadamia Gâteau

Meringue Soufflé With Berry Sauce

Cappuccino Mousse on Chocolate Shell

Apricot Bavarian

Dessert Cookbook

Glorious finales to savor, including a magnificient Neapolitan cake—it's adorned with slats of chocolate and pink candy curls.

Sherry-Pecan Torte
(pictured, page 41)

11 large eggs, separated
1 whole large egg
1½ cups granulated sugar
5 tablespoons dry sherry
2 cups ground pecans
⅔ cup fine dry bread crumbs
1 tablespoon all-purpose flour
¼ teaspoon cream of tartar
3 cups heavy cream
¼ cup confectioners' sugar
¾ cup seedless strawberry or raspberry jam
1 cup chopped pecans

1. Grease two 10-inch springform or round cake pans. Line each with a 10-inch round of waxed paper; grease and flour paper.

Page 41: Sherry-Pecan Torte.

Pages 42 and 43: (Clockwise from top right) Grape Cream Tart, Mrs. Sethre's Candy Pudding, Neapolitan Chocolate Box, Very Coconut Custard Tart, Chocolate-Ribbon Cheesecake, Apple Tatin With Custard Sauce.

Pages 44 and 45: (Clockwise from top right) Raspberry Black-Bottom Pie, Macadamia Gâteau, Meringue Soufflé With Berry Sauce, Cappuccino Mousse on Chocolate Shell, Apricot Bavarian.

2. Preheat oven to 275°F. In large bowl, with electric mixer at high speed, beat egg yolks and whole egg together until thick—5 minutes. Gradually add 1 cup granulated sugar, beating until mixture is thick and light. Beat in 3 tablespoons sherry.

3. Fold in ground pecans, bread crumbs and flour. In another bowl, beat egg whites and cream of tartar until foamy. Add remaining ½ cup granulated sugar, 1 tablespoon at a time, beating until stiff peaks form.

4. Stir about one-fourth of the whites into nut mixture; gently fold in remaining whites. Pour batter into prepared pans; smooth tops with spatula. Bake on two oven racks 50 minutes, or until top springs back when lightly touched. Cool cakes in pans on racks 30 minutes. Invert layers on cloth-covered rack; peel off waxed paper. Carefully invert again; cool completely.

5. In small bowl, with electric mixer, beat cream and confectioners' sugar until stiff. Gently fold in remaining 2 tablespoons sherry; refrigerate while cutting torte layers.

6. With long serrated knife, cut each layer horizontally in half. Place one layer, top side down, on serving plate; spread with ¼ cup jam, then ¾ cup whipped cream; continue layering torte, jam and cream, ending with torte, cut side down. Place strips of waxed paper around bottom of torte on plate. With half of remaining whipped cream, frost top and side of torte. Evenly coat side of torte with chopped pecans. Place remaining whipped cream in pastry bag fitted with ½-inch star tip; decoratively pipe around top edge of torte. Garnish with strawberry slices or raspberries, if desired. Store in refrigerator. Remove waxed-paper strips before serving.

Makes 16 to 20 servings.

Grape Cream Tart
(pictured, page 43)

2½ cups unsifted all-purpose flour
¾ cup (1½ sticks) chilled butter or margarine
½ teaspoon salt
6 to 7 tablespoons ice water
1 cup sour cream
2 large eggs
½ cup sugar
1 tablespoon Cognac or brandy
2½ pounds seedless grapes

1. Preheat over to 400°F. In food processor, combine 2¼ cups flour, the butter and salt; process until mixture resembles coarse crumbs. With processor running, gradually add ice water, process until pastry forms a ball. Divide dough in half. On lightly floured surface, roll half into an 11-inch round. Fit into a 9-by-2-inch fluted tart pan with removable bottom. Trim edge; refrigerate. Roll remaining half of pastry

to ⅛-inch-thick round. With small sharp knife, cut out leaf shapes; with back of knife, make veins on each leaf. Place leaves on waxed-paper-lined tray; refrigerate.

2. Bake tart shell 5 minutes. In medium bowl, whisk sour cream, eggs, sugar, remaining ¼ cup flour and the Cognac until well blended. Place grapes in tart shell; pour sour-cream mixture over grapes. Arrange pastry leaves on top. Bake 1 hour, or until pastry is golden and custard is set. Cool on wire rack; refrigerate. Remove pan rim; garnish tart with sugared grapes, if desired.

Makes 8 servings.

Neapolitan Chocolate Box

(pictured, page 43)

2¼ cups unsifted cake flour
1½ cups sugar
2 teaspoons baking powder
½ teaspoon salt
9 large eggs, separated
½ cup salad oil
½ cup milk
3 tablespoons unsweetened cocoa powder
3 tablespoons hot water
1 tablespoon grated lemon peel
¼ cup lemon juice
Red food color
Chocolate Buttercream (recipe follows)
Chocolate Slats (see box, page 48)
Pink Candy Curls (see box, page 48)

1. Grease three 8-inch square cake pans. Line bottoms with waxed paper; grease and flour waxed paper. In large bowl, combine flour, ¾ cup sugar, the baking powder and salt; mix well. Add egg yolks, oil and

milk; whisk until smooth. In small bowl, mix cocoa with hot water.

2. Preheat oven to 350°F. In large bowl, with electric mixer at high speed, beat egg whites until foamy. Gradually add remaining sugar, beating until stiff, moist peaks form; fold into egg-yolk mixture. In medium bowl, fold cocoa mixture into 3 cups batter; turn into a prepared pan. Fold lemon peel and juice into remaining batter; turn half of batter into a prepared pan. Add few drops red food color to remaining batter; turn into a prepared pan. Bake 25 minutes, or until cake tester inserted in center comes out clean. Cool on wire racks 5 minutes; invert. Remove waxed paper; cool.

3. Make Chocolate Buttercream.

4. Place pink cake layer, top side down, on serving plate. Spread with ⅔ cup buttercream. Top with yellow layer; spread with ⅔ cup buttercream; top with chocolate layer. Frost sides and top with remaining buttercream. Place Chocolate Slats around side, and Pink Candy Curls on top, if desired.

Makes 16 servings.

Chocolate Buttercream

1½ cups (3 sticks) butter, softened
2 cups confectioners' sugar
3 large egg yolks
1 cup (6 ounces) semisweet-chocolate pieces, melted

In large bowl, with electric mixer at high speed, cream butter and sugar until light and fluffy. Beat in egg yolks, one at a time. Gradually beat in chocolate until blended and spreadable. (If too soft, refrigerate until cold; beat until fluffy.)

Makes enough frosting for a 3-layer cake.

Mrs. Sethre's Candy Pudding

(pictured, page 43)

3 large eggs, separated
¼ teaspoon salt
⅛ teaspoon cream of tartar
1 cup sugar
1 tablespoon all-purpose flour
1 teaspoon baking powder
1 teaspoon vanilla extract
1 cup coarsely chopped pitted dates
1 cup coarsely chopped walnuts
½ cup semisweet-chocolate pieces
1 cup heavy cream, whipped

1. Lightly grease bottom of shallow 2-quart baking dish. In medium bowl, with electric mixer at high speed, beat egg whites with salt and cream of tartar until soft peaks form. At high speed, gradually beat in ¼ cup sugar, 1 tablespoon at a time, until stiff peaks form.

2. Preheat oven to 350°F. In large bowl, with electric mixer at high speed, beat egg yolks, remaining ¾ cup sugar, the flour, baking powder and vanilla until blended. Stir in chopped dates, chopped nuts and chocolate pieces. With rubber spatula, stir one-fourth of the egg whites into egg-yolk mixture; fold in remaining whites until no white streaks remain. Pour mixture into prepared dish.

3. Place dish in large roasting pan; add boiling water to come 1 inch up sides of pan. Bake 45 minutes, or until top of pudding is brown. Carefully remove dish from pan; cool on wire rack. Serve pudding at room temperature in dessert dishes or stemmed glasses; top with whipped cream.

Makes 8 servings.

Very Coconut Custard Tart

(pictured, pages 42 and 43)

1¾ cups unsifted all-purpose
　flour
¾ cup (1½ sticks) chilled
　butter or margarine, cut in
　pieces
½ teaspoon salt
4 to 5 tablespoons ice water
1 cup superfine sugar
2 large eggs
3 large eggs, separated
¼ teaspoon almond extract
1 cup heavy cream
3 cups firmly packed grated
　fresh coconut or 1½
　packages (7-ounce size)
　flaked coconut
¼ teaspoon cream of tartar
⅓ cup granulated sugar

1. In food processor, combine
1½ cups flour, ½ cup butter and the
salt; process until mixture resembles coarse crumbs. With processor
running, gradually add ice water;
process until pastry forms a ball.

2. Preheat oven to 350°F. On
lightly floured surface, roll pastry
into a 14-by-12-inch rectangle. Fit
into an 11-by-8-inch fluted tart pan
with removable bottom; fold edge
under. (Or roll into an 11-inch
round, and fit into 9-inch pie plate;
crimp edge.) Refrigerate.

3. In large bowl, with electric
mixer at high speed, beat remaining
butter and the superfine sugar until
light and fluffy. Beat in whole eggs
and egg yolks, one at a time. At low
speed, beat in remaining ¼ cup
flour, almond extract and cream; stir
in coconut. Pour into prepared tart
shell. Bake 45 minutes, or until center is firm; remove to wire rack.

4. In bowl, with electric mixer at
high speed, beat egg whites and
cream of tartar until foamy. Gradually beat in granulated sugar until
stiff peaks form. Spread one-third on
tart. With remainder in pastry bag
fitted with small star tip, pipe lattice
over top and a border around edge.
Bake 10 minutes, or until golden.
Makes 8 to 10 servings.

Chocolate-Ribbon Cheesecake

(pictured, page 42)

½ cup whole blanched
　almonds, ground
1 cup unsifted all-purpose
　flour
1 cup sugar
½ cup (1 stick) cold butter or
　margarine, cut in pieces
1 large egg
1 package (12 ounces)
　semisweet-chocolate pieces
2 tablespoons salad oil
3 packages (8 ounces each)
　cream cheese, softened
2 teaspoons grated lemon peel
3 tablespoons lemon juice
6 large egg whites
1 cup (½ pint) heavy cream
Whipped cream (optional)
Chocolate Butterflies (optional;
　see box below)

1. In food processor or medium
bowl, combine ground nuts, flour
and ¼ cup sugar. Add butter; process or cut in with pastry blender

---

How to Dress Up a Dessert

■ **Chocolate Slats:** In double
boiler or microwave, melt 1 cup
(6 ounces) semisweet-chocolate
pieces and 2 tablespoons shortening; stir until smooth. Line a large
baking sheet with foil; trace a 12-
inch square on foil. With spatula,
evenly spread chocolate within
square. Refrigerate 30 minutes;
let stand at room temperature 10
minutes. With sharp knife, cut
into thirty-six 4-by-1-inch rectangles. Refrigerate until firm. Carefully peel away foil; use chocolate
slats to decorate sides of Neapolitan Cake.

■ **Pink Candy Curls:** In double
boiler or microwave oven, melt 1

package (12 ounces) vanilla-flavor candy melting wafers; stir in a
few drops red food color to tint
pink. Line a 5-by-3-by-2-inch loaf
pan with foil. Pour mixture into
pan; refrigerate 30 minutes. Let
hardened candy loaf stand at
room temperature for 10 minutes. Remove from pan; carefully
pull away foil. Pull cheese plane
or vegetable parer along length of
loaf to make curls; arrange on top
of Neapolitan Cake.

■ **Chocolate Butterflies:** 1 cup
melted semisweet-chocolate
pieces. Place in pastry bag fitted
with 1/16-inch writing tip. Cover
baking sheet with waxed paper;
place a butterfly pattern under
waxed paper. Pipe melted chocolate along outline. Gently slide
pattern to another section of

waxed paper; pipe along outline.
Repeat with remaining chocolate.
Refrigerate 10 minutes, or until
firm. Gently peel off waxed paper.
To garnish Chocolate-Ribbon
Cheesecake, place two butterfly
halves together, antennae facing
in same direction, in whipped
cream.

■ **Chocolate Leaves:** Wash 12
lemon or mint leaves; dry with
paper towels. Brush with salad
oil. In top of double boiler, over
hot, not boiling, water, melt ½
cup semisweet- or milk-chocolate
pieces and 1 tablespoon butter or
margarine. Add 1 tablespoon light
corn syrup; stir until smooth.
Brush thick layer on back of each
leaf; place on waxed paper. Chill
until firm. When ready to serve,
peel leaves from chocolate.

until mixture resembles coarse crumbs. Add egg; process or stir until pastry forms a ball. Press into bottom and 2 inches up side of a 9-inch springform pan. Refrigerate while making filling.

2. In top of double boiler, melt chocolate and oil over hot, not boiling, water until smooth. Preheat over to 350°F. In large bowl, with electric mixer at medium speed, beat cream cheese, remaining sugar, the grated lemon peel and lemon juice until light and fluffy. Beat in egg whites, one at a time. At high speed, gradually beat in 1 cup cream until thick and fluffy.

3. Pour half of cheesecake mixture into prepared crust. Spoon half of chocolate mixture on top. Swirl gently with a knife. Repeat with remaining cheesecake mixture and chocolate.

4. Bake 55 minutes, or until edges are set and center is almost firm. Cool in pan on rack until room temperature. Refrigerate until thoroughly chilled—3 hours or overnight. With sharp knife, loosen edge of cake. Remove side of springform pan. If desired, pipe whipped cream decoratively around top edge; garnish with Chocolate Butterflies.
Makes 12 servings.

Apple Tatin With Custard Sauce
(pictured, page 42)

Custard Sauce (recipe follows)
½ cup rum
½ cup golden raisins
¼ cup currants
4 pounds Rome apples
2 teaspoons grated lemon peel
¼ cup lemon juice
½ cup sugar
¼ teaspoon ground allspice
¼ teaspoon ground nutmeg
⅓ cup butter or margarine, melted

1. Make Custard Sauce.

2. Lightly butter a 9-inch springform pan. In small saucepan, bring rum, raisins and currants to boiling. Remove mixture from heat; cover and let stand 15 minutes.

3. Preheat over to 375°F. Pare, core and thinly slice apples; place in large bowl, and toss with lemon peel and juice. Add sugar, allspice and nutmeg; mix well. Arrange one-fourth of prepared slices in springform pan in concentric circles, rounded side toward edge. Brush with some melted butter; sprinkle with 2 rounded tablespoons raisin-currant mixture. Repeat layering, ending with raisin-currant mixture.

4. Cover pan tightly with aluminum foil; bake 50 minutes. Remove foil; bake 15 minutes longer, or until apples are tender and light golden. Serve, at room temperature or chilled, with Custard Sauce.
Makes 8 servings.

Custard Sauce

½ cup sugar
1 tablespoon cornstarch
2 cups milk
2 tablespoons butter or margarine
3 large egg yolks
1 teaspoon vanilla extract
½ cup heavy cream

1. In medium saucepan, combine sugar and cornstarch; mix well. Gradually stir in milk until smooth; add butter. Bring to boiling, stirring constantly; boil 1 minute. Stir some of hot milk mixture into egg yolks; return to saucepan. Cook, stirring constantly, just until mixture boils.

2. Immediately strain custard through sieve into medium bowl; stir in vanilla. Place plastic directly on surface; refrigerate until completely cooled. (Custard may be made a day ahead.) Before serving, stir cream into custard.
Makes 2½ cups.

Macadamia Gâteau
(pictured, page 45)

4 large eggs
1¾ cups confectioners' sugar
1 cup unsifted all-purpose flour
2 teaspoons ground cinnamon
1 teaspoon vanilla extract
½ cup finely chopped macadamia nuts, lightly toasted
3 cups heavy cream
2 tablespoons rum
1 can (8 ounces) crushed pineapple, drained

1. Preheat oven to 375°F. Using a 9-inch square cake pan as a pattern, trace a square on parchment paper. Lightly grease paper; place on baking sheet. Repeat, making three more squares. In medium bowl, with whisk or electric mixer, beat eggs and 1½ cups confectioners' sugar until blended. Add flour, cinnamon and vanilla; mix until smooth.

2. With spatula, evenly spread ½ cup batter onto each square; sprinkle with 2 tablespoons chopped nuts. Bake 12 minutes, or until edges are lightly browned. With spatula, loosen cookies; quickly remove to wire rack; cool completely.

3. In medium bowl, with electric mixer at high speed, beat cream and remaining ¼ cup confectioners' sugar until stiff peaks form. Fold in rum. Place 1 cup whipped-cream mixture in pastry bag fitted with ¼-inch star tip; set aside. Fold pineapple into remaining cream mixture. Place one cookie on plate. Spread with one-third pineapple cream; repeat with remaining cookies and pineapple cream. Pipe plain whipped-cream mixture on top. Garnish with additional toasted macadamia nuts, if desired. Refrigerate at least 1 hour. (Cookies will soften and be easy to cut and serve.)
Makes 12 to 16 servings.
Note: Nine-inch round layers can be made instead of squares.

Raspberry Black-Bottom Pie

(pictured, page 45)

1¼ cups semisweet-chocolate
  pieces
¼ cup (½ stick) butter or
  margarine
1¼ cups crushed chocolate-
  wafer cookies (24 wafers)
⅓ cup ground walnuts
2 envelopes unflavored gelatine
¼ cup cold water
1¼ cups sugar
½ cup cornstarch
2 cups milk
4 large eggs, separated
¼ cup white or golden rum
1 teaspoon vanilla extract
2 packages (10 ounces each)
  frozen raspberries in syrup,
  thawed
2 tablespoons lemon juice
¼ teaspoon cream of tartar
Chocolate Leaves (optional; see
  box, page 48)

1. Preheat oven to 350°F. In small saucepan, melt ¼ cup chocolate pieces and the butter. Remove from heat; stir in cookie crumbs and nuts until well mixed. Line 9-inch pie plate evenly with crumb mixture; bake 12 minutes. Cool on wire rack.

2. In small cup, sprinkle gelatine over cold water; set aside. In medium saucepan, combine ½ cup sugar and ¼ cup cornstarch; mix well. Gradually stir in milk. Bring to boiling, stirring constantly; boil 1 minute, or until thickened. In small bowl, beat egg yolks and some of hot-milk mixture; return to saucepan. Over low heat, cook 1 minute longer.

3. In medium bowl, mix 1½ cups custard and remaining chocolate; stir until chocolate is melted. Pour chocolate mixture into pie shell; refrigerate. Stir softened gelatine into remaining custard in saucepan until melted. (If necessary, place pan over low heat to melt gelatine completely.) Place custard in large bowl;

stir in rum and vanilla extract. Refrigerate, stirring occasionally, about 30 minutes, or until consistency of unbeaten egg white.

4. Meanwhile, in food processor or blender, puree raspberries with syrup. In medium saucepan, combine ¼ cup sugar and remaining ¼ cup cornstarch; mix well. Gradually add raspberry puree and lemon juice. Over medium-high heat, bring to boiling, stirring constantly. Boil 1 minute, or until thickened and translucent; pour into bowl. Place plastic wrap directly on surface; refrigerate. When chilled, pour into pie shell; refrigerate.

5. In large bowl, with electric mixer at high speed, beat egg whites and cream of tartar until foamy. Beat in remaining ½ cup sugar, 2 tablespoons at a time, until stiff, moist peaks form; fold into reserved custard. Spoon over raspberry layer, mounding. Place Chocolate Leaves around edge of pie crust; refrigerate 2 hours, or until firm. Garnish top with fresh raspberries, if desired.

Makes 8 to 10 servings.

Meringue Soufflé With Berry Sauce

(pictured, pages 44 and 45)

Berry Sauce (recipe follows)
1¼ cups sugar
2 large eggs, separated
1 tablespoon cornstarch
1 teaspoon grated lemon peel
4 large egg whites, at room
  temperature
¼ teaspoon cream of tartar

1. Make Berry Sauce.

2. Preheat oven to 400°F. Line baking sheet with aluminum foil; lightly grease and sprinkle with 2 tablespoons sugar.

3. In medium bowl, whisk egg yolks, 2 tablespoons sugar, the cornstarch and lemon peel until frothy; set aside. In medium bowl, with electric mixer at high speed, beat 2

egg whites until foamy; gradually add ¼ cup sugar until stiff peaks form. Fold whites into yolk mixture; set soufflé mixture aside.

4. In bowl, at high speed, beat 4 egg whites and cream of tartar until foamy. Gradually add remaining ¾ cup sugar until stiff, moist peaks form. Place in pastry bag fitted with ½-inch star or plain tip.

5. Pipe meringue on prepared baking sheet in an 8-by-5-inch oval, filling in the center. Pipe three rows of meringue around top edge of oval; pipe two or three layers meringue on top of each row to make side 3 inches high. (If side starts to fall, support with wooden picks.) Pipe shell pattern around top and bottom of oval; quickly fill center with prepared soufflé mixture. Bake 12 minutes, or until meringue is golden. (Center mixture will be soft and runny.) Serve immediately with Berry Sauce.

Makes 6 servings.

Berry Sauce

2 packages (10 ounces each)
  frozen strawberries in heavy
  syrup, thawed
¼ cup seedless raspberry jam
2 tablespoons cassis
  (black currant liqueur)
2 tablespoons cornstarch
1 cup coarsely chopped fresh
  strawberries

1. In medium saucepan, combine thawed strawberries and syrup, jam, liqueur and cornstarch; stir until cornstarch is dissolved. Bring to boiling, stirring; cook 1 minute, or until slightly thickened.

2. Stir in chopped strawberries; refrigerate until cool. (May be made a day ahead.)

Makes 1½ cups.

■ Bake and freeze cream-puff shells to fill later with small, pop-top cans of vanilla pudding.

Cappuccino Mousse on Chocolate Shell

(pictured, page 44)

2 packages (12 ounces each)
  chocolate-flavor melting
  candy wafers (4 cups)
2 envelopes unflavored gelatine
¾ cup cold water
6 large eggs, separated
1½ cups sugar
⅓ cup coffee-flavored liqueur
1 tablespoon instant-espresso-
  coffee powder
1 tablespoon unsweetened
  cocoa powder
½ teaspoon ground cinnamon
2 cups heavy cream, whipped
  until stiff

1. In top of double boiler, over hot, not boiling, water, melt 12 ounces candy wafers. (Or place in a glass bowl; cook in microwave on HIGH 1 minute; stir. Cook on HIGH 30 seconds longer, or until melted.) Pour into a 6-cup plastic shell mold or shallow plastic bowl. Swirl chocolate to coat bottom and side of mold evenly. Chill in refrigerator about 1 minute, or until partially set. Swirl chocolate again to build up coating on side of mold. Repeat as necessary until chocolate is no longer fluid. Refrigerate mold about 30 minutes, or until hardened completely (bottom of mold will look frosty). Carefully unmold by gently pressing around edges of shell. Place on plate. Repeat with remaining wafers to make lid.

2. Sprinkle gelatine over cold water in top of double boiler. Stir in egg yolks and ½ cup sugar. Cook over simmering water, stirring constantly, until gelatine and sugar dissolve and mixture thickens slightly. Remove from heat; stir in liqueur and next 3 ingredients. Pour into large bowl set over larger bowl of ice and water. Chill, stirring occasionally, 15 minutes, or until consistency of unbeaten egg whites.

3. In larger bowl, with electric mixer at high speed, beat egg whites until foamy. Gradually beat in remaining 1 cup sugar, beating at high speed until stiff peaks form. Fold meringue and whipped cream into gelatine mixture. Spoon into shell, mounding; refrigerate 2 hours, or until set. To serve, place lid askew on top of mold and mousse.

Makes 12 to 16 servings.

Apricot Bavarian

(pictured, page 44)

Jelly Roll (recipe follows)
1 can (15 ounces) apricot
  halves in heavy syrup
¾ cup milk
2 envelopes unflavored gelatine
¾ cup sugar
4 large eggs, separated
¼ cup apricot liqueur
¼ teaspoon salt
1½ cups heavy cream, whipped
  until stiff

1. Make Jelly Roll.

2. Drain apricots, reserving ⅔ cup syrup. Puree apricots in blender or food processor; set aside. Place milk in top of double boiler; sprinkle gelatine over milk. Let stand 5 minutes, or until softened. Stir in ½ cup sugar, the egg yolks and reserved apricot syrup. Over simmering water, cook until gelatine and sugar dissolve and mixture thickens slightly. Remove from heat; stir in apricot puree and liqueur. Transfer to large bowl set in large bowl of ice water. Chill, stirring occasionally, until consistency of unbeaten egg whites—15 minutes.

3. In large bowl, with electric mixer at high speed, beat egg whites and salt until foamy. Gradually beat in remaining ¼ cup sugar until stiff peaks form. Spoon about ½ cup meringue into apricot mixture. Fold in remaining meringue and whipped cream until well blended.

4. Line a 10-cup mold or bowl with aluminum foil; butter foil. Cut Jelly Roll into ¼-inch slices. Line bottom and side of mold with slices, placed together without gaps. Spoon Bavarian mixture into mold; place leftover cake slices on top. Cover with plastic wrap; refrigerate several hours or overnight, until firm.

5. Remove plastic; invert onto plate. Remove foil. If desired, garnish with additional whipped cream, strawberries and mint.

Makes 12 servings.

Jelly Roll

5 large eggs, separated
1 teaspoon vanilla extract
⅓ cup granulated sugar
¼ teaspoon cream of tartar
½ teaspoon salt
⅓ cup unsifted all-purpose
  flour
⅓ cup cornstarch
Confectioners' sugar
¾ cup apricot preserves

1. Preheat oven to 375°F. Grease a 15½-by-10½-by-1-inch jelly-roll pan. Line pan with waxed paper; grease paper. In bowl, with electric mixer at medium-high speed, beat egg yolks, vanilla and 2 tablespoons granulated sugar about 5 minutes, or until thick and pale. In large bowl, at high speed, beat egg whites, cream of tartar and salt until foamy. Gradually beat in remaining granulated sugar until stiff peaks form. Stir about ½ cup meringue into egg-yolk mixture. Fold egg-yolk mixture into meringue. Sift flour and cornstarch over all; gently fold in until blended. Spread into pan; bake 12 minutes, or until toothpick inserted in center comes out clean.

2. Sift confectioners' sugar generously onto a towel. Loosen edges of cake; invert onto towel. Carefully remove waxed paper. With help of towel, roll up cake from long side. Place on wire rack; cool.

3. Carefully unroll cake. Spread preserves evenly over cake; carefully reroll without towel. Wrap with plastic wrap.

Makes 1 jelly roll.

Lite Eating: Luscious Low-Calorie Desserts

Fruit-Filled Meringue

¾ cup sugar
8 large egg whites, at room
temperature
¼ teaspoon cream of tartar
½ teaspoon almond extract
2 cups assorted fruit: kiwifruit,
grapes, peach slices and
raspberries
1 package (10 ounces) frozen
strawberries in light syrup,
pureed
1 tablespoon brandy

1. Preheat oven to 250°F. Line a baking sheet with aluminum foil; lightly grease. Sprinkle with 1 tablespoon sugar. In bowl, with electric mixer at high speed, beat egg whites, cream of tartar and almond extract until foamy. Gradually beat in remaining sugar until stiff peaks form. Fill pastry bag fitted with ½-inch star tip. Pipe 9-inch square; fill center. Pipe on edge to form rim. Bake 1 hour; turn off oven. Keep in oven 1½ hours or overnight.

2. Place on plate; arrange fruit inside. In pan, heat strawberries and brandy; serve with meringue.

Makes 8 servings; 135 calories each serving.

Raspberry-Drizzled Angel Cake

1 package (about 16 ounces)
angel-food cake mix
2 packages (3 ounces each)
reduced-calorie
raspberry-flavored gelatin
1 cup boiling water
1 cup cold water
2 cups nondairy whipped
topping
¾ cup confectioners' sugar
1 teaspoon grated lime peel
1 to 2 tablespoons lime juice

1. Bake cake as package label directs; cool. Cut in half horizontally. Place layers, cut side up, on baking sheet. With fork, prick at ½-inch intervals.

2. In medium bowl, combine gelatin and boiling water; add cold water. Pour 1½ cups gelatin into 8-inch square pan; refrigerate until firm. Spoon remaining gelatin over layers; refrigerate.

3. Place one layer, cut side up, on serving plate. Cut gelatin in pan into ½-inch cubes. Fold into whipped topping. Spoon onto layer on serving plate; top with remaining layer, cut side down.

4. In small bowl, blend confectioners' sugar, peel, and just enough lime juice to make spoonable. Spread on top of cake; garnish with lime slices, if desired.

Makes 16 servings; 166 calories each serving.

Strawberry-Chocolate Roll

4 large eggs, separated
Dash salt
½ cup sugar
½ cup self-rising cake flour
Unsweetened cocoa powder
1½ cups coarsely chopped
strawberries
1½ cups nondairy whipped
topping

1. Preheat oven to 325° F. Line a 15-by-10-by-½-inch pan with waxed paper. In bowl, with electric mixer at high speed, beat egg whites and salt until soft peaks form. Gradually beat in 6 tablespoons sugar until stiff peaks form; set aside.

2. In bowl, with electric mixer at medium-high speed, beat egg yolks and remaining 2 tablespoons sugar 5

minutes, or until thick. Fold in egg whites. Sift flour and 2 tablespoons cocoa powder over egg mixture; gently fold until blended. Spread in prepared pan. Bake 30 minutes, or until cake springs back when touched. Sprinkle cocoa onto kitchen towel; invert cake onto towel. Remove waxed paper; with aid of towel, roll up cake from long side. Cool on wire rack.

3. In bowl, fold berries into topping. Unroll cake; spread with strawberry cream; reroll without towel. Place cake on serving plate. If desired, sprinkle confectioners' sugar on top; decorate with additional topping and strawberry halves.

Makes 14 servings; 116 calories each serving.

Quick & Easy: All-Season Desserts

Quick Cassata

1 package (1 pound) frozen
   pound cake
2 cups ricotta cheese
½ cup mini semisweet-
   chocolate pieces
2 tablespoons almond-flavored
   liqueur
2 tablespoons confectioners'
   sugar
¼ cup seedless raspberry jam
1 tablespoon instant
   espresso-coffee powder
1 package (8 ounces) nondairy
   whipped topping
Sliced almonds
Crushed bittersweet almond-
   flavored Italian cookies

1. With long knife, cut frozen cake in four layers. In medium bowl, combine ricotta, chocolate pieces, liqueur and sugar.

2. Spread 1 tablespoon jam on one cut side of each layer. Place one layer on serving dish, jam side up. Cover jam with one-third of cheese mixture; top with another cake layer, jam side up. Repeat layering cheese mixture and cake, ending with cake layer, jam side down.

3. Stir coffee powder into whipped topping until blended. Frost sides and top of cake; garnish with sliced almonds and crushed cookies. Refrigerate cake until serving time.

Makes 12 servings.

Piña-Colada Tarts

1 cup sour cream
¼ cup crushed pineapple
¼ cup cream of coconut
2 tablespoons confectioners'
   sugar
2 tablespoons white rum
1 package (4 ounces) prepared
   graham-cracker tart shells (6)
½ cup flaked coconut, toasted
⅓ cup chopped toasted pecans

1. In medium bowl, combine sour cream, pineapple, cream of coconut, sugar and rum; mix well.

2. Carefully spoon about ¼ cup pineapple mixture into each tart shell. Top with coconut and pecans. Freeze until firm—about 1½ hours. If desired, garnish with pineapple chunks, mandarin oranges and mint.

Makes 6 servings.

Strawberries 'n' Cream Tart

1 package (17¼ ounces) frozen puff pastry, thawed
1 large egg, beaten
1 package (3½ ounces) vanilla-flavored instant-pudding-and-pie-filling mix
1 cup sour cream
¾ cup milk
2 tablespoons orange-flavored liqueur
1 tablespoon grated orange peel
½ cup nondairy whipped topping
1 cup thinly sliced strawberries
½ cup strawberry jelly, melted

1. Preheat oven to 375°F. On lightly floured surface, roll 1 sheet pastry to 12-by-10-inch rectangle. Cut lengthwise in half. Lightly brush surface of one half with beaten egg; place remaining half on top. Prick with fork; brush with egg. Roll remaining sheet into 12-by-10-inch rectangle; cut 12 (12-by-½-inch) strips. Form strips into four braids; attach ends. Place braid around edge of pastry. Using wooden picks, prop braids up. Bake 15 minutes, or until golden. Cool on wire rack.

2. In medium bowl, whisk pudding mix and next 4 ingredients until smooth. Fold in whipped topping. Spoon into pastry tart. Arrange strawberry slices, slightly overlapping, on top; brush with melted jelly. Refrigerate at least 1 hour. Garnish with mint, if desired.

Makes 12 servings.

■ Need whipped cream for a dessert but have none on hand? Don't panic. Instead, try this nifty trick: Beat one ripe banana with one to two egg whites until thick. Then spread generously over your favorite sweet treats and serve. Your family will think you are wonderfully creative!

Micro-Way: Luscious Cakes

Coconut-Lime Cake

2 packages (8.6 ounces each)
  microwave lemon- or
  yellow-cake mix
¼ cup cornstarch
1 tablespoon all-purpose flour
¾ cup sugar
¾ cup water
2 large egg yolks
1 tablespoon grated lime peel
⅓ cup lime juice
1 cup heavy cream
1 cup flaked coconut
Lime slices

1. Prepare cakes as package label
directs; remove from pans onto wire
racks, and cool completely.

2. In medium glass bowl, combine cornstarch, flour and sugar; mix
well. Gradually stir in water until
smooth. Cook on HIGH 4 minutes,
or until thickened and clear, stirring
after 2 minutes. Stir in egg yolks
until smooth. Gradually add peel
and juice. Place plastic wrap directly
on surface; refrigerate until completely cooled.

3. Cut each cake in half horizontally. In small bowl, with electric
mixer, beat heavy cream until stiff.
Fold ⅓ cup whipped cream into
lime mixture.

4. Place one cake layer, top side
down, on cake plate. Spread cut side
with ½ cup lime filling. Repeat with
remaining cake layers and filling;
place top layer right side up. Frost
side and top of cake with remaining
whipped cream. Sprinkle side and
top with coconut; garnish top of
cake with lime slices.
  Makes 12 servings.

Banana-Rum Cake

1½ cups finely chopped
  walnuts
1½ cups unsifted all-purpose
  flour
1 teaspoon baking powder
1 teaspoon baking soda
¼ teaspoon salt
¾ cup (1½ sticks) butter or
  margarine
1½ cups granulated sugar
3 large eggs
1 cup sour cream
1 cup mashed bananas
  (2 medium)
5 tablespoons rum
1 teaspoon vanilla extract
½ cup raisins
2 tablespoons butter or
  margarine
1 cup confectioners' sugar
1 to 2 tablespoons water

1. Grease a 12-cup microwave-
safe Bundt pan; sprinkle with ½ cup
nuts; set aside. On sheet of waxed
paper, combine flour, baking powder, soda and salt; mix well.

2. In large bowl of electric mixer,
cream ¾ cup butter and the granulated sugar. Beat in eggs, one at a
time, until light and fluffy. Beat in
sour cream, bananas, ¼ cup rum
and the vanilla. On low speed, beat
in flour mixture until blended. Stir
in raisins and remaining nuts. Spread
evenly in prepared pan.

3. Place pan on inverted microwave-safe cereal bowl; cook on ME-
DIUM 15 minutes, rotating quarter
turn every 5 minutes. Cook on
HIGH 5 minutes, rotating after 2

minutes. Let stand on counter 15 minutes. Invert onto serving plate.

4. In small glass bowl, melt 2 tablespoons butter on HIGH 1 minute. Stir in confectioners' sugar, remaining 1 tablespoon rum and the water until spoonable. Drizzle over cooled cake. Garnish with galax leaves and fresh orange slices, if desired.

Makes 12 to 16 servings.

Glazed Mocha Gâteau

1 cup unsifted all-purpose flour
1 teaspoon baking powder
¼ teaspoon salt
1 cup sugar
½ cup unsweetened cocoa powder
2 teaspoons instant-coffee powder
¾ cup milk
¾ cup (1½ sticks) butter or margarine, cut in pieces
1 large egg
3 squares (1 ounce each) semisweet chocolate, finely chopped
½ cup heavy cream
Fresh strawberries
Chopped nuts

1. Grease microwave-safe, 8½-inch round baking dish. Line bottom with two rounds of waxed paper; set aside. On sheet of waxed paper, combine flour, baking powder and salt; mix well.

2. In large glass bowl, combine sugar, cocoa powder and coffee powder; mix well. Gradually stir in milk; add butter. Cook on HIGH 2 minutes, or until butter melts. Whisk in egg; stir in flour mixture until smooth. Spread evenly in prepared dish; place on inverted microwave-safe cereal bowl.

Note: Recipes were tested in 600- to 700-watt microwave ovens.

3. Cook on MEDIUM 8 minutes, rotating quarter turn after 4 minutes. Cook on HIGH 2 minutes, or until center is set. (Top may still be moist in some places; it will dry on standing.) Let stand 5 minutes. Invert onto 8-inch cardboard round.

4. In small glass bowl, cook chopped chocolate and cream on MEDIUM 3 minutes, stirring once. Continue stirring until chocolate is melted and mixture is smooth; let cool slightly.

5. Dip strawberries in chocolate glaze; place on waxed-paper-lined tray. Place cake on wire rack; pour remaining glaze over top and down side. Coat side with nuts; garnish with chocolate-dipped strawberries.

Makes 8 servings.

Apple Kuchen

1¼ cups unsifted all-purpose flour
½ cup sugar
1½ teaspoons baking powder
¼ teaspoon salt
½ cup (1 stick) butter or margarine
1 large egg
¼ cup milk
1 teaspoon vanilla extract
1½ pounds Granny Smith apples
1 teaspoon ground cinnamon
⅓ cup peach preserves
Mint sprig
Whipped cream

1. Grease microwave-safe, apple-shape cake dish or 13-by-9-by-2-inch baking dish. In medium bowl, combine flour, ¼ cup sugar, the baking powder and salt; mix well. With pastry blender or two knives, cut in ¼ cup butter until coarse crumbs form. With fork, stir in egg, milk and vanilla just until dough sticks together. Spread dough evenly in prepared pan.

2. Pare and core apples; thinly slice. Arrange slices in concentric circles on top of dough. In small glass bowl, cook remaining butter on HIGH 1 minute; stir in cinnamon and remaining ¼ cup sugar. Brush over apple slices.

3. Cook on MEDIUM 10 minutes, rotating a quarter turn after 5 minutes. Cook on HIGH 5 minutes. Let stand on counter 5 minutes. In small glass bowl, cook preserves on HIGH 2 minutes, or until melted. Brush over top of kuchen. Garnish with mint; serve with whipped cream.

Makes 8 servings.

■ To test whether a dish or utensil is microwave-safe, place it in the microwave and cook on HIGH for 15 seconds. If the dish or utensil is very warm to the touch, it should not be used in the microwave oven.

April

Our simple but superb recipes show off chicken's versatility. The sampling below gives a clue to the wide range of dishes in this chapter. The feast starts with luscious apricot-glazed Cornish hens and then offers chicken that's been roasted, chopped, sauced, or stuffed—all in savory new ways!

Glazed Cornish Hens With Pineapple Chutney

Chili-Cheese Chicken in Black-Bean Sauce

Seafood-Filled Roast Chicken

Jumbo Chicken Ravioli With Parsley Sauce

Chicken Liver Frittata

Ham-Stuffed Chicken Wings

Mexican Chicken in Baked Tortilla Basket

Apple-Brandy Chicken

Chicken Moussaka in Phyllo

Cheese-Stuffed Chicken Breasts With Sopapillas

Creamy Asparagus-and-Chicken Soup

Chicken Cookbook

Irresistible chicken dishes to savor—some with an international flair! Try our ravioli or moussaka or our chicken tossed in a salad and served in a Mexican tortilla.

Glazed Cornish Hens With Pineapple Chutney
(pictured, page 59)

2 Cornish hens, halved (1½ pounds each)
½ teaspoon salt
¼ teaspoon pepper
½ cup apricot preserves
1 tablespoon apricot liqueur or water
Pineapple Chutney (recipe follows)

1. Preheat oven to 375°F. Place hens, skin side up, in roasting pan; sprinkle with salt and pepper. In small saucepan, heat preserves and

---

Page 59: Glazed Cornish Hens With Pineapple Chutney.

Pages 60 and 61: (Clockwise from top right) Seafood-Filled Roast Chicken, Jumbo Chicken Ravioli With Parsley Sauce, Chicken Liver Frittata, Ham-Stuffed Chicken Wings, Chili-Cheese Chicken in Black-Bean Sauce.

Pages 62 and 63: (Clockwise from top center) Mexican Chicken in Baked Tortilla Basket, Apple-Brandy Chicken, Chicken Moussaka in Phyllo, Cheese-Stuffed Chicken Breasts With Sopapillas, Creamy Asparagus-and-Chicken Soup.

liqueur until melted. Brush mixture on hens. Roast, basting with pan juices every 15 minutes, 45 minutes, or until tender.

2. Make Pineapple Chutney.

3. Place hens on warm serving platter. Serve with sugar snap peas, and garnish with red-onion flowers, if desired. Serve chutney warm or cold with roasted hens.

Makes 4 to 6 servings.

Pineapple Chutney

1 cup cider vinegar
1 cup firmly packed light-brown sugar
¼ cup pared and thinly sliced ginger root
1 tablespoon mustard seeds
⅛ teaspoon crushed red-pepper flakes
½ teaspoon salt
1 fresh pineapple, cored and cut in 1-inch pieces (4 cups)
½ cup golden raisins
2 red onions, cut in ½-inch wedges
1 red pepper, cut in 1-inch pieces

In 5-quart Dutch oven, combine first 6 ingredients. Bring to boiling; simmer, uncovered, 5 minutes. Add pineapple and raisins. Cook over medium-high heat 20 minutes, or until thick and syrupy. Add onions and red pepper; simmer 10 minutes, or until thick. Serve warm or cold.

Makes about 8 cups.

Chicken Liver Frittata
(pictured, page 60)

¼ pound bacon, chopped
1 pound chicken livers, washed and halved
¼ cup anise-flavored liqueur
1 teaspoon cornstarch
½ teaspoon salt
⅛ teaspoon pepper
¼ teaspoon crushed anise seeds
8 large eggs
½ cup crème fraîche or sour cream
¼ pound asparagus, cut in 2-inch pieces
½ cup chopped red pepper

1. In 10-inch, nonstick skillet, cook bacon until crisp. Remove bacon and all but 2 tablespoons drippings; reserve bacon and remaining drippings. Add livers to skillet; sauté about 5 minutes, or until just pink inside. Mix liqueur with cornstarch, ¼ teaspoon salt, the pepper and anise. Pour over livers. Bring to boiling, stirring constantly. Cook 1 to 2 minutes, or until thickened; remove. Clean skillet.

2. In bowl, beat eggs, crème fraîche and remaining ¼ teaspoon salt. Heat reserved drippings in skillet. Add egg mixture; cook, stirring gently, until partially set on bottom. Place livers in center of omelet. Arrange last 2 ingredients around livers. Sprinkle with reserved bacon. Cover; cook over medium-low heat 10 minutes, or until top is set.

Makes 4 to 6 servings.

Seafood-Filled Roast Chicken

(pictured, page 61)

2 pounds (24 to 30) large fresh
   mussels
1 cup white wine
2 tablespoons salad oil
¼ cup (½ stick) butter or
   margarine
2 large onions, chopped
3 medium celery stalks, thinly
   sliced
1 package (8 ounces)
   cornbread-stuffing mix
½ cup water
2 large tomatoes, coarsely
   chopped
¼ cup chopped parsley
1 teaspoon dried thyme leaves
½ teaspoon salt
⅛ teaspoon pepper
7- to 8- pound roasting chicken
3 tablespoons all-purpose flour
1 can (about 14 ounces)
   chicken broth

1. Check mussels; discard any not tightly closed. With brush, scrub mussels to remove sand. With scissors, remove and discard "beard." Place mussels in large bowl; cover with cold water. Let stand 30 minutes. Drain and rinse well. In a large skillet, over high heat, steam mussels in wine 4 minutes, or until they open. Remove from heat; cool. Set aside 12 mussels for garnish; keep covered. Remove and discard shells from remaining mussels. Toss mussels in oil. Set aside.

2. In medium skillet, over medium-high heat, melt butter. Add half of onion and half of celery; sauté 3 minutes. Stir in mussels, stuffing mix, water, 1 chopped tomato and next 4 ingredients.

3. Preheat oven to 350°F. Spoon some stuffing in neck cavity. Bring neck skin over stuffing; secure with poultry pins. Spoon remaining stuffing into body cavity—do not pack. Place any extra stuffing in baking dish; cover, and bake during last 30 minutes of baking time. Close body cavity with poultry pins; lace with string and tie legs together. Scatter remaining half of chopped onion and sliced celery in bottom of roasting pan, and place chicken on top. Roast 2 hours, or until chicken is golden and meat thermometer registers 170°F.

4. Place chicken on heated platter and remove pins and laces; keep warm. Strain pan drippings into bowl; discard vegetables. Skim off all but 2 tablespoons fat; return drippings to pan. Stir in flour until smooth. Whisk in chicken broth; boil 3 minutes, stirring constantly until thickened and smooth. Arrange reserved mussels-in-shell around chicken. Garnish with remaining chopped tomato. Serve with gravy.

Makes 8 servings.

Jumbo Chicken Ravioli With Parsley Sauce

(pictured, page 61)

Parsley Sauce (recipe follows)
6 boneless chicken thighs (1½
   pounds), coarsely chopped
1 cup coarsely chopped ham
1 package (8 ounces)
   mozzarella cheese, coarsely
   chopped
¼ cup fresh basil or 1
   teaspoon dried basil leaves
¼ teaspooon dried sage leaves
½ cup pine nuts, chopped
1 package (16 ounces) egg-roll
   wrappers (24)
2 large egg yolks, slightly
   beaten

1. Make Parsley Sauce; keep sauce warm.

2. In food processor, finely chop chicken, ham and cheese, half at a time. Place in large bowl. Add basil, sage and pine nuts; mix well.

3. Spoon rounded ⅓ cup chicken filling onto center of each of 12 egg-roll wrappers; spread to within 1 inch of edge. Brush beaten egg yolk over exposed portion of wrappers; cover with another wrapper. Press edges to seal. Using pastry wheel, trim off ½ inch from wrapper edges.

4. In large skillet, bring 2 inches salted water to boiling. Cook ravioli, two at a time, for 3 minutes. With slotted spoon or spatula, remove ravioli to heated casserole. Cover; keep warm. Spoon Parsley Sauce over ravioli. If desired, sprinkle with shredded Parmesan cheese and toasted pine nuts.

Makes 6 servings.

Parsley Sauce

¼ cup unsifted all-purpose
   flour
1 cup milk
1 cup (10½ ounces) condensed
   chicken broth
1 large clove garlic, crushed
¾ cup parsley leaves
¼ cup grated Parmesan cheese
⅛ teaspoon pepper
Dash ground nutmeg

1. In medium saucepan, whisk flour into milk. Stir in broth and garlic. Bring to boiling, stirring constantly; boil 1 minute, until thickened and smooth.

2. In food processor, puree parsley with ½ cup white sauce. Stir puree, Parmesan, pepper and nutmeg into remaining white sauce. Cook over low heat 1 minute.

Makes 2¼ cups sauce.

Chili-Cheese Chicken in Black-Bean Sauce

(pictured, page 60)

4 large whole chicken breasts, halved (4 pounds)
1½ cups (6 ounces) shredded fontina or Monterey Jack cheese
1 cup fresh bread crumbs (about 3 slices)
1 can (4 ounces) chopped green chiles
¼ cup slivered almonds
1¼ teaspoons chili powder
¼ teaspoon salt
⅛ teaspoon pepper
Cooked rice
Black-Bean Sauce (recipe follows)

1. Preheat oven to 350°F. With sharp knife, cut a deep pocket the length of each chicken-breast half between tenderloin and top portion of meat.

2. In medium bowl, mix cheese, bread crumbs, chiles, almonds and ½ teaspoon chili powder until combined. Spoon about ¼ cup filling into each pocket; secure with metal skewers or wooden picks.

3. Place chicken in shallow roasting pan; sprinkle with remaining chili powder, the salt and pepper. Roast 30 minutes; if crisp skin is desired, broil 3 minutes longer.

4. Make Black-Bean Sauce.

5. Remove skewers; place chicken on bed of cooked rice. Spoon some of Black-Bean Sauce over chicken; serve remaining sauce with chicken. If desired, garnish platter with lime wedge and sprig of cilantro (fresh coriander).

Makes 6 servings.

■ For an easier job of shredding soft cheeses such as Monterey Jack or mozzarella, place the cheese in freezer until it is firm but knife can still be inserted in center of cheese.

Black-Bean Sauce

2 tablespoons salad oil
2 cups 1-inch-wide slices red, green and yellow peppers
2 medium cloves garlic, crushed
1 can (15 ounces) black beans, undrained
2 tablespoons minced cilantro (fresh coriander) leaves
½ cup chicken broth
1 tablespoon cornstarch

In large skillet, heat oil. Add peppers and garlic; sauté 5 minutes. Stir in beans and cilantro. In measuring cup, blend broth with cornstarch. Add to skillet. Bring to boiling, stirring constantly; simmer 1 minute, until thickened and smooth.

Makes about 4 cups sauce.

Ham-Stuffed Chicken Wings

(pictured, page 60)

16 to 20 chicken wings (3 pounds)
¼ pound boiled ham, coarsely chopped
1 package (3 ounces) cream cheese, softened
2 green onions, coarsely chopped
2 tablespoons cilantro (fresh coriander) leaves
½ cup chopped, seeded, pared cucumber
½ teaspoon paprika
¼ teaspoon salt
⅛ teaspoon pepper

1. Loosen skin and meat around bones to form pockets in chicken wings; set aside.

2. Place ham, cream cheese, green onions and cilantro in container of food processor. Process on high about 30 seconds, or until pureed. Stir in cucumber. Spoon mixture in a pastry bag fitted with a ½-inch plain tip.

3. Preheat broiler. Pipe about 1 tablespoon ham mixture into pocket of each chicken wing. Bring wing tip over end, securing filling. Place in shallow roasting pan. Sprinkle with paprika, salt and pepper. Broil 6 inches from heat, 5 minutes. Reduce oven temperature to 375°F. Roast for 15 minutes, or until the chicken wings are done.

Makes 8 servings.

Mexican Chicken in Baked Tortilla Basket

(pictured, pages 62 and 63)

Salad oil
2 packages (12½ ounces each) 8-inch flour tortillas
Water
2 large heads Boston lettuce, washed and crisped
1 large ripe avocado
2 tablespoons lemon juice
1 large cucumber, unpared
1 jar (6 ounces) marinated artichoke hearts
¼ cup prepared chili sauce
1 tablespoon picante or taco sauce
½ teaspoon ground cumin
2 cups 2-inch strips cooked chicken
2 ripe tomatoes, cut in wedges
½ cup ripe pitted olives
½ red onion, cut crosswise into rings

1. Brush a large baking sheet with oil. Invert a 3-quart metal bowl onto sheet; cover outside of bowl with aluminum foil. Brush foil with oil. Preheat oven to 350°F.

2. Brush both sides of a tortilla with water and then oil. Place over side of prepared bowl, extending half of tortilla over baking sheet. Repeat with enough tortillas to cover side of bowl; with hands, press tortillas firmly to attach to one another. Brush and attach additional tortillas to cover curve of bowl. Bake tortilla basket 25 to 30 minutes, turning

baking sheet a half-turn once during baking. Loosely cover with foil if browning unevenly.

3. Cool basket completely on baking sheet. Invert serving platter over basket; gently invert baking sheet to place basket on platter. Remove baking sheet, bowl and foil. Line basket with lettuce leaves.

4. Pare, seed and cut avocado in ½-inch-thick slices. Place in small bowl; toss with lemon juice; set aside. With fork, score peel of cucumber all around lengthwise; cut crosswise into thin rounds.

5. In large bowl, drain marinade from artichoke hearts; add chili sauce, picante sauce and cumin to marinade; mix well. Add artichoke hearts, cucumber and remaining ingredients; toss to coat well with dressing. Add avocado; toss again. Fill basket with mixture; serve immediately, breaking off pieces of basket to serve with each portion.

Makes 8 servings.

Apple-Brandy Chicken
(pictured, page 63)

2 tablespoons butter or margarine
2 tablespoons salad oil
1 (3½- to 4-pound) chicken, cut in 8 pieces
½ teaspoon salt
¼ teaspoon pepper
½ pound mushrooms, quartered
2 medium leeks, coarsely chopped
1 can (about 14 ounces) chicken broth
¼ cup apple-flavored brandy
½ pound medium shrimp, shelled, tail section intact
1 unpared Granny Smith apple, cored and cut in ¼-inch wedges
1 tablespoon lemon juice
2 tablespoons cornstarch

1. In large skillet, over medium-high heat, melt butter in oil. Sprinkle chicken with salt and pepper. Brown chicken pieces, half at a time, on both sides—about 10 minutes. Remove to platter as they brown.

2. Remove all but 2 tablespoons drippings. Add mushrooms and leeks; sauté 3 minutes. Add 1½ cups chicken broth and the brandy, stirring to loosen brown bits. Return chicken to skillet; bring to boiling. Reduce heat; simmer, covered, 20 minutes. Add shrimp, apple and lemon juice; cook, covered, 3 minutes longer, or until tender.

3. In bowl, blend remaining chicken broth with cornstarch. Stir into liquid in skillet. Bring to boiling, stirring constantly. Cook 1 minute, or until sauce is thickened and smooth.

Makes 4 servings.

Chicken Moussaka in Phyllo
(pictured, page 63)

6 tablespoons salad oil
1 pound boneless chicken breasts, skinned and cut in ½-inch pieces
1 medium eggplant, cut in ½-inch cubes
1 medium onion, chopped
2 medium cloves garlic, crushed
1 cup (6 ounces) crumbled feta cheese
½ cup minced parsley
¼ cup pine nuts
1 teaspoon dried oregano leaves
½ teaspoon salt
¼ teaspoon pepper
½ cup (1 stick) butter or margarine
2 tablespoons all-purpose flour
1 cup milk
2 large egg yolks
6 sheets (15 by 10 inches) phyllo dough

1. In large skillet, heat 2 tablespoons oil over medium heat; cook chicken 5 minutes, or until golden-brown. Transfer to bowl. Heat remaining ¼ cup oil; add eggplant, onion and garlic; cook 5 minutes, or until eggplant is tender. Stir in cheese, parsley, nuts, oregano, salt and pepper. Return chicken to skillet; keep warm.

2. Make sauce: In medium saucepan, melt 2 tablespoons butter; blend in flour. Gradually add milk; cook, stirring constantly, until thickened. In small bowl, quickly whisk some of the hot-milk mixture into egg yolks. Return all to saucepan; mix well. Set aside.

3. Preheat oven to 350°F. Assemble crust: Work with one pastry sheet at a time, keeping remaining sheets covered with plastic wrap to prevent drying out. Brush one pastry sheet with melted butter; fold in half crosswise. With short side of pastry facing you, place folded pastry in a 9-inch pie plate, leaving 5 inches of dough hanging over one side of dish. Fold over edge; bunch dough to form a rim. Brush with butter. Repeat with remaining pastry sheets, overlapping each sheet slightly.

4. Spoon chicken mixture into prepared phyllo crust. Pour sauce over mixture at edge of dish. Bake 25 minutes, or until pastry is golden-brown. Let stand 10 minutes before serving. If desired, garnish with tomato rose and parsley leaves.

Makes 6 to 8 servings.

■ To make a tomato rose, cut a ½-inch-wide strip of skin from a firm red tomato. The longer you make the strip the bigger your rose will be. Starting in center, wrap strip, skin side at bottom, with toothpick. Arrange with cucumber peel leaves. Refrigerate, covered with damp towel.

Cheese-Stuffed Chicken Breasts With Sopapillas

(pictured, page 62)

½ cup chopped parsley
⅓ cup chopped cilantro (fresh coriander) leaves
¼ cup shredded Monterey Jack cheese
¼ cup ricotta cheese
1 tablespoon grated Parmesan cheese
1 large clove garlic, crushed
4 chicken breast halves (8 ounces each)
½ cup apple jelly
¼ cup lime juice
Sopapillas (recipe follows)

1. Preheat oven to 375°F. In small bowl, combine parsley, ¼ cup cilantro, the cheeses and garlic.

2. With fingers, make a 1-inch pocket on rounded side of each chicken breast by carefully loosening skin. Spoon 2 rounded tablespoons filling into each pocket. Place chicken, skin side up, in roasting pan. Roast 25 minutes, or until tender and golden. (If desired, broil 2 minutes for crisp skin.)

3. In small saucepan, melt apple jelly; add lime juice and remaining cilantro. Brush over chicken. If desired, garnish with cilantro. Serve with Sopapillas.

Makes 4 servings.

Sopapillas

2 cups unsifted all-purpose flour
¾ teaspoon baking powder
1 teaspoon salt
½ teaspoon sugar
½ cup warm water
2 tablespoons salad oil
2 tablespoons milk
Oil for frying

1. In medium bowl, combine flour, baking powder, salt and sugar. With wooden spoon, stir in water, oil and milk until mixture forms a dough. Turn out onto lightly floured surface; knead 3 minutes, or until smooth. Cover dough with bowl; let rest 15 minutes.

2. In deep-fat fryer or large saucepan, heat 2 inches oil to 375°F. Divide dough into eight equal pieces. On lightly floured surface, roll each into a 5-inch round. Fry sopapillas, two at a time, 30 seconds. Turn; fry until golden. Drain on paper towels; serve warm.

Makes 8 servings.

Creamy Asparagus- and-Chicken Soup

(pictured, page 62)

2 whole chicken breasts (about 1¾ pounds)
1 medium onion, quartered
2 large celery stalks, cut up
3 cups water
1½ teaspoons salt
¼ teaspoon pepper
1½ pounds asparagus
2 cups half-and-half
2 tablespoons butter or margarine
2 tablespoons chopped parsley

1. In 3-quart saucepan, combine chicken, onion, celery, water, salt and pepper. Bring to boiling; simmer, covered, 20 minutes. Remove chicken, reserving broth; cool slightly. Remove and discard bones and skin; cut meat into thin strips.

2. Remove tough ends of asparagus stalks. Using vegetable peeler, scrape skin and scales from lower part of stalk only. Cut asparagus into 2-inch pieces; add to reserved chicken broth. Bring to boiling; simmer, covered, 10 minutes. Remove saucepan from heat.

3. In food processor or blender, puree asparagus-broth mixture, one-third at a time. Return puree to saucepan. Stir in chicken breast strips, half-and-half and butter. Continue to cook until heated through—5 minutes. Sprinkle with parsley.

Makes 4 servings.

Castilian Chicken

¼ cup unsifted all-purpose flour
½ teaspoon salt
⅛ teaspoon freshly ground pepper
8 chicken thighs, washed and patted dry
2 tablespoons salad oil
1 medium onion, chopped
1 medium tomato, chopped
½ cup water
1 cup raisins
½ cup sliced pimiento-stuffed olives
½ cup sherry
3-inch stick cinnamon
Cooked rice

1. On waxed paper, combine flour, salt and pepper. Dredge chicken in flour mixture; shake off excess.

2. In large skillet, heat oil over medium heat. Brown chicken on all sides—9 minutes in all. Remove; drain on paper towels. Pour off all but 1 tablespoon drippings. Add onion and tomato; sauté 3 minutes, or until onion is tender.

3. Return chicken to pan; add water, raisins, olives, sherry and cinnamon stick. Cover; simmer for 30 minutes, or until the chicken is tender. Remove and discard cinnamon stick; serve chicken over rice.

Makes 4 servings.

■ Allow a roasted chicken to stand 10 minutes before carving to keep chicken from losing its internal juices. Be sure to cover the chicken loosely with foil to keep warm.

Stuffed Grape Leaves

½ pound boneless chicken breasts, skinned
½ cup chopped walnuts
¼ cup uncooked long-grain rice
¼ cup currants
⅓ cup minced mint leaves
2 tablespoons minced parsley
1½ teaspoons grated lemon peel
¼ teaspoon ground allspice
2¼ cups chicken broth or water
1 jar (16 ounces) grape leaves
¼ cup olive oil
¼ cup lemon juice

1. In food processor, finely chop chicken; transfer to medium bowl. Add walnuts, rice, currants, 2 tablespoons mint, the parsley, lemon peel, allspice and ¼ cup chicken broth; mix ingredients well.

2. Drain grape leaves; rinse in cold water, and pat dry. Place 1 leaf, shiny side down, on wooden board. Spoon 1 level tablespoon filling near base of leaf. Fold over sides of leaf to cover filling. Then roll up, jelly-roll fashion, to form a neat package. Repeat with remaining filling and about 20 leaves.

3. Place two to three unfilled leaves in bottom of 2-quart saucepan. Arrange a layer of stuffed leaves, seam side down, in bottom of pan, placing close together. Cover layer with several more unfilled leaves. Repeat layers. Cover top layer with more unfilled leaves. To prevent filled leaves from opening, set a plate over leaves, and weight with several cans. Pour remaining broth over leaves. Bring to boiling. Simmer, uncovered, 30 minutes, or until chicken and rice are cooked. Cool to room temperature; drain off liquid.

4. In shallow casserole, arrange stuffed grape leaves in single layer. In small bowl, whisk together oil, lemon juice and remaining mint; pour over grape leaves. Cover with plastic wrap; refrigerate several hours or overnight. If desired, serve stuffed leaves with remaining marinade or plain yogurt.

Makes about 20 stuffed leaves.

Almond-Coated Chicken Legs With Orange-Honey Sauce

1 cup toasted slivered almonds
¾ cup grated Parmesan cheese
1 teaspoon paprika
¾ teaspoon garlic powder
½ teaspoon salt
⅛ teaspoon ground red pepper
½ cup lemon juice
6 whole-leg quarters of chicken
Orange-Honey Sauce (recipe follows)

1. Preheat oven to 400°F. On waxed paper, combine first 6 ingredients; mix well. Pour lemon juice into pie plate.

2. Dip chicken into juice; coat with almond mixture. Place in ungreased jelly-roll pan; bake 45 minutes, or until fork-tender and golden-brown. Serve with Orange-Honey Sauce.

Makes 6 servings.

Orange-Honey Sauce

½ cup orange juice
¼ cup honey
3 tablespoons cider vinegar
3 tablespoons lemon juice
1 tablespoon grated orange peel
2 teaspoons cornstarch
½ teaspoon dry mustard
1 green onion, thinly sliced

In small saucepan, combine all ingredients except onion. Bring to boiling, stirring constantly; simmer 1 minute, or until slightly thickened and smooth. Stir in onion.

Makes ¾ cup.

Athenian Chicken Rolls

¾ cup (1½ sticks) butter or margarine
2 medium onions, finely chopped
1 celery stalk, finely chopped
2 cups chopped cooked chicken
1 cup chicken broth
2 tablespoons minced parsley
1 teaspoon dried oregano leaves
½ teaspoon salt
⅛ teaspoon pepper
½ pound feta cheese, crumbled
2 large eggs, beaten
12 sheets (15 by 10 inches) phyllo dough

1. In large skillet, over medium heat, melt 2 tablespoons butter; cook onions and celery 5 minutes, or until tender. Stir in next 6 ingredients. Cook 5 minutes, or until liquid is absorbed; stir in cheese. Cool completely; stir in eggs.

2. Preheat oven to 400°F. Melt remaining butter; with long side of one sheet of phyllo facing you, brush lightly with butter. Place another sheet of phyllo over first; lightly brush with butter. Repeat with four more sheets phyllo, using one-third of butter. Spread half of chicken mixture over length of one long side; roll up, jelly-roll fashion, beginning with filling side. Tuck in ends to enclose filling. Repeat with remaining phyllo, chicken mixture and one-third of butter.

3. Place rolls on large jelly-roll pan. Brush with remaining butter. Bake in top third of oven 30 minutes, or until browned and crisp. Cool slightly; cut in thick slices.

Makes 6 servings.

■ Does your recipe call for cubed cooked chicken or turkey? To measure, here's a good rule of thumb: One pound of boneless meat yields two cups cubed.

Lite Eating: Spring Chicken Favorites

Poultry Primavera

1 medium spaghetti squash
   (about 3 pounds)
¼ cup reduced-calorie
   margarine
1 pound boneless chicken
   breasts, skinned and
   cut in ½-inch strips
½ pound mushrooms, sliced
2 medium carrots, pared and
   thinly sliced
4 green onions, cut in
   2-inch pieces
½ pound snow pea pods
¼ cup all-purpose flour
2 cups skim milk
¼ cup grated Parmesan
   cheese
¼ cup chopped pimiento
½ teaspoon salt
⅛ teaspoon pepper

1. Preheat oven to 350°F. Cut squash in half lengthwise; discard seeds. Place halves, cut side down, in roasting pan. Add 1 inch water; cover with aluminum foil. Bake 45 minutes, or until tender.

2. In large skillet, over medium heat, melt margarine. Add chicken; sauté 3 minutes. Add mushrooms and carrots; sauté 3 minutes. Add green onions and snow peas; sauté 2 minutes. Stir in flour; gradually add milk. Cook, stirring constantly, until thickened and smooth. Stir in cheese, pimiento, salt and pepper.

3. With spoon, scrape squash lengthwise into strands. Arrange on platter; spoon primavera on top.

Makes 4 servings; 309 calories each serving.

Chicken Jambalaya

2 tablespoons reduced-calorie
  margarine
1 pound boneless chicken
  breasts, skinned and cut in
  2-inch pieces
1 medium onion, chopped
1 medium green pepper, cut in
  ½-inch pieces
1 large clove garlic, crushed
1 cup uncooked rice
1 can (16 ounces) whole
  tomatoes
1 can (about 14 ounces)
  chicken broth
¼ cup chopped parsley
1 teaspoon dried basil leaves
1 teaspoon hot-red-pepper sauce
½ pound large shrimp, shelled,
  tails intact
1 cup frozen peas

1. In large skillet, over medium
heat, melt margarine. Add chicken,
onion, pepper and garlic; sauté 5
minutes. Add rice, and cook 3 minutes, stirring often.

2. Add tomatoes and their liquid
and next 4 ingredients; bring to boiling, and simmer, covered, 15 minutes. Add shrimp and peas; simmer,
covered, 3 minutes, until shrimp are
cooked and chicken is tender.

Makes 6 servings; 245 calories
each serving.

■ To brown chicken without
steaming it, heat oil or butter in
skillet over medium heat. Add
chicken (do not crowd pan) skin
side down, and do not move or
turn until browned; turn only
once. When meat loses contact
with the pan and is replaced on
the same side, valuable juices are
lost and meat toughens. Avoid
further loss of juices by using
tongs or a spatula to turn chicken.

Cucumber Chicken

2 medium cucumbers, unpared
1 chicken-flavored bouillon
  cube
1 cup water
⅛ teaspoon garlic powder
4 boneless chicken-breast
  halves, skinned (1¼ pounds)
1 cup plain low-fat yogurt
1½ teaspoons lemon juice
1 tablespoon cornstarch
½ teaspoon dried dillweed

1. With tip of vegetable parer,
score cucumbers lengthwise all
around; cut in half lengthwise. Remove seeds; cut crosswise in ¼-inch
slices; set aside. In large skillet, dissolve bouillon in water; add garlic
powder, and bring to boiling. Add
cucumbers and chicken; poach 5

minutes, until chicken is tender. Remove cucumbers and chicken; place
on serving platter.

2. In bowl, combine yogurt,
lemon juice, cornstarch and dillweed; blend into broth in skillet.
Cook, stirring until thickened and
smooth. Spoon over chicken and cucumbers. If desired, garnish with
fresh dill and lemon.

Makes 4 servings; 190 calories
each serving.

■ To store purchased chicken,
remove tight plastic wrap; rewrap chicken in waxed or
butcher's paper to allow chicken
to breathe.

Quick & Easy:
Savory Chicken Dishes

Chicken Curry

2 tablespoons butter or
  margarine
1 small onion, finely chopped
1 medium clove garlic, crushed
3 tablespoons all-purpose flour
1 teaspoon curry powder
½ teaspoon salt
⅛ teaspoon pepper
1 can (about 14 ounces)
  chicken broth
1 unpared medium apple,
  cored and thinly sliced
½ medium green pepper,
  thinly sliced
2 cups cubed cooked chicken
½ cup raisins

1. In large heavy saucepan, over medium heat, melt butter. Add onion and garlic and sauté until tender—5 minutes. Blend in next 4 ingredients. Cook over low heat, stirring constantly, until bubbly. Remove from heat; stir in chicken broth. Add apple and green pepper.

2. Cook over medium heat, stirring constantly, until thickened and smooth. Stir in chicken and raisins; heat through. If desired, serve with rice, chutney and toasted coconut.

Makes 4 servings.

Sichuan Chicken

½ cup water
¼ cup soy sauce
¼ cup white-wine
  Worcestershire sauce
1 tablespoon cornstarch
1 teaspoon sugar
½ teaspoon ground ginger
1 pound boneless chicken
  cutlets, cut in ½-inch cubes
2 tablespoons salad oil
¼ to ½ teaspoon crushed
  red-pepper flakes
½ pound asparagus spears, cut
  in 2-inch pieces
½ cup cashews
Cooked rice

1. In medium bowl, combine first 7 ingredients; toss to blend. Marinate 15 minutes.

2. In large skillet or wok, heat oil over medium-high heat. Add red-pepper flakes; stir-fry until black.

With slotted spoon, drain chicken, and place in skillet; reserve marinade. Stir-fry 2 minutes.

3. Add reserved marinade; over medium-low heat, cook, covered, 2 minutes, or until tender. Add asparagus; stir-fry 1 minute. Stir in nuts. Serve over rice.

Makes 4 servings.

Bacon-Onion
Drumsticks

¼ cup imitation bacon bits
⅓ cup fine dry seasoned bread
  crumbs
1½ teaspoons instant minced
  onion
8 chicken drumsticks
1¾ cups prepared ranch
  dressing
2 tablespoons butter or
  margarine, melted

1. Preheat oven to 400°F. Line a baking sheet with aluminum foil; set aside. Reserve 2 tablespoons bacon bits. On sheet of waxed paper, combine crumbs, remaining bacon bits and onion. Brush drumsticks with ¼ cup dressing; coat with crumb mixture. Place on baking sheet; drizzle with butter; bake 30 minutes.

2. Place remaining dressing in small bowl; sprinkle with reserved bacon bits. Serve as a dip for drumsticks. Place drumsticks on platter; if desired, garnish with green-leaf lettuce and tomato wedges.

Makes 4 servings.

Micro-Way: Chicken Around the World

Tex-Mex Cornish Hens

½ cup (1 stick) butter or margarine
1 small onion, chopped
1 small green pepper, cut in thin strips
1 small red pepper, cut in thin strips
1 can (8 ounces) whole-kernel corn, drained
3 cups cornbread-stuffing mix
1 cup chicken broth
½ teaspoon poultry seasoning
½ teaspoon salt
2 (1 pound each) Cornish hens, halved
1 teaspoon paprika

1. In microwave-safe, 13-by-9-by-2-inch baking dish, cook ¼ cup butter, the onion, pepper strips and corn on HIGH 3 minutes, stirring once. Add cornbread-stuffing mix, chicken broth, poultry seasoning and salt; mix well.

2. Place Cornish hens, skin side up and with thickest portion toward edge of dish, on top of stuffing mixture. In small bowl, melt remaining ¼ cup butter; stir in paprika, and brush butter mixture over Cornish hens. Cover hens with waxed paper; cook on HIGH 15 minutes, rotating dish once. Let stand 5 minutes before serving.

Makes 4 servings.

Poulet Normande

¼ cup (½ stick) butter or margarine
2 medium Granny Smith apples, pared, cored and cut in ½-inch pieces
1 medium celery stalk, sliced
2 medium shallots, finely chopped
½ cup apple cider or juice
2 tablespoons cornstarch
1 cup chicken broth
½ cup heavy cream
6 boneless chicken breast halves, skinned (2¼ pounds)
Chopped parsley
Cooked red new potatoes

1. In microwave-safe, 13-by-9-by-2-inch baking dish, cook butter, apples, celery and shallots on HIGH 4 minutes, stirring once. In small bowl, blend cider with cornstarch;

stir into apple mixture. Add broth and cream; stir until blended.

2. Place chicken breasts in sauce, with thicker portions toward edge of dish. Cover with plastic wrap, turning back one corner to vent. Cook on HIGH 8 minutes, or until chicken is cooked, stirring sauce and rotating dish twice. Sprinkle chicken with parsley; serve with red new potatoes.

Makes 6 servings.

Chicken Wings Satay

½ cup creamy peanut butter
¼ cup soy sauce
3 tablespoons lime juice
2 tablespoons brown sugar
2 medium cloves garlic,
 crushed
½ teaspoon ground cumin
½ teaspoon ground coriander
¼ teaspoon crushed
 red-pepper flakes
12 chicken wings (2 pounds)
Cooked rice
Sliced green onions

1. In microwave-safe, 13-by-9-by-2-inch baking dish, blend peanut butter with soy sauce, lime juice, brown sugar, garlic, cumin, coriander and pepper flakes. Toss chicken wings in peanut-butter mixture; arrange with thick side toward edge of dish. Cover with plastic wrap; refrigerate 3 hours or overnight.

2. Turn back one corner of plastic wrap to vent; cook on HIGH 10 minutes, rotating dish once. Serve over cooked rice tossed with green onions as first course. If desired, garnish chicken with carrot curls and onion flowers.

Makes 6 servings.

Spanish Chicken Stew

2 tablespoons olive oil
1 medium onion, cut in
 wedges
1 green pepper, cut in 1-inch
 pieces
1 medium clove garlic, crushed
1 can (29 ounces) whole
 tomatoes in puree
½ cup chicken broth
½ teaspoon salt
½ teaspoon dried thyme leaves
½ teaspoon turmeric
1½ pounds boneless chicken
 thighs, cut in 2-inch pieces
½ pound boiled ham, cut in
 ¼-inch strips
2 jars (7 ounces each)
 marinated artichoke hearts,
 drained
1 cup frozen peas
½ cup sliced pitted black olives

1. In microwave-safe, 3-quart casserole, cook oil, onion, pepper and garlic on HIGH 2 minutes. Add tomatoes, broth, salt, thyme and turmeric; mix well. Stir in chicken. Cover with plastic wrap, turning back one corner to vent. Cook on HIGH 10 minutes, stirring twice.

2. Add ham, artichoke hearts, peas and olives; cover; cook on HIGH 3 minutes. If desired, serve over cooked noodles or rice.

Makes 8 servings.

■ An ice cube tray is the key to never-fail carrot curls. Use a vegetable peeler to cut long strips of carrot; roll them up, and fit each into an ice cube tray compartment. Fill with cold water, and store in refrigerator until serving time; then drain tray, and adorn plates with carrot curls.

May

Entertain effortlessly from start to finish. These simple yet sensational recipes get you out of the kitchen—and into your party—in no time flat! And you'll be serving eye-catching dishes, like the Almond Chiffon Bundt Cake with strawberries gently cascading down its sides. The photographs and the tantalizing titles below give an inkling of this cookbook's contents. And there are even more recipes. So get ready for a sensational get-together.

Almond Chiffon Bundt Cake

Tutti-Frutti Punch

Upside-Down Lemon Meringue Pie

Ham-and-Cheese-Stuffed Rye Bread

Zucchini Fritters With Red-Pepper Mayonnaise

Grilled Beef With Mixed Vegetables

Caviar Torte

Marinated Steak Kebabs

Cincinnati-Style Chili

Nectarine Shortcake

Potato Salad Primavera

Summer Get-Together Cookbook

Serve a fabulous meal with almost no preparation, thanks to our simple recipes.

Tutti-Frutti Punch

(pictured, page 77)

3 packages (10 ounces each) frozen strawberries in syrup, thawed
1 can (46 ounces) pineapple juice, chilled
½ gallon orange juice, chilled
1 quart apple juice, chilled
1 can (12 ounces) frozen piña-colada mix, thawed
2 quarts ginger ale, club soda or lemon-lime soda, chilled
Fresh pineapple wedges
Orange slices

1. In blender or food processor, puree strawberries; press through a fine sieve or a food mill to remove seeds. In large punch bowl, combine strawberry puree, fruit juices and piña-colada mix; mix well. Refrigerate until ready to serve.

2. Just before serving, add soda. Garnish punch with fresh fruit. Serve over ice.

Makes 8 quarts (sixty [½-cup] servings).

Page 77: Almond Chiffon Bundt Cake, Tutti-Frutti Punch.

Pages 78 and 79: (Clockwise from top right) Upside-Down Lemon Meringue Pie, Grilled Beef With Mixed Vegetables, Zucchini Fritters With Red-Pepper Mayonnaise, Ham-and-Cheese-Stuffed Rye Bread.

Pages 80 and 81: (Clockwise from top right) Caviar Torte, Marinated Steak Kebabs, Potato Salad Primavera, Nectarine Shortcake, Cincinnati-Style Chili.

Almond Chiffon Bundt Cake

(pictured, page 77)

1½ cups sifted cake flour
1 cup granulated sugar
2 teaspoons baking powder
½ teaspoon salt
½ cup (2 ounces) finely chopped, toasted almonds
¾ cup milk
⅓ cup salad oil
6 large eggs, separated
½ teaspoon almond extract
1 tube (3½ ounces) almond paste (⅓ cup)
¼ teaspoon cream of tartar
2 cups confectioners' sugar
2 tablespoons light corn syrup
1 pint strawberries, hulled
Mint sprigs

1. Preheat oven to 325°F. Grease and flour bottom only of a 12-cup Bundt pan. In large bowl, sift together flour, ¾ cup sugar, the baking powder and salt; stir in nuts. Add ½ cup milk, the oil, egg yolks and extract. With wire whisk, mix until batter is smooth. Remove about 1 cup mixture to a small bowl; blend in almond paste until smooth. Return to egg-yolk mixture.

2. In large bowl, with electric mixer at high speed, beat egg whites and cream of tartar until foamy. Gradually add remaining ¼ cup granulated sugar, beating until stiff peaks form. Stir one-fourth of meringue into yolk mixture to lighten; gently fold in remainder until no white streaks remain. Pour batter into prepared pan.

3. Bake 1 hour, or until cake tester inserted in center comes out clean. Invert pan onto soda bottle; cool completely.

4. To unmold: Using a long, sharp knife, gently loosen cake from sides and center tube of pan. Invert and unmold onto wire rack; place rack over large baking sheet.

5. In small bowl, stir confectioners' sugar, corn syrup and 3 to 4 tablespoons milk until of spoonable consistency. Pour glaze over cake; if necessary, spread with spatula to cover. Transfer cake to serving plate. Arrange strawberries in center hole and over top and side of cake, halving berries if large. Garnish with mint sprigs.

Makes 12 servings.

Upside-Down Lemon Meringue Pie

(pictured, page 79)

4 large eggs, separated
¼ teaspoon cream of tartar
2 cups sugar
⅓ cup cornstarch
1½ cups water
2 tablespoons grated lemon peel
¼ cup lemon juice
1 tablespoon butter or margarine
1 cup heavy cream
Lemon slices

1. Day before: Preheat oven to 250°F. Line large baking sheet with aluminum foil; trace an 8½-inch circle on foil. Place egg yolks in small bowl; cover with plastic wrap; refrigerate. In large bowl, with electric mixer at high speed, beat egg whites with cream of tartar until foamy. Gradually beat in ¾ cup sugar, 2 tablespoons at a time, until mixture is very stiff and sugar is dissolved. Spread one-third of meringue evenly over circle. Spoon remaining meringue around top edge of circle, smoothing with spatula and large spoon, until edge is 1½ inches high. Bake 1 hour; turn off oven. Let meringue stand in oven overnight to completely dry out.

2. Next day: In medium saucepan, combine cornstarch and remaining 1¼ cups sugar; mix well. Gradually stir in water until smooth. Over medium-high heat, bring to boiling, stirring constantly; remove from heat. Stir some of hot mixture into reserved egg yolks; mix well. Return yolk mixture to saucepan; cook, stirring, 1 minute. Remove from heat; stir in lemon peel, lemon juice and butter. Cool until room temperature; pour into baked meringue shell; refrigerate 1 hour.

3. Before serving, in small bowl, with electric mixer at high speed, beat cream until stiff peaks form. Place in pastry bag fitted with ½-inch star tip. Decoratively pipe on top of meringue shell. Garnish with lemon slices.

Makes 12 servings.

Grilled Beef With Mixed Vegetables

(pictured, pages 78 and 79)

2 pounds boneless top-round steak, 1½ inches thick
1 tablespoon Cajun- or Creole-seasoning mix (see *Note*)
2 cups baby carrots, trimmed and pared
1 cup medium mushrooms, halved
1 small green pepper, cut in strips
1 small yellow pepper, cut in strips
1 cup coarsely chopped cucumber
⅓ cup salad oil
2 tablespoons red-wine vinegar
¼ cup smoky-flavored barbecue sauce
1 medium clove garlic, peeled

1. Rub both sides of steak with seasoning mix; place on rack in broiler pan or on grill rack. Broil 6 inches from heat, 8 minutes on each side for medium rare; keep warm. Place carrots, mushrooms and peppers on broiler pan. Cook 5 minutes, or until tender; keep warm.

2. In food processor or blender, puree half of cucumber with oil, vinegar, barbecue sauce and garlic; stir in remaining cucumber. Thinly slice meat across grain, on diagonal.

Spoon some sauce over each portion; serve with grilled vegetables.
Makes 4 to 6 servings.

Note: Available in specialty food stores, or combine 2 teaspoons paprika, 1 teaspoon each onion and garlic powder, ½ teaspoon dried thyme leaves, ½ teaspoon salt and ¼ teaspoon pepper.

Ham-and-Cheese-Stuffed Rye Bread

(pictured, page 78)

10-inch round loaf rye bread (about 3½ pounds)
2 packages (10 ounces each) frozen mixed vegetables, thawed
½ pound boiled ham, cut in thin strips
2 cups (½ pound) shredded Swiss cheese
1 cup (¼ pound) finely shredded Parmesan cheese
2 large eggs, lightly beaten
1 cup sour cream
1 cup mayonnaise
1 package (1.4 ounces) vegetable-soup-and-recipe mix

1. Preheat oven to 350°F. Cut 1-inch-thick slice from top of bread; reserve for another use. With fork, carefully scoop out and coarsely chop soft inside, leaving ½-inch shell. Lightly toast 2 cups crumbs; reserve remainder for another use.

2. In large bowl, mix 2 cups crumbs, vegetables, ham, cheeses, eggs, sour cream, mayonnaise and soup mix until well combined. Spoon into bread shell; cover top with aluminum foil. Place on baking sheet. Bake 1 hour, or until cheeses melt and mixture is hot. Let stand 20 minutes before slicing.

Makes 6 to 8 servings.

Summer Get-Together Cookbook

Zucchini Fritters

(pictured, page 78)

Red-Pepper Mayonnaise (recipe
follows)
3 large eggs
¼ cup unsifted all-purpose
flour
¼ teaspoon salt
⅛ teaspoon pepper
2 tablespoons grated onion
1 medium green zucchini,
shredded
1 medium yellow zucchini,
shredded
1 large carrot, shredded
¼ cup salad oil

1. Make Red-Pepper Mayonnaise.
2. In large bowl, beat eggs, flour,
salt and pepper; stir in vegetables;
mix well.
3. In large skillet, heat oil. Drop
batter by tablespoons into hot oil.
Cook about 1 minute on each side,
or until golden. Drain on paper-
towel-lined tray. Serve immediately
with Red-Pepper Mayonnaise.
Makes 2 dozen fritters.

Red-Pepper Mayonnaise

½ cup mayonnaise
1 jar (7 ounces) roasted red
peppers, drained
1 teaspoon red-wine vinegar
1 medium clove garlic, crushed

In food processor or blender,
puree mayonnaise, red peppers, vinegar and garlic until smooth. Cover,
and refrigerate.
Makes 1 cup.

■ Don't let the last few tablespoons of mayonnaise go to
waste! Turn them into tonight's
tasty salad dressing instead: Add
vinegar (start with a teaspoon,
and add more as needed) and
spices to taste. Shake well, and
toss with greens.

Caviar Torte

(pictured, page 81)

8 hard-cooked large eggs,
peeled and quartered
¼ cup mayonnaise
¼ cup chopped parsley
¼ teaspoon salt
¼ teaspoon pepper
2 tablespoons coarse
Dijon-style mustard
1 cup minced green onions
(1 large bunch)
2 packages (5 ounces each)
frozen cooked shrimp,
thawed (2 cups)
4 packages (3 ounces each)
cream cheese, at room
temperature
½ cup bacon bits
¼ cup sherry or Marsala wine
½ cup sour cream
1 jar (2 ounces) red caviar
1 jar (2 ounces) black caviar
1 jar (2 ounces) golden caviar
Chopped parsley
Melba toast

1. Butter bottom and side of 9-
inch springform pan. In food processor, process eggs, mayonnaise, ¼
cup parsley, the salt, pepper and
mustard until well mixed. Spread in
prepared pan. Sprinkle half of green
onions over mixture.
2. In food processor, process
shrimp, 3 ounces cream cheese, the
bacon bits and wine until smooth;
spread over onions. Sprinkle remaining onions over shrimp mixture.
3. In food processor, process remaining cream cheese until smooth;
blend in sour cream. Pour over
green onion layer. Cover top of pan
with plastic wrap; refrigerate 3
hours or overnight—until firm.
4. With sharp knife or metal spatula, carefully loosen torte from pan.
Remove side of pan; place torte on
serving dish. Spread caviar in desired fashion on top of cream-cheese
layer. Press chopped parsley around
top edge of torte. Serve torte with
Melba toast.
Makes 16 to 20 servings.

Marinated Steak Kebabs

(pictured, page 81)

1 pound boneless chuck, 1½
inches thick

Marinade
¾ cup prepared barbecue
sauce
½ cup water
⅓ cup salad oil
3 tablespoons lemon juice
1 small onion, grated
2 large cloves garlic, crushed
2 teaspoons dried oregano
leaves, crushed
¾ teaspoons fennel seed,
crushed

1 large zucchini
1 pint cherry tomatoes
8 (12-inch) metal or wooden
skewers

1. Place steak in freezer until partially frozen—about 15 minutes.
2. Make marinade: In medium
bowl, combine barbecue sauce,
water, oil, lemon juice, onion, garlic,
oregano and fennel; set aside.
3. With sharp knife, slice partially
frozen steak against the grain into
4-by-1½-by-¼-inch strips.
4. Trim and discard stem end
from zucchini; slice lengthwise in
eight ¼-inch strips.
5. In large shallow baking dish,
layer zucchini and meat strips; brush
generously with marinade between
layers. Prick cherry tomatoes several times with tines of fork; place in
pan with meat. Brush with marinade. Cover dish with plastic wrap;
refrigerate 4 hours or overnight.
6. To assemble kebabs, layer a
strip of meat over a slice of zucchini
and thread onto skewer in an S-
shape (see photograph, page 81),
threading tomato between loops;
place cherry tomato on end of a
12-inch metal or wooden skewer.
Repeat to make 8 kebabs in all. (Add
any remaining kebab ingredients to
ends of skewers.)

7. Prepare outdoor grill, or line broiler pan with foil. Grill, 6 inches from heat, 10 to 12 minutes, turning after 5 or 6 minutes. If desired, serve with parsleyed rice.

Makes 8 kebabs.

Potato Salad Primavera
(pictured, page 80)

2 pounds medium red potatoes, quartered
1 pound asparagus, cut in 2-inch lengths
1 package (10 ounces) frozen peas
1 small red pepper, cut in strips
1 small yellow pepper, cut in strips
¾ cup heavy cream
½ cup mayonnaise
1 small red onion, minced
2 tablespoons lemon juice
1 tablespoon Dijon-style mustard
1 small clove garlic, crushed
¾ teaspoon salt
½ teaspoon freshly ground pepper
¼ cup minced parsley
¼ cup minced fresh dill
Lettuce leaves

1. Cover potatoes with salted water. Cook 12 minutes, or until tender; drain. Place in large bowl; keep warm. In boiling water, cook asparagus, peas and peppers 2 minutes, or until just tender; drain. Add vegetables to bowl containing potatoes, and cover.

2. In medium saucepan, combine cream, mayonnaise, onion, lemon juice, mustard, garlic, salt and pepper. Cook, stirring, until boiling; stir in parsley and dill. Pour sauce over vegetables; toss well to coat evenly. Arrange lettuce on platter, and top with potato salad.

Makes 6 to 8 servings.

Feta-Lamb Kebabs With Peperonata

Peperonata
¼ cup olive oil
3 small green peppers, sliced into ½-inch strips
3 small red peppers, sliced into ½-inch strips
2 medium red onions, cut into ¼-inch wedges
2 medium cloves garlic, crushed
½ cup quartered pitted black olives
1 teaspoon dried basil leaves

Kebabs
1½ pounds ground lamb
1 small eggplant, finely chopped (about ¾ pound)
1 small onion, finely chopped
½ cup fine dry bread crumbs
1 large egg
¾ cup crumbled feta cheese (4 ounces)
2 tablespoons chopped parsley
1 teaspoon dried rosemary leaves, crumbled
½ teaspoon salt
¼ teaspoon pepper
7 (10-inch) metal skewers

1. Make peperonata: In large skillet, heat oil over medium heat. Add peppers, onions and garlic; sauté 10 minutes. Add olives and basil; cook 5 minutes longer; set aside. (May be made up to two days ahead and refrigerated. Reheat while cooking kebabs.)

2. Make kebabs: In large bowl, using wooden spoon or hands, combine lamb, eggplant, onion, bread crumbs, egg, cheese, parsley, rosemary, salt and pepper; mix well. With hands, form mixture into 28 (2-inch) meatballs (about 1 rounded tablespoon each). On each of seven 10-inch metal skewers, thread four meatballs.

3. Broil kebabs 6 inches from heat, 15 minutes, turning after 7 minutes. Serve with peperonata.

Makes 7 servings.

Cincinnati-Style Chili
(pictured, pages 80 and 81)

2 tablespoons salad oil
1½ pounds boneless pork butt, cut in ½-inch cubes
2 pounds ground beef
1 large onion, chopped
1 to 2 jalapeño peppers, seeded and minced
2 medium cloves garlic, crushed
1 can (28 ounces) crushed tomatoes
1 can (12 ounces) beer
½ cup water
2 packages (1.25 ounces each) chili-seasoning mix
½ teaspoon ground cinnamon
½ teaspoon ground allspice
½ teaspoon salt
Cooked pasta

1. In large skillet or saucepan, heat 2 tablespoons oil. Cook pork 5 minutes, or until evenly browned. With slotted spoon, remove to large bowl. Cook beef 5 minutes, or until browned; remove to bowl. Add onion, peppers and garlic to pan; cook 3 minutes, or until tender.

2. Return all meat to pan. Add tomatoes, beer, water, seasoning mix, spices and salt. Simmer, partially covered and stirring occasionally, 45 minutes. Serve over pasta. If desired, sprinkle with shredded Cheddar cheese.

Makes 8 servings.

■ Add salad dressings to leafy greens just before serving them so that they won't wilt. And do as the French do: Mix the dressing in the bottom of the salad bowl, cross the serving spoon and fork over it and set the washed and crisped greens on top. Place damp paper towels over the greens; cover with plastic wrap. To serve, remove spoon and fork, and toss the salad for perfectly dressed, crisp greens.

Summer Get-Together Cookbook

Poached Salmon With Corn Salsa

2 large salmon steaks, 1 inch thick (¾ pound each)
¾ cup dry white wine
¾ cup water
½ cup coarsely chopped celery leaves
1 teaspoon salt
1 cup fresh or frozen corn kernels
1 large tomato, seeded and chopped
2 tablespoons minced red onion
2 tablespoons minced cilantro (fresh coriander) leaves
2 teaspoons minced jalapeño pepper
1 medium clove garlic, crushed
¼ teaspoon ground cumin
3 tablespoons lemon juice
2 tablespoons salad oil

1. With sharp paring knife, remove skin from salmon steaks, taking care not to cut flesh of fish. Cut away and discard all bones; divide each salmon steak lengthwise into two pieces. Wrap thin end around thicker portion, forming a medallion; secure with a wooden pick. Repeat entire procedure with other half of steak and remaining salmon steak.

2. In medium skillet, combine wine, water, celery leaves and ½ teaspoon salt. Place salmon medallions in water mixture. Heat just until simmering; cover; cook 3 minutes. Remove pan from heat. Let medallions stand in poaching liquid until room temperature.

3. Make salsa: In medium bowl, combine corn, tomato, onion, cilantro, pepper, garlic, cumin, remaining ½ teaspoon salt, the lemon juice and oil; mix well.

4. Drain fish; arrange on serving platter. Spoon 2 tablespoons salsa over each medallion; serve remaining salsa with fish.

Makes 4 servings.

Nectarine Shortcake

(pictured, page 80)

1½ pounds ripe nectarines, sliced
¾ cup granulated sugar
2½ cups unsifted all-purpose flour
4 teaspoons baking powder
1 cup (2 sticks) butter or margarine, cut in pieces
1 cup sour cream
2 large eggs
1 teaspoon vanilla extract
1 cup blueberries
2 cups heavy cream
½ cup confectioners' sugar

1. In medium bowl, toss nectarine slices with ½ cup granulated sugar; set aside. Preheat oven to 450°F. In medium bowl, combine flour, baking powder and remaining ¼ cup granulated sugar; mix well. With pastry blender or two knives, cut in ¾ cup butter until mixture resembles coarse crumbs. In small bowl, blend sour cream, eggs and vanilla; with fork, stir mixture into flour mixture until just moistened. (Dough will be soft.)

2. On lightly floured surface, with well-floured hands, knead dough 10 times. Roll dough into a 9-inch square. Cut into nine 3-inch squares. With broad spatula, place squares onto large ungreased baking sheet. Bake 12 minutes, or until biscuit squares are golden.

3. While biscuit squares are still warm, split in half horizontally; spread cut side of bottom of each biscuit with remaining ¼ cup butter. Toss blueberries with nectarines. In large bowl, with electric mixer at high speed, beat cream and confectioners' sugar until stiff peaks form. Place about ⅓ cup whipped cream on bottom half of each biscuit; top each with about ⅓ cup fruit mixture. Place remaining half biscuits on top of fruit; garnish with remaining whipped cream and, if desired, a nectarine slice.

Makes 9 servings.

Peach Mousse

1 can (29 ounces) peach halves, drained and pureed
1 envelope unflavored gelatine
4 large eggs, separated
½ cup granulated sugar
⅓ cup lime juice
¼ cup confectioners' sugar
1 cup heavy cream
2 tablespoons rum

1. Fold 26-inch piece of foil in thirds lengthwise; with string, tie collar around a 1-quart soufflé dish, to form 2-inch rim above top.

2. In small cup, place ¼ cup peach puree. Sprinkle with gelatine; set aside to soften. In double-boiler top, combine egg yolks, remaining peach puree, granulated sugar and lime juice; mix well. Cook over hot, not boiling, water, stirring constantly, 8 minutes, or until hot. Stir in softened gelatine; continue to cook, stirring, until gelatine is dissolved. Place in medium bowl set over larger bowl of ice and water for 30 minutes, or until gelatine mixture begins to mound.

3. In large bowl, with electric mixer at high speed, beat egg whites until foamy. Add 2 tablespoons confectioners' sugar; beat until stiff peaks form. With same beaters, in a small bowl, beat heavy cream, remaining 2 tablespoons confectioners' sugar and the rum until stiff peaks form. Fold beaten egg whites and the cream into thickened puree until no white streaks remain.

4. Spoon into dish. Refrigerate 4 hours or overnight. Remove collar; if desired, garnish with whipped cream and lime slices.

Makes 10 to 12 servings.

■ If you forget whether a refrigerated egg is raw or cooked, carefully spin it on a counter. If the egg wobbles, it's raw; if it twirls evenly, it's cooked.

White-Chocolate Petal Cake

1 bar (6 ounces) white chocolate, grated
½ cup boiling water
2½ cups sifted cake flour
¾ teaspoon baking soda
½ teaspoon salt
¾ cup (1½ sticks) butter or margarine, at room temperature
1 cup sugar
3 large eggs, separated
1 teaspoon vanilla extract
¾ cup buttermilk
1 cup raspberry jam
White-Chocolate Buttercream (recipe follows)

1. Preheat oven to 350°F. Grease two 9-inch round cake pans. Line bottom with waxed paper; grease and flour paper. In medium bowl, combine grated chocolate and boiling water; whisk until chocolate is melted; cool to room temperature. On waxed paper, sift together flour, baking soda and salt; set aside.

2. In large bowl, with electric mixer at high speed, cream butter with ⅔ cup sugar until light and fluffy. Beat in egg yolks, one at a time. Beat in vanilla and cooled chocolate mixture. Alternately add one-fourth of flour mixture with one-third of buttermilk, beginning and ending with flour mixture. Beat at low speed 1 minute, or until mixture is smooth.

3. In small bowl, with electric mixer at high speed, beat egg whites until foamy. Gradually beat in remaining ⅓ cup sugar, beating until stiff peaks form. Fold into batter; spread batter evenly in pans.

4. Bake 35 minutes, or until cake tester inserted in center comes out clean. Cool cakes in pans on wire racks 5 minutes. Loosen cake edges; invert onto rack. Remove waxed paper; cool completely.

5. Using a long serrated knife, with wooden picks as a guide, slice each cake horizontally in half.

Spread cut side of each of three layers with ⅓ cup jam. Place one layer on serving plate, jam side up. Stack layers with jam side up, placing plain layer, cut side down, on top. Frost side and top of cake with White-Chocolate Buttercream.

Makes 12 to 16 servings.

White-Chocolate Buttercream

3 large egg whites
2 cups confectioners' sugar
1 cup (2 sticks) butter, at room temperature, cut in pieces
1 bar (6 ounces) white chocolate, melted and cooled
2 tablespoons white crème de cacao

1. In top of double boiler, set over simmering water, combine egg whites and sugar. Whisk constantly until mixture is very warm. Transfer to large bowl of electric mixer; at high speed, beat 5 minutes, or until stiff peaks form and meringue is room temperature.

2. At medium speed, add butter, a few pieces at a time, beating until each portion is well mixed before adding more. At high speed, beat until very thick. (If room is too warm and mixture is thin, set bowl over ice water, or refrigerate; beat until thick.) Gradually beat in melted chocolate and crème de cacao; beat until smooth.

Makes enough frosting for one 9-inch cake.

Kahlúa-Nut Dessert Sauce

1 cup heavy cream
1 cup milk
½ cup sugar
½ cup Kahlúa or other coffee-flavored liqueur
½ cup lightly toasted hazelnuts

In medium saucepan, over medium-high heat, bring cream, milk and sugar to boiling. Reduce heat; simmer, uncovered, stirring frequently, until mixture turns a very light caramel color—about 30 minutes. Stir in Kahlúa and nuts; simmer 30 seconds longer. Serve warm or at room temperature with ice cream.

Makes about 1⅓ cups.

Angel Ice Cream Cake

10-inch baked angel-food cake
1 quart strawberry ice cream, softened
2 cups peach ice cream, softened
2 cups heavy cream
½ cup confectioners' sugar
½ teaspoon almond extract
2 peaches, sliced
6 strawberries

1. Freeze cake until firm—about 2 hours or overnight. With a long serrated knife and using toothpicks as a guide, slice cake into four equal layers. Spread 2 cups strawberry ice cream on bottom layer. Add second layer; spread with peach ice cream. Add third layer, and spread with remaining strawberry ice cream. Top with fourth layer. Cover cake with plastic wrap; freeze until very firm.

2. About 1 hour before serving, whip cream: In large bowl of electric mixer, combine heavy cream, confectioners' sugar and almond extract; beat until stiff.

3. Transfer cake to serving plate. Spread about three-fourths of the cream on top and side of cake. Fill pastry bag fitted with ½-inch star tip with the remaining cream; pipe rosettes on top. Garnish with fruit.

Makes 12 servings.

Note: Cake may be frosted with whipped cream and frozen. Freeze in covered cake holder. Thaw 1 hour in refrigerator. Garnish with fruit just before serving.

Lite Eating: Elegant Dishes

Stained-Glass Veal Roast

4½-pound boneless veal breast
1 medium onion,
    chopped
1 large clove garlic,
    crushed
1 teaspoon salt
1 teaspoon dried thyme
    leaves
¼ teaspoon pepper
2 medium carrots, pared
1 medium green pepper
1 medium red pepper
1 medium turnip, pared
1 small fennel bulb, with fern
2 large eggs, beaten
¼ cup grated Parmesan cheese
1 can (about 14 ounces)
    chicken broth

1. Open natural pocket in veal; fold back flap so that meat is of even thickness. In small bowl, combine onion, garlic, salt, thyme and pepper; spread over veal. Preheat oven to 350°F.

2. Cut carrots, peppers, turnip and fennel bulb in long, ½-inch-wide strips; reserve fennel fern for garnishing. Toss strips with eggs and cheese. Arrange vegetables lengthwise over middle of veal. Fold one long side of meat over vegetables; roll up so that seam is on bottom. Tie with kitchen string.

3. Place meat in roasting pan; add broth. Cover with aluminum foil. Bake 1 hour and 45 minutes. Uncover; bake 30 minutes longer. Transfer roast to platter; cut off strings. Garnish with fennel fern.

Makes 12 servings; 288 calories each serving.

Asparagus Guacamole

1 pound asparagus, chopped
    and cooked
1 small red pepper, chopped
1 green onion, chopped
2 tablespoons chopped canned
    green chiles
1 small clove garlic, crushed
3 tablespoons lime juice
½ teaspoon salt
1 large cucumber, unpared
1 large yellow pepper, cut in
    strips
1 large jicama, cut in strips

1. In food processor, puree asparagus; place in bowl. Add next 6 ingredients; mix. Cover; chill.

2. With fork, score cucumber lengthwise all around; cut into thin rounds. Serve with pepper and jicama strips as "dippers."

Makes 8 appetizer servings; 43 calories each serving.

Strawberry-Swirl Cheesecake

⅔ cup sugar
4 teaspoons cornstarch
1 package (10 ounces) quick-
    thaw frozen strawberries
    in light syrup, thawed
Nonstick cooking spray
2 packages (8 ounces each)
    reduced-calorie cream cheese
2 containers (16 ounces each)
    low-fat cottage cheese
3 large eggs
1 teaspoon vanilla extract
½ cup chopped pistachios
1 pint strawberries, halved

1. In a saucepan, combine 2 tablespoons sugar and the cornstarch. Strain juice from berries; place 3 tablespoons juice in small cup; reserve. Place remainder in food processor with berries; puree. Stir into cornstarch mixture. Bring to boiling, stirring; boil 1 minute. Transfer mixture to medium bowl; cover with plastic wrap. Refrigerate.

2. Preheat oven to 500°F. Grease 9-inch springform pan with nonstick cooking spray; sprinkle with flour. Wrap heavy-duty aluminum foil under and up outside of pan to prevent leaks; set pan aside. In food processor, puree cream cheese with cottage cheese. Add eggs, remaining sugar, reserved 3 tablespoons strawberry juice and vanilla extract; process to blend.

3. Pour mixture into prepared pan; place pan on baking sheet. Spoon thickened puree in lines on top of cheesecake mixture; with spatula, swirl puree.

4. Bake 10 minutes; reduce heat to 250°F. Bake 50 minutes longer, or until center is just set. Cool in pan on wire rack; refrigerate 3 hours or overnight. Remove foil and side of pan. Pat nuts onto side of cake; top with strawberries.

Makes 16 servings; 218 calories each serving.

Right: (clockwise from right)
Asparagus Guacamole,
Stained-Glass Veal Roast,
Strawberry-Swirl Cheesecake.

Quick & Easy: Oriental Dinner

SPICY LONDON BROIL
WITH EASY "FRIED RICE"
SESAME STIR-FRIED BROCCOLI
ORANGE-GINGER PARFAITS

■ Make parfaits first; refrigerate. Prepare rice and slice steak; keep warm. Prepare broccoli.

Spicy London Broil With Easy "Fried Rice"

2 tablespoons salad oil
½ cup chopped red pepper
4 green onions, cut in 1½-inch diagonal slices
2 ounces mushrooms, sliced
1 cup chicken broth
3 tablespoons soy sauce
½ teaspoon ground ginger
1⅓ cups precooked rice
1 pound flank steak
3 tablespoons prepared plum sauce
1 teaspoon salt
½ teaspoon garlic powder
¼ teaspoon pepper

1. In 10-inch skillet, heat oil over medium heat. Sauté pepper, onions and mushrooms until tender-crisp—3 minutes. Add broth, soy sauce and ginger; bring to boiling. Stir in rice. Cover; let stand 5 minutes.

2. Brush each side of steak with half of plum sauce; sprinkle each side with ½ teaspoon salt, ¼ teaspoon garlic power and ⅛ teaspoon pepper. Broil 3 inches from heat for 3 minutes on each side.
Makes 4 servings.

Sesame Stir-Fried Broccoli

1 tablespoon salad oil
½ pound broccoli flowerets
¼ teaspoon salt
Dash sugar
2 tablespoons water
1 tablespoon toasted sesame seeds

In skillet, heat oil over medium-high heat, and stir-fry broccoli 2 minutes. Add salt, sugar and water; cover and cook until tender—about 2 minutes. Toss with sesame seeds.
Makes 4 servings.

Orange-Ginger Parfaits

4 teaspoons chopped candied ginger root
4 containers (4 ounces each) prepared vanilla-flavored pudding
1 can (11 ounces) mandarin-orange slices, drained
4 teaspoons wheat germ
Non-dairy whipped topping
Fresh mint sprigs

Stir 1 teaspoon ginger into each pudding. In parfait glasses, make 2 layers of pudding, oranges and wheat germ; add third layer of pudding. Top with topping and mint.
Makes 4 servings.

Micro-Way: Children's Cakes

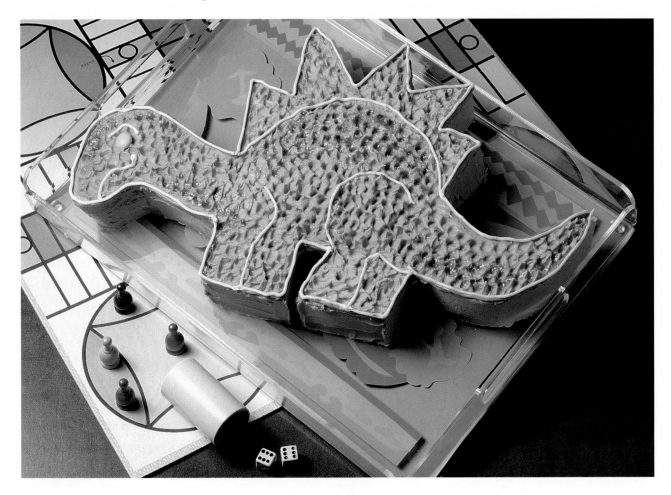

Lemony Dinosaur Cake

2 packages (8.6 ounces each) microwave lemon-cake mix
⅔ cup peach nectar
⅔ cup sour cream
⅔ cup salad oil
2 large eggs
½ cup peach preserves
½ cup (1 stick) butter or margarine
1 package (1 pound) confectioners' sugar
6 tablespoons lemon juice
Green food color
Candy-coated chocolate candy

1. Prepare and bake cake mix as package label directs, except to add ⅓ cup peach nectar, ⅓ cup sour cream, ⅓ cup oil and 1 egg to contents of each package. Invert cakes on wire rack; let cool completely. With sharp knife, cut each cake in half horizontally. In small bowl, cook peach preserves on HIGH 1 minute; spread preserves on cut side of two layers of cake. Top each of these layers with remaining cake layers, cut side down.

2. (See *Note*, next column.) Place pattern pieces over cake layers; cut out and assemble cake, as pictured above, on large tray, attaching tail,

head, feet and spikes with wooden picks. In large bowl with electric mixer at high speed, cream butter, confectioners' sugar and lemon juice until frosting mixture is fluffy. Place ⅓ cup frosting into pastry bag fitted with writing tip; tint remaining frosting green.

3. Spread cake with green frosting, making rough surface. With white frosting, pipe outline and any details of dinosaur. Add candy pieces for the eye.

Makes 10 to 12 servings.

Note: To cut out and assemble Lemony Dinosaur Cake, use dinosaur diagram given on page 250.

Giant Cookie Treat

¾ cup shortening
1 cup firmly packed
   light-brown sugar
1 large egg
¼ cup water
1 teaspoon vanilla extract
3 cups uncooked rolled oats
1 cup unsifted all-purpose
   flour
½ teaspoon baking soda
1 cup flaked coconut
1 cup candy-coated chocolate
   candies
½ cup prepared fudge sauce
2 pints vanilla ice cream

1. Grease two microwave-safe, shallow 10-inch round baking dishes. Line bottoms and sides with waxed paper, leaving one inch of paper extending over edge of dish; grease. In large bowl, with electric mixer at high speed, cream shortening, brown sugar, egg, water and vanilla until light and fluffy. Stir in oats, flour, baking soda, ½ cup coconut and ½ cup chocolate candies; mix well.

2. Press half of dough into each prepared dish; sprinkle ¼ cup coconut over each. Cook, one dish at a time, on MEDIUM 8 to 10 minutes, or until cookie appears dry on top, rotating after 4 minutes. Press ¼ cup chocolate candies into top of warm, baked cookie; let stand on counter 10 minutes. Repeat with remaining dish. When cooled, remove cookies by grasping edges of waxed paper; remove paper.

3. In small bowl, heat fudge sauce on HIGH 1 to 2 minutes, or until warm. Place 4 scoops ice cream on each cookie; top with fudge sauce. Cut each into four wedges.

Makes 8 servings.

■ If a stick of butter is too cold to be creamed easily, pop it in the microwave at low-to-medium power for 10 to 15 seconds.

Brownie-Sundae Delight

1 cup sugar
¾ cup (1½ sticks) butter or
    margarine
5 tablespoons water
1½ packages (12-ounce size)
    semisweet-chocolate pieces
    (3 cups)
4 large eggs
2 teaspoons vanilla extract
1½ cups unsifted all-purpose
    flour
¾ teaspoon baking soda
1 cup chopped walnuts
¼ teaspoon salt
2 pints ice cream
1 container (12 ounces) frozen
    nondairy whipped topping,
    thawed
Multicolor sprinkles
Maraschino cherries

1. Grease three microwave-safe, 8-inch round baking dishes. Line each with two waxed-paper rounds. In large bowl, combine sugar, butter and water; cook on HIGH 5 minutes, or until boiling, stirring once. Add chocolate; stir until melted. Whisk in eggs, one at a time; add vanilla. Stir in flour, baking soda, walnuts and salt; mix well.

2. Pour one-third batter into each dish. Cook, one dish at a time, on MEDIUM 6 minutes, rotating once. Cook on HIGH 1 minute. Let stand 10 minutes. Invert layers onto paper-lined tray; remove paper rounds. Cool.

3. Place one layer in 8-inch springform pan. Slightly soften 1 pint ice cream on MEDIUM 30 seconds. Spread on top of layer. Cover with second layer and remaining ice cream. Top with last layer; freeze until firm.

4. Remove pan; fill pastry bag fitted with star tip with 1 cup whipped topping. Frost cake with remaining whipped topping. Pipe topping on edge of cake; garnish with colored sprinkles and cherries.

Makes 12 servings.

Crunchy Chocolate-Chip Cake

2 cups unsifted all-purpose flour
2 teaspoons baking soda
2 teaspoons ground cinnamon
1½ cups salad oil
1 cup granulated sugar
1 cup light-brown sugar
4 large eggs
2 cups shredded carrots
⅔ cup mini semisweet-
    chocolate pieces
2 packages (8 ounces each)
    cream cheese
¼ cup butter or margarine
2 cups confectioners' sugar
1 teaspoon vanilla extract

1. Grease two microwave-safe, 8-inch square baking dishes. Line with waxed paper; grease paper. On another sheet of paper, combine flour, soda and cinnamon. In large bowl, beat oil, granulated sugar, ½ cup light-brown sugar and the eggs until thick and light. Gradually beat in flour mixture; stir in carrots. Spread evenly into prepared dishes; sprinkle each with ⅓ cup chocolate pieces.

2. Cover corners of dishes with foil. Cook, one dish at a time, on MEDIUM 10 minutes; remove foil; rotate. Cook on MEDIUM 5 minutes longer. Rotate; cook on HIGH 2 minutes, or until center is set. Let stand 5 minutes. Repeat. Invert 1 cake layer onto serving plate; cool.

3. Place cream cheese and butter in bowl; heat on LOW 1 minute to soften. Beat in confectioners' sugar, remaining ½ cup light-brown sugar and vanilla until fluffy. Frost 1 layer with 1 cup frosting. Top with second layer; frost. If desired, sprinkle with additional chocolate pieces.

Makes 12 servings.

■ Need to store cookies? Empty coffee or shortening cans make excellent containers for storing batches of homemade cookies. Separate layers of cookies with paper toweling. To take cookies along in lunch boxes, use small cans with plastic lids to keep cookies fresh.

June

For effortless summer entertaining or quick family meals, choose from our nine mouth-watering menus. (Five of the entrées are listed below and pictured with their accompaniments.) And you'll even find an easy-to-follow work plan for getting each meal ready—in just 30 minutes. Start the timer!

Super Supper Hero

Cashew-Parmesan Fish Fillets

Zuppa de Pesce

Stuffed Salisbury Steak

Chicken Yakitori

30-Minute Supper Cookbook

It takes only a few moments' preparation to delight family or guests with any of these easy summer meals.

STUFFED SALISBURY STEAK
CRISP ROLLS
HERBED CORN ON THE COB
APRICOT CREAM
ASSORTED COOKIES

■ Make dessert first; place in freezer. Prepare corn. While corn cooks, shape steak ovals. Broil steaks with corn during last 10 minutes of cooking time.

Stuffed Salisbury Steak

(pictured, pages 98 and 99)

3 pounds ground beef
1 package (2.5 ounces) onion-and-mushroom soup-and-recipe mix (2 envelopes)
1 roasted large red pepper, cut in six strips
3 ounces provolone cheese, cut in 3-by-½-by-¼-inch strips
6 strips boiled ham (3 ounces), 3-by-1½-by-¼ inches

1. Preheat broiler or barbecue grill. In large bowl, gently mix beef with soup mix. Divide mixture into four large ovals. With thumb, make an indentation in one side of oval; fill each with a strip of pepper, cheese and ham. Press meat around filling to seal, and reshape ovals, if necessary.

2. Broil or grill, 6 inches from heat, 5 minutes. Turn; grill 5 minutes longer for medium-rare.

Makes 6 servings.

Herbed Corn on the Cob

(pictured, pages 98 and 99)

6 ears corn on the cob, husked and washed
½ cup (1 stick) butter or margarine, melted
2 tablespoons prepared horseradish
2 tablespoons minced fresh dill or 2 teaspoons dried dillweed
½ teaspoon salt
¼ teaspoon pepper

1. Prepare barbecue grill, or preheat oven to 400°F. Place each ear of corn on a large sheet of heavy-duty aluminum foil. In small glass measure, combine butter, horseradish, dill, salt and pepper. Brush on corn, dividing among ears. Wrap foil around ears, twisting foil at ends to keep in drippings.

2. Grill corn, 6 inches from heat, turning occasionally, 15 to 20 minutes; or bake 30 minutes, or until corn is tender.

Makes 6 servings.

Apricot Cream

(pictured, pages 98 and 99)

1 package (3 ounces) apricot-flavored gelatin
¾ cup boiling water
½ cup cold water
Ice cubes
1 pint vanilla ice cream, softened slightly
1 teaspoon vanilla extract
2 small apricots, pitted and sliced

1. In medium bowl, completely dissolve gelatin in ¾ cup boiling water. Combine ½ cup cold water with ice cubes to make 1¼ cups ice and water. Add to gelatin, stirring until consistency of unbeaten egg whites. If necessary, remove any unmelted ice.

2. With whisk, blend ice cream and vanilla into gelatin until smooth—about 30 seconds. Spoon

---

Page 95: Super Supper Hero, Spiced Shoestring Potatoes, Quick Tortoni.

Pages 96 and 97: Cashew-Parmesan Fish Fillets, Broiled Tomato Wedges, Asparagus With Quick Hollandaise, Strawberries With Zabaglione; (inset) Zuppa de Pesce, "Quilted" Cheesy Cornbread, Assorted Fruits and Cheeses.

Pages 98 and 99: Stuffed Salisbury Steak, Crisp Rolls, Herbed Corn on the Cob, Apricot Cream, Assorted Cookies; (inset) Chicken Yakitori, Sweet-and-Sour Rice, Oriental Salad, Lemon Tarts, Lime Tea.

mixture evenly into six dessert glasses; place in freezer 20 minutes, or until set. Remove from freezer, and refrigerate until serving time. Garnish with apricot slices.

Makes 6 servings.

CASHEW-PARMESAN FISH FILLETS
ASPARAGUS WITH QUICK
HOLLANDAISE
BROILED TOMATO WEDGES
STRAWBERRIES WITH
ZABAGLIONE

■ Make zabaglione; refrigerate. Prepare hollandaise; keep warm. Coat fish; while it bakes, prepare tomatoes. Keep fish warm while tomatoes broil; cook asparagus.

Cashew-Parmesan Fish Fillets
(pictured, pages 96 and 97)

3 tablespoons butter or
  margarine
1 large egg
¾ cup grated Romano cheese
2 tablespoons all-purpose flour
6 fillets (4 ounces each) sole
  or turbot
3 tablespoons salad oil
½ cup chopped cashews
Lemon wedges

1. Preheat oven to 425°F. In jelly-roll pan or large, shallow, rimmed baking pan, melt butter in oven. Meanwhile, in pie plate, beat egg slightly. On waxed paper, combine cheese and flour. Dip each fillet in egg; coat both sides with cheese mixture.

2. Remove pan from oven; add oil to butter; swirl to blend. Arrange fillets in pan, turning to coat with butter mixture. Sprinkle with nuts. Bake on top rack 10 minutes. Garnish with lemon wedges.

Makes 6 servings.

Asparagus With Quick Hollandaise
(pictured, pages 96 and 97)

1½ pounds fresh asparagus
1 cup mayonnaise
2 large egg yolks
2 tablespoons lemon juice
1 to 2 tablespoons hot water

1. In large skillet, bring 1 inch salted water to boiling. Add asparagus; reduce heat. Simmer, covered, 5 minutes, or until just tender; drain.

2. In small, heavy saucepan, combine mayonnaise, egg yolks and lemon juice; mix well. Over medium-low heat, cook, stirring, 2 minutes or until warm. Slowly stir in hot water until desired consistency. Pour over asparagus.

Makes 6 servings.

Broiled Tomato Wedges
(pictured, pages 96 and 97)

¼ cup (½ stick) butter or
  margarine
4 medium tomatoes, cut in 6
  wedges
½ teaspoon salt
¼ teaspoon freshly ground
  pepper

Melt butter in shallow baking pan. Add tomatoes; turn to coat on all sides. Broil, 4 inches from heat, 5 minutes, or until hot. Sprinkle with salt and pepper.

Makes 6 servings.

Strawberries With Zabaglione
(pictured, page 97)

1 box (2.8 ounces)
  whipped-topping mix
  (2 envelopes)
½ cup cold milk
⅓ cup sherry
1 large egg yolk
1 quart strawberries, hulled

In small bowl, with electric mixer at medium speed, beat topping mix and milk until thick and fluffy. At low speed, gradually beat in sherry and egg yolk. Serve over berries.

Makes 6 servings.

■ Crown it with Caviar—Add visual and edible magic out of a little jar of caviar!

—Top deviled egg with caviar.

—Stuff avocado half with shrimp salad; pass mayonnaise seasoned with lemon juice and a spoonful or two of caviar. Garnish with additional caviar.

—Gently top an 8-ounce block of cream cheese with 2 tablespoons red caviar. Trim sides with chopped green onions. Let guests spread on crackers.

ZUPPA DE PESCE
"QUILTED" CHEESY CORNBREAD
ASSORTED FRUITS AND CHEESES

■ Let fruits and cheeses come to room temperature. Prepare cornbread; while cornbread bakes, make Zuppa de Pesce. Arrange fruit-and-cheese platter; place crackers on platter with fruits and cheeses.

Zuppa de Pesce
(pictured, page 96, inset)

2 tablespoons salad oil
½ pound chorizo sausage, cut in ½-inch diagonal slices
1 medium onion, chopped
1 large red pepper, chopped
2 cans (about 14 ounces each) chicken broth
1½ cups water
2 tablespoons lemon juice
1 package (8 ounces) linguini
1 pound little-neck clams, well scrubbed
¼ cup chopped parsley

In 5-quart saucepan, heat oil over medium heat. Cook sausage 3 minutes, or until browned. Add onion and red pepper; sauté 3 minutes. Stir in chicken broth, water and lemon juice; bring to boiling. Add linguini; cook, partially covered, 5 minutes. Add clams. Reduce heat; simmer, covered, 5 minutes, or until clams are opened and linguini is tender. Sprinkle with parsley.
Makes 8 servings.

"Quilted" Cheesy Cornbread
(pictured, page 96, inset)

1 package (8½ ounces) corn-muffin mix
1 large egg
¾ cup sour cream
¼ cup chopped pimiento
¼ cup finely chopped green pepper
½ teaspoon garlic powder
¼ pound fontina cheese, cut into ten ¼-inch-thick strips

Preheat oven to 400°F. Line 8-inch square pan with aluminum foil; grease foil. In medium bowl, combine muffin mix, egg, sour cream, pimiento, pepper and garlic powder; mix well. Spread evenly in prepared pan. Arrange cheese strips in crosswise rows, 1 inch apart, in "quilt" pattern on top of batter (see photograph, page 96). Bake 20 minutes, or until lightly browned.
Makes 8 servings.

Assorted Fruits and Cheeses
(pictured, page 96, inset)

8 peaches, nectarines, pears or apples, cut in slices
1 bunch each green and red grapes
½ pound Cheddar or Gorgonzola cheese
½ pound wedge Brie
Assorted crackers

Arrange ingredients on a platter. Cover with plastic wrap. Leave at room temperature 30 minutes.
Makes 8 servings.

CHICKEN YAKITORI
SWEET-AND-SOUR RICE
ORIENTAL SALAD
LEMON TARTS
LIME TEA

■ Prepare chicken; set aside. Sauté vegetables for rice, and make salad dressing. While rice and chicken cook, assemble tarts. Cut lettuce; top with dressing.

Chicken Yakitori
(pictured, page 99, inset)

1½ pounds boneless chicken breasts, skinned and cut in 1-inch cubes
1 medium green pepper, cut in 1-inch squares
1 medium red pepper, cut in 1-inch squares
1 jar (15 ounces) baby corn, drained
⅓ cup teriyaki sauce
⅓ cup honey
1 medium clove garlic, crushed
¼ teaspoon ground ginger

1. Preheat broiler or barbecue grill. Arrange chicken and vegetables on eight long wooden or metal skewers. In small bowl, combine teriyaki sauce, honey, garlic and ginger. Brush on meat and vegetables.
2. Broil or grill skewered chicken, 6 inches from heat, basting and turning occasionally, 12 to 15 minutes, or until meat is tender.
Makes 4 servings (2 skewers each serving).

■ Here's a way to get a headstart on meals. When cooked chicken is needed for salads, casseroles or other dishes, try poaching it in the microwave: Place skinless pieces in a microwave-safe baking dish and sprinkle chicken with two tablespoons broth or water per piece. Cover with microwave-safe plastic wrap and cook four to eight minutes per pound on HIGH, or until juices run clear. Rearrange once or twice during cooking; let stand, covered, for three minutes. Besides being a real time-saver, this method yields wonderfully succulent chicken.

Sweet-and-Sour Rice

(pictured, page 99, inset)

1 tablespoon salad oil
1 package (4.6 ounces) long-grain rice with Oriental seasoning
4 green onions, cut in 1-inch pieces
1 can (8 ounces) sliced water chestnuts, drained
1⅓ cups water

In medium skillet, heat oil over medium heat. Add rice, green onions and water chestnuts; sauté 3 minutes. Add water and seasoning packet from rice package; bring to boiling. Simmer, covered, 10 minutes, or until rice is tender.
Makes 4 servings.

Oriental Salad

(pictured, page 99, inset)

1 medium head iceberg lettuce
½ cup bottled Oriental-style dressing
2 tablespoons soy sauce
¼ teaspoon ground ginger

Cut lettuce into four wedges. In small bowl, combine dressing, soy sauce and ginger. Pour dressing over lettuce.
Makes 4 servings.

Lemon Tarts

(pictured, page 99, inset)

8 (3-inch) soft oatmeal cookies
Confectioners' sugar
½ cup canned lemon-pie filling

Using a 1-inch rounded cookie cutter, remove and discard a 1-inch-diameter round from center of 4 cookies; sprinkle top of cut cookies with confectioners' sugar. Spread 2 tablespoons lemon filling on each of the remaining cookies; top with cut cookie, sugared side up.
Makes 4 servings.

SUPER SUPPER HERO
SPICED SHOESTRING POTATOES
QUICK TORTONI

■ Make tortoni; place in freezer. Make eggplant mixture for hero sandwich. Prepare shoestring potatoes; assemble hero sandwich while potatoes cook.

Super Supper Hero

(pictured, page 95)

½ cup olive oil
¾ pound eggplant, cut in ½-inch cubes
1 medium red onion, sliced
1 medium green pepper, cut in strips
1 medium red pepper, cut in strips
1 medium yellow pepper, cut in strips
½ cup sun-dried tomatoes
1 teaspoon dried oregano leaves
½ teaspoon salt
⅛ teaspoon pepper
1 large loaf Italian bread, 14-by-4-by-4 inches
Lettuce leaves, washed and crisped
½ pound sliced boiled ham
½ pound sliced salami
½ pound sliced turkey breast
½ pound sliced mozzarella cheese

1. In skillet, heat oil over medium-high heat. Add eggplant, onion and peppers. Sauté, stirring, 5 minutes, or until vegetables are tender. Add sun-dried tomatoes, oregano, salt and pepper.
2. Cut bread in half horizontally. Arrange lettuce on bottom half of bread. Arrange cold cuts and cheese over lettuce. Place pepper mixture on top. Cover with top half of bread. Place long skewers into sandwich to

mark off servings. Use serrated knife to cut between skewers.
Makes 8 servings.

Spiced Shoestring Potatoes

(pictured, page 95)

1 bag (20 ounces) frozen shoestring potatoes
½ cup grated Parmesan cheese
1 tablespoon salt-free herb blend

Preheat oven to 425°F. Arrange potatoes in single layer on aluminum-foil-lined baking sheet or jelly-roll pan. Bake potatoes 5 minutes; toss with cheese and herb blend. Bake 5 minutes longer, or until crisp and golden-brown.
Makes 8 servings.

Quick Tortoni

(pictured, page 95)

10 paper or foil muffin-pan liners
1 cup frozen non-dairy whipped topping, thawed
1 pint vanilla ice cream, slightly softened
¼ cup mini semisweet-chocolate pieces
2 tablespoons almond-flavored liqueur or ½ teaspoon almond extract
¼ cup crushed almond cookies

Place paper liners in muffin pan; set aside. In medium bowl, fold whipped topping into ice cream. Stir in chocolate and liqueur. Spoon into paper liners, dividing evenly. Sprinkle tops of tortoni with cookie crumbs. Freeze 30 minutes, until firm, or ready to serve.
Makes 10 servings.

> TORTELLINI PRIMAVERA
> WITH GORGONZOLA SAUCE
> SAVORY LAVASH
> MARINATED BERRIES

■ Heat water for pasta. Prepare and marinate berries. Cook pasta; prepare vegetables. Warm lavash. Toss pasta with other ingredients.

Tortellini Primavera With Gorgonzola Sauce

1 package (8 ounces) spinach-cheese tortellini
1 package (8 ounces) cheese tortellini
2 tablespoons olive oil
½ pound snow pea pods, trimmed
¼ pound mushrooms, sliced
2 medium carrots, thinly sliced
2 green onions, cut in 2-inch pieces
1 large clove garlic, crushed
½ teaspoon salt
1 cup light cream
¼ pound Gorgonzola cheese, crumbled
¼ cup (½ stick) butter or margarine
¼ teaspoon cracked pepper

1. Cook tortellini as package label directs; drain. Return to saucepan; cover.
2. In large skillet, heat oil. Over high heat, sauté pea pods, mushrooms, carrots, onions, garlic and salt 3 minutes, or until tender-crisp.
3. Toss vegetable mixture with tortellini in saucepan; add cream, half of cheese and the butter and pepper. Over medium heat, cook until mixture is heated through. Sprinkle remaining cheese on top. Serve immediately.
Makes 4 servings.

Savory Lavash

1 package (6 ounces) round sesame lavash (8 pieces)
2 teaspoons olive oil
2 teaspoons grated Parmesan cheese

Preheat oven to 350°F. Place lavash in single layer on baking sheet; brush lightly with oil, and sprinkle with cheese. Bake 5 minutes, or until golden-brown.
Makes 4 servings.

Marinated Berries

1 pint fresh strawberries
½ pint fresh blueberries
½ cup almond-flavored liqueur
4 gaufrettes

Hull strawberries; slice each in half. In medium bowl, combine all berries and liqueur. Marinate 15 minutes. Spoon into wine glasses; serve with gaufrettes.
Makes 4 servings.

> STUFFED BEEF ROLL
> LIME-THYME POTATOES
> EASY FRUIT DIP

■ Prepare vegetables; assemble roll. Prepare potatoes. While beef and potatoes cook, prepare dip, and cut fruit.

Stuffed Beef Roll

1 medium zucchini
1 medium carrot
2 pounds lean ground beef
1 tablespoon salt-free herb blend
3 green onions, cut in half crosswise
¼ pound thinly sliced Cheddar Cheese

1. Preheat oven to 450°F. Cut zucchini and carrot in long, ¼-inch-thick strips. On 15-inch-long heavy-duty aluminum foil, pat beef into a 12-by-10-inch rectangle. Top with herb blend. Place zucchini, carrot and onions lengthwise in center. Top with half of cheese.
2. Using foil, lift and roll up meat over vegetables. Press meat together at ends to seal. Roll off foil; place beef roll, seam side down, in roasting pan. Bake 15 minutes; top with remaining cheese. Bake 5 minutes.
Makes 8 servings.

Lime-Thyme Potatoes

¼ cup (½ stick) butter or margarine, melted
1 teaspoon grated lime peel
1 tablespoon lime juice
1 teaspoon dried thyme leaves
3 large baking potatoes
¼ cup grated Romano cheese
Paprika
½ teaspoon salt

Preheat oven to 450°F. In bowl, combine first 4 ingredients. Cut potatoes lengthwise into eighths; toss in mixture. Place, skin side down, on aluminum-foil-lined baking sheet. Top with cheese, paprika and salt. Bake 20 minutes, or until tender.
Makes 4 to 6 servings.

Easy Fruit Dip

1 cup sour cream
¼ cup firmly packed brown sugar
¼ teaspoon ground cinnamon
Dash ground nutmeg
Assorted seasonal bite-size fruits and fruit pieces

In medium bowl, combine first 4 ingredients. Serve with fruit.
Makes 1 cup.

SCALLOPS WITH ITALIAN PASTA
CRISP SOUR-DOUGH LOAF
CRUNCHY CRÈME PARFAITS

■ Heat water for pasta; prepare parfaits while pasta cooks. Prepare bread. While bread bakes, make sauce for pasta.

Scallops With Italian Pasta

1 package (about 6 ounces) pasta-salad mix with Italian seasoning
2 tablespoons butter or margarine
2 tablespoons olive oil
¼ cup pine nuts
1 pound bay scallops
¼ cup thinly sliced sun-dried tomatoes
¼ cup dry white wine

1. Cook pasta as package label directs; drain. Reserve seasoning packet.
2. In large skillet, melt butter in olive oil. Add pine nuts; sauté 1 minute. Add scallops; cook 2 minutes, or until tender. Stir in contents of reserved seasoning packet, tomatoes and wine. Cook 1 minute. Toss pasta with scallop mixture.
Makes 4 servings.

Crisp Sour-Dough Loaf

¾ cup (1½ sticks) unsalted butter or margarine, softened
1 (1 pound) round sour-dough loaf
¼ pound prosciutto or ham, coarsely chopped
½ cup grated Romano or Parmesan cheese
2 tablespoons snipped fresh chives

1. Melt 2 tablespoons butter; set aside. Preheat oven to 400°F. Cut round loaf, not quite all the way through, into eight wedges.
2. In food processor, combine remaining butter, the ham, cheese, and chives; process until ham is finely chopped and mixture is blended.
3. Spread ham mixture evenly over cut sides of bread wedges. Brush crust with melted butter; place on aluminum-foil-lined baking sheet. Bake 10 minutes.
Makes 8 servings.

Crunchy Crème Parfaits

2 tablespoons cream liqueur
About 1 cup milk
1 package (3.8 ounces) instant vanilla-flavored pudding-and-pie-filling mix
1 cup sour cream
¼ cup crushed macaroon cookies

Place liqueur in 1-cup glass measure. Add milk to make 1 cup. In large bowl, combine milk mixture and pudding mix. With wire whisk or electric mixer, beat until blended and thickened. With rubber spatula, fold in sour cream until blended. Spoon half of the pudding into four parfait glasses. Sprinkle 1 tablespoon crushed cookies over each. Top with remaining pudding. If desired, garnish with whipped topping.
Makes 4 servings.

CURRY-FRUITED TURKEY SALAD
BISCUITS
CHOCOLATE-ALMOND-FILLED CRÊPES
FRUITED ICED TEA

■ Fill and roll crêpes; garnish and refrigerate. Make turkey salad; arrange on platter.

Curry-Fruited Turkey Salad

1½ cups plain yogurt
3 tablespoons lemon juice
2 teaspoons curry powder
1½ tablespoons snipped fennel fern or ½ teaspoon crushed fennel seed
3 cups cubed cooked turkey
1 medium red apple, cored and cut in 1-inch chunks
1 medium ripe avocado, peeled, pitted and cut in 1-inch chunks
1 medium fennel bulb, thinly sliced (2 cups)
½ cup smoked almonds
½ cup chopped dates or raisins
Lettuce leaves

In large bowl, whisk first 4 ingredients until blended. Add turkey, apple, avocado, sliced fennel, almonds, and dates; toss until evenly coated. Serve on lettuce.
Makes 6 to 8 servings.

Chocolate-Almond-Filled Crêpes

1 package (3 ounces) cream cheese, softened
1 cup sour cream
1 bar (8 ounces) milk chocolate with almonds, coarsely chopped, melted and cooled
1 container (8 ounces) frozen non-dairy whipped topping, thawed
8 prepared 8-inch crêpes
½ cup raspberries

1. In bowl, with electric mixer at medium speed, beat cream cheese until smooth. Beat in next 2 ingredients until blended. With rubber spatula, fold in 2 cups topping.
2. Spread ½ cup mixture over each crêpe; roll up, jelly-roll fashion. Place, seam side down, on plate. Garnish with remaining topping and the raspberries.
Makes 8 servings.

Lite Eating: Father's Day Dinner

NONALCOHOLIC CHAMPAGNE
CHICKEN TONNATO
MOLDED CUCUMBER SALAD
CRANAPPLES WITH RASPBERRY
SHERBET

Chicken Tonnato

1¼ cups dry white wine
¼ teaspoon salt
¼ teaspoon dried thyme leaves
2 whole boneless chicken
  breasts, skinned and halved
  (1½ pounds)

Tonnato Sauce
¼ cup drained water-packed
  canned tuna
¼ cup reduced-calorie
  mayonnaise
1 small onion, coarsely
  chopped
1 small celery stalk, coarsely
  chopped
1 anchovy, oil pressed out on
  paper towel
1 tablespoon lemon juice

Leaf lettuce, washed and
  crisped

1. In medium skillet, heat first 3 ingredients to simmer; add chicken and cover. Poach 10 minutes; turn. Cover; poach 5 minutes longer, or until fork-tender. Place in glass bowl. Add poaching liquid. Cool.

2. Meanwhile, in blender, puree sauce ingredients. Set aside.

3. Remove chicken from poaching liquid; place on wire rack. Spread sauce over chicken. Arrange on lettuce-lined plates. If desired, garnish with green-onion flowers, capers and pepper strips.

Makes 4 servings; 220 calories each serving.

Molded Cucumber Salad

1 package (.6 ounce) sugar-
  free lemon-flavored gelatin
1 cup boiling water
1 small unpared cucumber,
  seeded
1 small onion
Cold water
2 tablespoons white vinegar
¼ teaspoon salt
Leaf lettuce, crisped

1. In medium bowl, dissolve gelatin in boiling water; set aside.

2. Shred cucumber and onion over small bowl. Squeeze liquid from cucumber and onion into 2-cup glass measuring cup; reserve vegetables. Add enough cold water to vegetable liquid to make 1½ cups; add to dissolved gelatin with vinegar and salt.

3. Chill until gelatin is the consistency of unbeaten egg white. Stir in reserved cucumber and onion. Pour into 1-quart mold. Refrigerate until firm—2 to 3 hours.

4. To serve, unmold on lettuce leaves; garnish with cucumber slices, if desired.

Makes 4 servings; 20 calories each serving.

Cranapples With Raspberry Sherbet

2 cups reduced-calorie
  cranberry-apple juice
4 medium apples, pared and
  cored
½ pint raspberry sherbet

1. In medium saucepan, bring juice to boiling. Add apples, and reduce heat; simmer until just tender. Transfer apples and juice to glass bowl; refrigerate at least 1 hour.

2. To serve, place an apple on a dessert dish; top with small (¼ cup) scoop of sherbet, and drizzle with poaching liquid. Garnish with mint, if desired.

Makes 4 servings; 169 calories each serving.

■ Garnish Chicken Tonnato with green-onion flowers. Trim root and green part of onion to make a 3-inch piece. Lay onion on its side, and cut through one end to within 1 inch of other end, cutting many times. Place onions in ice water; cover, and refrigerate until onions open.

Quick & Easy: Summer Salads in a Jiffy

Chicken-Antipasto Toss

2 whole boneless chicken
 breasts, skinned and split
 (about 1¼ pounds)
2 cups water
1½ teaspoons salt
½ cup olive oil
⅓ cup red-wine vinegar
2 tablespoons minced fresh
 basil or 1 teaspoon dried
 basil leaves
1 tablespoon minced parsley
1 medium clove garlic, minced
1 teaspoon sugar
¼ teaspoon pepper
2 jars (7 ounces each)
 marinated artichoke hearts,
 drained
1 package (9 ounces) bite-size
 balls of mozzarella
¾ cup sun-dried tomatoes
1 medium zucchini, thinly
 sliced
1 cup sliced mushrooms
½ cup sliced pitted ripe olives
Green-leaf lettuce leaves,
 washed and crisped

1. In large skillet, bring chicken, water and ½ teaspoon salt to boiling. Simmer, covered, 10 minutes or until tender. Remove chicken; cool slightly. Cut into 1½-inch pieces.

2. In bowl, combine oil, vinegar, basil, parsley, garlic, sugar, remaining 1 teaspoon salt and the pepper; mix. Add chicken, artichokes and next 5 ingredients; toss gently.

3. Spoon onto lettuce-lined platter; if desired, garnish with basil leaves.

Makes 6 to 8 servings.

Left: (From top) Warm Shrimp and Pasta, Smoked-Turkey-and-Cucumber Salad, Chicken-Antipasto Toss.

Warm Shrimp and Pasta

2 tablespoons salad oil
1 pound jumbo shrimp,
 shelled, deveined and cut in
 half lengthwise
1 cup chopped tomatoes
1 cup diagonally sliced celery
1 medium clove garlic, minced
1 package (1 ounce) creamy
 herb salad-dressing mix
1 cup sour cream
½ cup mayonnaise
½ cup water
1 pound warm, cooked whole
 wheat pasta shells

1. In large skillet, heat oil over medium heat; add shrimp, tomatoes, celery and garlic and sauté 3 minutes, or until shrimp are cooked.

2. In large bowl, combine salad-dressing mix, sour cream, mayonnaise and water. Stir in pasta; arrange on platter. Spoon shrimp mixture on top. If desired, garnish with radicchio "cups" filled with celery leaves.

Makes 4 servings.

Smoked-Turkey-and-Cucumber Salad

⅓ cup walnut oil
⅓ cup raspberry vinegar
2 teaspoons grated orange peel
1 teaspoon sugar
1 teaspoon salt
¼ teaspoon pepper
1 large or 2 medium hot-house
 cucumbers
Lettuce leaves
2 packages (6 ounces each)
 smoked turkey breast
 (16 slices)
8 sprigs watercress
8 leaves Belgian endive
1 cup fresh raspberries

1. In large bowl, combine oil, vinegar, orange peel, sugar, salt and pepper. Cut cucumber in half lengthwise. Scoop out and discard seeds. Cut halves crosswise into thin slices. Add to dressing; toss to coat. Arrange on lettuce leaves on one side of platter.

2. Roll two slices of turkey into cone shape. Place sprig of watercress and endive leaf in cone. Secure with wooden pick, if necessary. Repeat with remaining turkey, watercress and endive. Arrange on platter with more lettuce leaves and the raspberries.

Makes 4 servings.

■ There are some days when we have little energy and few ideas for dinner except fast-food takeout. Next time you're feeling unimaginative, try one of these handy alternatives to cardboard cuisine:

—Confetti Rice: Combine 3 cups cooked rice with 1 cup cubed baked ham, ¼ cup each sliced green onion, sliced celery and chopped red pepper. Stir in ¾ cup mayonnaise and 2 teaspoons each seasoned salt and dried parsley flakes. Chill. Serve an ice cream-scoopful on a fruit-salad plate.

—Buttered Garlic Noodles with Tuna: Combine ¼ cup melted butter or margarine, ½ teaspoon each garlic powder and spiced salt and one 6½-ounce can of tuna, drained. Toss with 8-ounce package of noodles, cooked and drained. Garnish with ¼ cup shredded Cheddar cheese.

Micro-Way: Extra-Fast Entrées

Crab-and-Corn Bisque

2 tablespoons butter or
  margarine
1 small onion, chopped
1 small red pepper, chopped
1 large celery stalk, chopped
¼ teaspoon dried thyme
  leaves
⅛ to ¼ teaspoon ground red
  pepper
1 can (10¾ ounces) condensed
  cream-of-potato soup
2 cups milk
1 can (17 ounces) creamed
  corn
1 package (12 ounces) surimi
  (fish and crab blend)
Toast rounds

1. In microwave-safe 3-quart glass casserole, melt butter on HIGH 1 minute. Add onion, pepper, celery, thyme and ground red pepper. Cover with plastic wrap; turn back one corner to vent. Cook on HIGH 5 minutes, stirring once.

2. Stir in soup, milk, corn and surimi. Cover; vent. Cook on HIGH 7 minutes, or until boiling. Serve with toast rounds.

Makes 8 servings.

■ Blanch fresh vegetables quickly and easily in your microwave. Rinse and place them in a flat microwave-safe dish; cook until tender-crisp. This enhances color and locks in nutrients.

Scallops in Mushroom-Cream Sauce

**2 tablespoons butter or
    margarine**
4 green onions, chopped
**¼ pound medium mushrooms,
    sliced**
1 large carrot, shredded
½ cup milk
**2 tablespoons white wine or
    lemon juice**
**1 package (1 ounce)
    white-sauce mix**
1 pound bay scallops
**1 cup (4 ounces) shredded
    Swiss cheese**
Chopped parsley

1. In microwave-safe 2-quart glass casserole, melt butter on HIGH 1 minute. Add onions, mushrooms and carrot; cover with plastic wrap and turn back one corner to vent. Cook on HIGH 3 minutes, stirring once. Stir in milk, wine and white-sauce mix until blended. Cover and vent; cook on HIGH 3 minutes, stirring once.

2. Stir in scallops; cover and vent. Cook on HIGH 2 minutes. Add cheese; stir until melted. Spoon into four large or eight small scallop shells. Sprinkle with parsley. If desired, garnish with lemon twists.

Makes 4 luncheon or 8 appetizer servings.

■ If scallops seem strong or old in aroma, add 1 tablespoon lemon juice, sherry or brandy to the dish or add a generous dash of ground ginger.

■ Get more juice from a lemon by warming it in the microwave before squeezing. Heat on HIGH one minute, or until lemon is warm to the touch.

July

Rev up your summer cooking
with the luscious fresh flavor of fruit.
Here colorful twists with tropical
sauces, appetizers, main dishes
and tangy desserts offer light,
refreshing choices for a
warm-weather meal.
Some of the selections are
listed below and pictured
on the next five pages.

Watermelon Fruit Basket With Sabayon Dip

Warm Fruited Brie

Brandied Peach Chicken

Cantaloupe-Vegetable Cups

Curried Papaya Baby-Back Ribs

Apricot-Shrimp Kebabs

Raspberry-Chocolate Pie

Apricot Meringue Pie

Almond Fruit Torte

Fruit Cookbook

Dazzle your guests. Try glossing ribs with a tantalizing tropical fruit sauce, and toss melon balls into your salad, too.

Warm Fruited Brie

(pictured, page 113)

1 package (15 ounces)
    refrigerated all-ready piecrust
2-pound wheel Brie cheese,
    about 8 inches in diameter
2 peaches, pitted and sliced
1 cup green grapes
1 cup (½ pint) raspberries
2 cups apple juice
2 tablespoons cornstarch

1. Preheat oven to 400°F. On large ungreased baking sheet, unfold one round pastry. Place Brie in center; decoratively flute pastry edge to within ½ inch of cheese. Remove cheese; with fork, prick pastry. Bake pastry 10 minutes.

2. Meanwhile, on another baking sheet, unfold second round of pastry. With tip of paring knife, cut out 2-inch-long leaf shapes; mark veins in leaves with back of knife. Bake leaves 5 minutes, or until golden-brown. Cool on wire rack.

3. Remove fluted pastry round from oven; lower heat to 350°F. Place Brie on pastry round; arrange peach slices around top edge of cheese; place grapes and raspberries in center. Bake 10 minutes.

4. Meanwhile, in small saucepan, blend apple juice with cornstarch. Bring to boiling, stirring constantly; cook, 1 minute, until clear and thickened. Place pastry leaves on baked Brie; brush leaves and fruit with apple-juice glaze. Allow to stand 15 minutes, until cheese softens. Carefully transfer pastry and cheese to serving board. With cheese knife, cut through fruit, cheese and pastry into wedges.

Makes 24 wedges.

Page 113: Watermelon Fruit Basket With Sabayon Dip, Warm Fruited Brie.

Pages 114 and 115: (Clockwise from top right) Curried Papaya Baby-Back Ribs, Apricot-Shrimp Kebabs, Brandied Peach Chicken, Cantaloupe-Vegetable Cups.

Pages 116 and 117: (Clockwise from top) Raspberry-Chocolate Pie, Almond Fruit Torte, Apricot Meringue Pie.

Watermelon Fruit Basket With Sabayon Dip

(pictured, page 113)

½ watermelon, cut crosswise
    (10 by 8 inches)
8 to 10 cups assorted summer
    fruits
Sabayon Dip (recipe follows)

1. With a long, sharp knife, remove a 1½-inch slice from cut end of melon; cut slice crosswise in half. With paring knife, remove flesh; reserve. Discard half of rind. Using edge of bowl of a tablespoon as a guide, cut edges of remaining half rind in scallop pattern to form basket handle. Place a wooden pick in handle ends; set aside.

2. Place knife between fruit and rind, to about 2 inches from outside edges of melon; slide knife around diameter to loosen flesh. Remove melon in large chunks; set aside. Cut a small slice from bottom of melon so that melon will stand upright.

3. With paring knife, cut scallop on top edge of rind, using spoon as a guide. With paper towels, absorb juice in melon bottom. Place on serving plate; attach prepared handle. Fill with melon and other fruits; serve with Sabayon Dip.

Makes 12 to 14 servings.

Sabayon Dip

1 cup sugar
6 large egg yolks
1 tablespoon grated orange
    peel
½ cup champagne

1. In top of double boiler set over hot water, over medium heat, combine sugar, egg yolks and orange peel. With portable electric mixer at medium speed, beat 10 minutes, until mixture is light and it falls from beaters in a thick ribbon.

2. Over low heat, with mixer at low speed, blend in champagne. At high speed, beat until sauce is frothy and thick. Serve immediately.

Makes 2½ cups.

Curried Papaya Baby-Back Ribs

(pictured, page 115)

3 pounds pork baby-back
    spareribs
1 cup rice vinegar
¾ teaspoon salt
⅛ teaspoon pepper
2 tablespoons salad oil
¼ cup thinly sliced green
    onion
1 tablespoon minced ginger
    root
2 large cloves garlic,
    crushed
1 tablespoon curry powder
½ cup firmly packed
    light-brown sugar
1 tablespoon tomato paste
1 teaspoon mustard seeds
1 ripe papaya, pared, seeded
    and coarsely chopped

1. Place ribs in large roasting pan. Pour ½ cup vinegar over ribs; turn to coat both sides. Sprinkle with ½ teaspoon salt and the pepper. Let stand 30 minutes.

2. Meanwhile, in medium saucepan, heat oil over medium heat. Add green onion, ginger and garlic; sauté 1 minute, until onion is just tender. Stir in curry powder; cook, stirring, 30 seconds longer. Add remaining ½ cup vinegar, sugar, tomato paste, mustard seeds and ¼ teaspoon salt. Cook, stirring, until smooth. Add papaya; simmer 10 minutes, until mixture thickens slightly.

3. Broil or grill ribs, 6 inches from heat, 30 minutes, or until almost done. Baste both sides of ribs with sauce; cook 10 minutes longer, or until done and well glazed.

4. Pass remaining sauce, placed in papaya half, if desired. If desired, garnish platter with carrot and green-onion curls and lime slices.
Makes 4 servings, 2 cups sauce.

Apricot-Shrimp Kebabs

(pictured, page 115)

1 jar (10 ounces) preserved
    kumquats
1 teaspoon grated lemon peel
¼ cup lemon juice
1 large clove garlic, crushed
Dash hot-red-pepper sauce
½ cup salad oil
½ teaspoon salt
1 pound medium shrimp,
    peeled and deveined
8 large apricots, pitted and
    quartered
1 can (8 ounces) whole water
    chestnuts, drained
¼ pound snow peas, blanched
⅓ cup apricot preserves

1. Make marinade: Drain syrup from kumquats into medium bowl. Stir in lemon peel and juice, garlic, pepper sauce, oil and salt; set aside.

2. Soak eighteen 12-inch wooden skewers in water at least 1 hour; drain. Alternately thread shrimp, apricots, water chestnuts, snow peas and kumquats onto skewers. Place kebabs in single layer in roasting pan; pour marinade over kebabs. Cover; refrigerate 1 hour.

3. Drain kebabs; reserve marinade. Broil or grill kebabs, 6 inches from heat, 2 minutes. Turn; cook 2 minutes longer, or until shrimp are just firm.

4. In saucepan, combine reserved marinade with preserves. Cook until preserves are melted, stirring occasionally; serve with kebabs.
Makes 18 kebabs.

Brandied Peach Chicken

(pictured, page 114)

½ cup peach nectar
½ cup brandy
¼ cup olive oil
2 medium shallots, minced
2 tablespoons light-brown
    sugar
1 teaspoon salt
¼ teaspoon pepper
4-pound chicken, halved
1 jar (12 ounces) peach
    preserves
4 plums, pitted and sliced
1 cup seedless green grapes,
    halved

1. In shallow baking dish, combine nectar, brandy, oil, shallots, sugar, salt and pepper. Place chicken halves in marinade mixture, turning to coat. Refrigerate, covered, several hours or overnight, turning chicken occasionally.

2. Preheat oven to 350°F. Drain chicken, reserving marinade; place, skin side down, in baking dish. Bake 30 minutes, basting occasionally with reserved marinade, and turning after 15 minutes, or until chicken is browned and juices run clear when leg is pierced. If desired, broil chicken until skin is crisp and browned.

3. In medium saucepan, combine remaining marinade, preserves, plums and grapes. Over medium heat, bring to boiling. Spoon part of sauce over chicken; serve remaining sauce with chicken.
Makes 4 servings.

■ Whether you bake, broil, or grill meats, be sure to use tongs, not a fork, to turn the meat. The tines of a fork will pierce meat, allowing the flavorful juices—those that keep the meat moist and succulent—to run out, making the meat tougher.

Plum Duckling

4- to 5-pound duckling
Salt and pepper
2 tablespoons salad oil
1¼ pounds purple plums,
    pitted and coarsely
    chopped
1 cup sugar
½ cup white vinegar
½ cup orange juice

1. Cut duckling in half length-wise, through breastbone and back. Sprinkle inside lightly with salt and pepper. With fork, prick skin well, being careful not to pierce meat.
2. In large skillet, heat oil over medium-high heat; add duck, skin side down, and sauté until evenly browned. Drain off excess fat as it accumulates.
3. Preheat oven to 450°F. In medium saucepan, combine plums, sugar, vinegar and orange juice; bring to boiling. Simmer 10 minutes, or until the plums are tender. Place mixture in food processor; puree.
4. Place duckling, skin side up, on rack in roasting pan. Bake 30 minutes; reduce heat to 400°F. Brush generously with plum sauce; bake 15 minutes longer. Brush again with sauce just before serving; serve remaining sauce with duckling.
Makes 4 servings.

■ Fruit salads are good first courses, side dishes and desserts. Because most fruits are sweet enough without extra sugar added, they are ideal to serve to dieting guests. For more sweetness, though, honey, syrup and preserves can be added. And a small amount of fruit-flavored liqueur, rum, brandy or a simple sugar syrup infused with flavor from vanilla beans adds a sophisticated touch to a mélange of favorite seasonal fruits.

Cantaloupe-Vegetable Cups

(pictured, page 114)

¾ cup salad oil
⅓ cup white-wine vinegar
⅓ cup sugar
1 tablespoon grated onion
1 teaspoon paprika
½ teaspoon dry mustard
½ teaspoon celery salt
½ teaspoon salt
½ pound green beans, stems
    removed
1 large red or green pear,
    cored and cut in 1-inch
    pieces
1 large red pepper, cut in strips
½ pound seedless green grapes
½ medium cantaloupe, cut in
    ½-inch balls
1 small red onion, sliced into
    rings
6 small heads Bibb lettuce
6 slices bacon, cooked and
    crumbled

1. Make dressing: In jar with tight-fitting lid, combine oil, vinegar, sugar, grated onion, paprika, mustard, celery salt and salt. Shake vigorously until blended. Set aside.
2. Cut beans in half crosswise. In medium saucepan, bring 2 inches water to boiling. Cook beans 3 minutes; drain. Rinse with cold water; drain. In large bowl, combine beans, pear, pepper, grapes, cantaloupe and red onion; toss with dressing. Cover; refrigerate 30 minutes.
3. On each of 6 salad plates, spread open a head of lettuce. Spoon 1 cup salad mixture in center; sprinkle with bacon. Garnish with frosted grapes, if desired. (See *Note,* below.)
Makes 6 servings.

Note: In custard cup, beat 1 large egg white lightly with fork until thin, not frothy. With small brush, coat each grape in a small cluster with egg white. Using a teaspoon, over a bowl, lightly sprinkle each grape cluster on all sides with sugar; shake off excess. Dry on wire rack.

Glazed Fruit Kebabs

¾ cup bottled chutney
¼ cup butter or margarine
1 tablespoon raspberry vinegar
½ teaspoon ground ginger
¼ teaspoon ground cinnamon
8 pineapple wedges
1 unpared orange, quartered
8 slices melon (cantaloupe,
    honeydew or casaba), about
    2 inches long
2 unpeeled peaches, halved
    and pitted

1. In small saucepan, combine chutney, butter, vinegar, ginger and cinnamon. Cook, stirring, until butter is melted.
2. Meanwhile, thread fruit on four skewers; brush with chutney glaze. Cook, 4 inches from heat, about 5 minutes, or until heated through. Brush with glaze several times during cooking. Serve remaining glaze with kebabs. Serve with grilled fish, chicken or pork.
Makes 4 servings.

Crunchy Grilled Bananas

Juice of 1 lime
¼ cup shredded coconut
¼ cup chopped macadamia
    nuts
4 large bananas, cut in 2-inch
    pieces
¼ cup butter or margarine,
    melted

1. Place lime juice in pie plate. In another pie plate, combine coconut and nuts. Toss banana pieces in lime juice. Brush each piece with butter; roll in coconut mixture. Thread banana pieces onto skewers.
2. Cook, 4 inches from heat, on coolest part of grill, turning several times, until coconut is golden—about 10 minutes. Serve with ice cream or sherbet.
Makes 4 servings.

Apricot Meringue Pie

(pictured, page 116)

6 large eggs, separated
½ cup superfine sugar
¼ cup apricot-flavored liqueur
¼ cup (½ stick) butter or
** margarine, melted**
½ cup sifted cake flour
3 pints vanilla ice cream,
** slightly softened**
½ pound (about 3) apricots,
** cut in ¼-inch pieces**
Apricot Sauce (recipe follows)
⅛ teaspoon cream of tartar
¾ cup granulated sugar

1. Day before serving: Preheat oven to 350°F. Grease 9-inch round cake pan. Line bottom with waxed paper; grease and flour paper. In top of double boiler set over simmering water, whisk egg yolks with superfine sugar until sugar dissolves and mixture is warm. Remove from heat. Transfer to large bowl of electric mixer. At high speed, beat 5 minutes, or until thick and pale. Slowly beat in 2 tablespoons liqueur. In small bowl, blend ½ cup yolk mixture with butter; fold flour, then butter mixture into yolk mixture. Pour into prepared pan; bake 15 minutes, or until cake tester inserted in center comes out clean. (Layer will be thin.) Loosen edge; invert onto wire rack. Remove waxed paper; cool completely. Place in 9-inch pie plate, pressing into plate to form shallow bowl. (See *Note.*)

2. In large bowl, combine ice cream, apricots and remaining 2 tablespoons liqueur. Spoon into prepared cake-bowl, mounding mixture in center. Cover with plastic wrap; freeze overnight or until hard.

3. Make Apricot Sauce.

4. Before serving: Preheat oven to 500°F. In large bowl of electric mixer, at high speed, beat egg whites and cream of tartar until foamy. Gradually beat in granulated sugar, 2 tablespoons at a time, until stiff peaks form. Spread about half meringue over ice-cream mixture

and cake. Using pastry bag fitted with ¾-inch star tip, pipe remaining meringue on top of pie. Bake 5 minutes, or until golden. Serve immediately with Apricot Sauce.

Makes 8 to 10 servings.

Note: A purchased sponge-cake may be used. Cut a 1-inch layer from cake; fit and press into pie plate.

Apricot Sauce

¾ pound apricots, coarsely
** chopped (about 5)**
½ cup apricot nectar
¼ cup sugar
2 tablespoons apricot-flavored
** liqueur**

In medium saucepan, combine apricots, nectar and sugar. Bring to boiling; simmer, uncovered, 8 minutes, or until apricots are tender. Stir in liqueur; puree in food processor or blender. Cover; refrigerate.

Makes 1½ cups sauce.

Almond Fruit Torte

(pictured, pages 116 and 117)

6 large eggs, separated
1 cup granulated sugar
1 teaspoon almond extract
¾ cup sifted cake flour
⅓ cup (1½ ounces) finely
** ground almonds**
1 teaspoon baking powder
⅛ teaspoon salt
⅓ cup confectioners' sugar
2 cups heavy cream
2 tablespoons almond-flavored
** liqueur**
2 kiwifruit, pared and sliced
1 cup sliced strawberries
Assorted berries
Sliced starfruit

1. Line a 15½-by-10½-by-1-inch jelly-roll pan with waxed paper, extending paper 1 inch over short ends. Grease paper. Preheat oven to 350°F. In large bowl of electric

mixer, at medium-high speed, beat egg yolks, ½ cup granulated sugar and almond extract, about 5 minutes until thick and pale. Meanwhile, on another sheet of waxed paper, combine flour, almonds, baking powder and salt. Fold flour mixture into yolk mixture; set aside.

2. In large bowl, with clean beaters, beat egg whites until foamy. At high speed, gradually beat in remaining ½ cup granulated sugar, beating until stiff peaks form. Stir about one-fourth of the meringue into yolk mixture to lighten. Fold in remaining meringue. Spread batter into prepared pan.

3. Bake 15 minutes, or until cake springs back when lightly touched. Sprinkle a kitchen towel with 1 tablespoon confectioners' sugar. When cake is done, with knife, loosen edges; invert onto towel. Remove pan and waxed paper. With serrated knife, trim crusts of cake. Cool on towel on wire rack.

4. Meanwhile, prepare filling: In small bowl of electric mixer, combine cream, remaining confectioners' sugar and the liqueur. At high speed, beat until stiff. Spread whipped cream over top of cooled cake. Cut cake crosswise into thirds, making three 10-by-5-inch pieces. Arrange kiwifruit on one layer; place on serving platter. Place second cake layer over kiwifruit, cream side up. Arrange strawberries on top. Place third layer over all. Arrange berries and starfruit on top.

Makes 10 servings.

■ Did you know that extra egg whites can be kept in a sealed jar in your refrigerator for up to one year? You can also freeze, defrost and refreeze them. A helpful note: One egg white is approximately an eighth of a cup, or two tablespoons.

Raspberry-Chocolate Pie

(pictured, page 117)

1 package (15 ounces) refrigerated all-ready piecrust
2 cups heavy cream
1½ cups (9 ounces) semisweet-chocolate pieces
3 tablespoons butter or margarine, softened
2 tablespoons brandy
3 cups raspberries
½ cup granulated sugar
1½ cups orange juice
4 teaspoons cornstarch
¼ cup confectioners' sugar

1. Preheat oven to 425°F. Fit one round pastry into 9-inch pie plate; trim pastry edge even with plate rim. Unfold second round pastry. With 1-inch star cutter, cut out about 30 stars. Brush pastry edge with water; place stars, overlapping, on dampened rim, pressing to secure. Line bottom of pie with aluminum foil; fill with metal pie weights, or uncooked beans or rice. Bake 15 minutes. Reduce heat to 375°F. Remove weights and foil; bake 10 minutes longer, or until crust is golden. Cool completely on wire rack.

2. Make filling: In medium saucepan, over medium heat, heat 1 cup cream and the chocolate until chocolate melts; stir until mixture is smooth. Remove from heat; add butter and brandy. Stir until butter melts. Transfer mixture to large bowl of electric mixer. Refrigerate until cold, about 45 minutes, stirring occasionally. At medium-high speed, beat chocolate mixture until soft peaks form. Pour into prepared pie shell. Cover loosely with plastic wrap; refrigerate.

3. Make sauce: In medium saucepan, combine 1½ cups raspberries with granulated sugar. Bring to boiling; simmer 5 minutes, or until thickened. In small bowl, blend orange juice with cornstarch; stir into raspberry mixture. Bring to boiling, and cook, stirring, 1 minute, until mixture is clear and thickened. Pour through fine sieve into bowl. Cover; refrigerate until cold. Pour half of raspberry sauce over chocolate layer in pie shell; refrigerate until set. Stir ½ cup raspberries into remaining sauce; set aside.

4. In large bowl, combine remaining 1 cup cream and the confectioners' sugar; at high speed, beat until stiff. Spread half of cream mixture over raspberry layer in pie; pipe or spread remainder on top. Arrange remaining raspberries on top of cream. Refrigerate until ready to serve; top each serving with sauce.

Makes 8 servings, 1 cup sauce.

Banana Cream Tartlets

1 cup plus 3 tablespoons unsifted all-purpose flour
½ teaspoon salt
¼ cup (½ stick) cold butter or margarine, cut in pieces
2 tablespoons shortening
3 to 4 tablespoons cold water
2 large eggs
⅔ cup sugar
1⅓ cups milk
2 tablespoons rum
1 teaspoon instant coffee powder
1 teaspoon vanilla extract
2 medium bananas, sliced
1½ cups sweetened whipped cream

1. In food processor, combine 1 cup flour and the salt. Add 3 tablespoons butter and the shortening; process until mixture resembles coarse crumbs. With processor running, add water; process until pastry forms a ball. Flatten ball into a disk; wrap in plastic wrap. Refrigerate 20 minutes.

2. Preheat oven to 425°F. On lightly floured surface, roll dough ⅛-inch thick. Using 4-inch biscuit cutter, cut out 8 rounds. Fit each round into a 2½-by-1½-inch muffin-pan cup or tart pan. Place a paper cupcake liner in each; fill with metal pie weights or uncooked beans or rice. Bake 10 minutes; remove liners and weights. Reduce heat to 375°F; bake pastry 8 minutes longer, or until golden. Cool completely in pan on wire rack.

3. In large bowl of electric mixer, at high speed, beat eggs with sugar until thick and pale—5 minutes. At medium speed, beat in remaining flour. In medium saucepan, heat milk to boiling. With mixer running, slowly pour hot milk into egg mixture; beat until blended. Pour mixture into clean saucepan. Over medium-high heat, cook, stirring, until boiling. Simmer, stirring, 2 minutes, or until custard is very thick. Remove from heat; stir in the remaining 1 tablespoon butter.

4. In small bowl, combine rum, coffee powder and vanilla; stir into custard. Cover surface with plastic wrap; refrigerate until cold.

5. To serve: Evenly divide custard among prepared tart shells. Arrange banana slices on top, reserving 8 slices; pipe whipped cream over bananas. Place a reserved banana slice on top of each tart.

Makes 8 tarts.

Three-Fruit Clafouti

2 large nectarines, cut in ½-inch wedges
½ cup blueberries
½ cup raspberries
⅔ cup granulated sugar
1½ cups milk
1 cup cream
4 large eggs
1¼ cups unsifted all-purpose flour
2 tablespoons brandy
1 teaspoon vanilla extract
Confectioners' sugar

1. Preheat oven to 375°F. Grease a 10-inch quiche dish; arrange fruit in bottom. Sprinkle with ⅓ cup granulated sugar; set aside.

2. In blender, combine milk, cream, eggs and remaining ⅓ cup granulated sugar. Process 30 seconds; add flour, brandy and vanilla. Process 1 minute, or until smooth; pour over fruit. Bake 40 minutes, or until puffed and golden. Sprinkle with confectioners' sugar; if desired, serve with additional cream.

Makes 8 servings.

Frozen Kiwi Dream

3 medium kiwifruit, pared
1 can (6 ounces) frozen lemonade concentrate (do not thaw)
1 cup cold water
¾ cup light rum
1 tablespoon Triple Sec (orange-flavored liqueur)
4 cups crushed ice or small ice cubes

1. Cut kiwifruit in ½-inch pieces; set aside.

2. Into blender container, spoon frozen lemonade concentrate; add water, rum and Triple Sec. Blend until smooth—about 30 seconds. With motor running, gradually add ice. Add kiwifruit pieces; blend until smooth. Serve in stemmed glasses; garnish each glass with crosswise slices of unpared kiwifruit.

Makes 6 servings.

■ "Should I sift flour before or after measuring it?" is a commonly asked question among home bakers. The answer lies in the recipe. "One cup sifted flour" means you should sift first; "one cup flour, sifted" indicates that you should measure first.

Papaya Upside-Down Cake

7 tablespoons butter or margarine, at room temperature
½ cup firmly packed light-brown sugar
1 large ripe papaya
3 tablespoons pine nuts
¼ teaspoon salt
1⅓ cups unsifted all-purpose flour
¾ cup granulated sugar
1¾ teaspoons baking powder
½ cup milk
1 large egg, beaten
1 tablespoon dark rum
½ teaspoon vanilla extract

1. Preheat oven to 375°F. Lightly grease sides of an 8-inch round cake pan. Set aside.

2. In small skillet, over low heat, melt 4 tablespoons butter; add brown sugar; stir until sugar is dissolved. Pour into prepared pan; cool 5 minutes.

3. Pare papaya; slice in half lengthwise; remove seeds. Cut papaya crosswise into ¼-inch-thick slices; arrange, overlapping in petal fashion, over sugar mixture, leaving center area clear.

4. In small skillet, over medium heat, shake pine nuts until lightly browned. Spoon over papaya slices and sugar mixture in center of pan.

5. In medium bowl, with wooden spoon, combine remaining 3 tablespoons butter with salt, flour, sugar, baking powder, milk, egg, rum and vanilla; pour batter over papaya and pine nuts, spreading evenly to edges of pan. Bake 30 minutes or until cake tester inserted in center comes out clean.

6. Cool on wire rack 5 minutes; invert cake onto serving plate; let stand 5 minutes before removing pan. If desired, serve cake warm with vanilla ice cream.

Makes 8 servings.

Poached Pears

1½ cups water
¼ cup grenadine
½ teaspoon ground ginger
4 medium Bosc pears, peeled, with stems

1. In medium saucepan, combine water, grenadine and ginger; bring to boiling. Remove cores from bottom ends of pears. Add pears to syrup; reduce heat and simmer, uncovered, until tender—about 20 minutes. Turn and baste pears with cooking liquid as they poach to distribute color evenly.

2. Remove pears with slotted spoon to serving dish. Return liquid to boiling and reduce to about 1 cup. Pour syrup over pears; cool, then chill in refrigerator. Garnish with lemon twists.

Makes 4 servings.

Strawberry Fluff

1 pint fresh strawberries, hulled
2 large egg whites, at room temperature
¼ cup sugar
1 tablespoon lemon juice
1 tablespoon orange-flavored liqueur

1. Thinly slice ¼ cup strawberries; cover, and set aside. Coarsely chop remaining berries, and freeze until firm.

2. In medium bowl, with portable mixer, beat egg whites at high speed until foamy. Gradually beat in sugar, 1 tablespoon at a time, until soft peaks form; beat in lemon juice.

3. In food processor or blender, puree frozen strawberries. Add puree, 1 tablespoon at a time, to egg whites; beat until nearly double in volume—5 minutes. Beat in liqueur. Spoon into stemmed glasses; garnish with sliced strawberries.

Makes 4 servings.

Lite Eating:
Tangy Oriental Dinner

MANDARIN VEAL
WITH GREEN-ONION RICE
CITRUS-CUCUMBER SALAD
FROZEN FRUIT TERRINE
WITH ALMOND SAUCE

Mandarin Veal With Green-Onion Rice

1 tablespoon salad oil
¾ pound lean boneless veal
1 small onion, cut in wedges
1 large clove garlic, crushed
1 cup chicken broth
⅓ cup white vinegar
¼ cup sugar
1 tablespoon soy sauce
½ teaspoon ground ginger
½ pound broccoli
1 medium red pepper, cubed
4 teaspoons cornstarch
¼ cup pineapple juice
2 cups fresh pineapple chunks
1 can (11 ounces) mandarin-orange segments, drained
1 cup whole water chestnuts, drained and halved
3 cups cooked rice
3 green onions, minced

1. In skillet, heat oil over medium-high heat; brown veal in hot oil. Remove veal; set aside. Add onion and garlic to pan; sauté 3 minutes. Add next 5 ingredients and veal. Cover; simmer 20 minutes.
2. Meanwhile, cut broccoli into flowerets; cut stalk into ¼-inch-thick slices. Add broccoli and pepper to veal mixture; cook 3 minutes.

In small bowl, blend cornstarch with pineapple juice; stir into veal mixture. Bring to boiling, stirring constantly. Cook 1 minute, until thickened and smooth. Add fruit and water chestnuts; heat through.
3. Toss rice with green onions, and serve with veal.
Makes 6 servings; 350 calories each serving.

Citrus-Cucumber Salad

1 large pink grapefruit, peeled
6 cucumbers, coarsely chopped
2 tablespoons soy sauce
1 tablespoon toasted sesame seeds
Radicchio leaves

1. Over bowl, section grapefruit, catching juice. Add sections, cucumber, soy sauce and sesame seeds; toss to combine.
2. Place in serving bowl lined with radicchio leaves. If desired, garnish with strips of grapefruit peel.
Makes 6 servings; 30 calories each serving.

■ You can make perfect melon balls with just a set of metal measuring spoons! Cut a melon in half; remove and discard seeds. Start with inside edge of spoon and cut into melon with a circular motion to form balls. Use the tablespoon for large balls, the teaspoon for small.

Frozen Fruit Terrine With Almond Sauce

1 package (12 ounces) frozen raspberries, partially thawed
½ cup sugar
6 kiwifruit, pared
2 medium-size ripe papaya, pared, halved and seeded
1 tablespoon lime juice
1 package (1.1 ounces) reduced-calorie vanilla-flavored instant-pudding-and-pie-filling mix
2½ cups skim milk
¼ teaspoon almond extract

1. Line an 8-by-4-inch loaf pan with aluminum foil. In blender, puree raspberries with ¼ cup sugar. Pour into pan; freeze 1 hour.
2. Puree kiwifruit with 2 tablespoons sugar. Pour over raspberry layer; freeze 1 hour. Puree papaya with 2 tablespoons sugar and the lime juice; pour over kiwifruit layer. Freeze overnight or until firm.
3. Unmold terrine onto platter; garnish with additional kiwifruit slices, if desired. Refrigerate ½ hour, or until soft enough to slice.
4. Blend pudding mix, milk and almond extract. Serve with terrine.
Makes 10 servings; 150 calories each serving.

Right: (Clockwise from top) Mandarin Veal With Green-Onion Rice, Frozen Fruit Terrine With Almond Sauce, Citrus-Cucumber Salad.

Quick & Easy: Fruited Side Dishes

Pear and Red-Potato Salad

2½ pounds medium
   red-skinned potatoes
3 pears, cored and sliced
2 medium celery stalks, thinly
   sliced
⅔ cup bottled red-wine
   vinaigrette dressing
2 tablespoons chopped parsley
1 green onion, minced
½ teaspoon salt
Lettuce leaves, washed and
   crisped

1. In covered saucepan, cook potatoes, covered with water, 15 minutes, or until tender. Drain; rinse with cold water until cool. (Do not allow to sit in water.)

2. Quarter potatoes. In large bowl, combine with pears and next 5 ingredients. Toss until coated; serve in lettuce-lined bowl.
   Makes 6 servings.

Rum-Splashed Fruit Brochettes

2 firm bananas, peeled and cut
   into 2-inch pieces
2 nectarines, cut into 1-inch
   wedges
2 unpeeled oranges, quartered
1 Golden Delicious apple,
   cored and cut into 1-inch
   wedges
1 unpeeled lime, quartered
¼ cup rum
⅓ cup sugar
3 cups 2½-inch French-bread
   cubes
½ cup (1 stick) butter or
   margarine, melted

1. Prepare grill for barbecuing.

2. In bowl, toss fruit with rum and 3 tablespoons sugar.

3. Brush bread with butter; sprinkle with remaining sugar. Thread fruit and bread on four 15-inch skewers; reserve liquid from fruit.

4. Grill brochettes, 6 inches from heat; turn frequently and brush with fruit liquid until lightly caramelized, about 5 minutes.
   Makes 4 servings.

Polynesian Vegetables

1 jar (12 ounces) apricot
   preserves
¼ cup red-wine vinegar
2 tablespoons soy sauce
1 teaspoon to 1 tablespoon
   grated ginger root
¼ teaspoon garlic powder
¾ teaspoon salt
1 small red onion, cut into
   ½-inch wedges
1 green pepper, cut into 1-inch
   pieces
1 yellow pepper, cut into
   1-inch pieces
1 medium pineapple, pared
   and cut into 1-inch pieces
2 tomatoes, cut into ½-inch
   wedges

1. Prepare grill for barbecuing.

2. In skillet, combine first 6 ingredients. Add onion and peppers.

3. Place skillet on grill 6 inches from heat. Cook, stirring until vegetables are tender-crisp. Add pineapple and tomatoes; heat through.
   Makes 6 servings.

■ Embellish party punches with jumbo "fruit cubes"—juices frozen with cherries or lemon or lime slices in muffin-pan cups. They look pretty, taste better and last longer than regular ice cubes.

Micro-Way: Fruit Desserts

Tropical Bavarian

2 packages (2.6 ounces each)
    Bambini cookies or other
    crisp ladyfinger cookies
1 can (29 ounces) apricot
    halves
2 envelopes unflavored
    gelatine
¾ cup milk
3 large eggs, separated
½ cup sugar
2 teaspoons grated lemon peel
⅓ cup lemon juice
3 tablespoons apricot-flavored
    brandy
½ cup heavy cream
12 strawberries, hulled

1. Cut cookies to measure 2¾ inches. Arrange around sides of 9-by-5-inch loaf pan. Drain apricots; reserve ¼ cup syrup. Coarsely chop half the apricots; set aside.

2. In small bowl, sprinkle gelatine over ½ cup milk; let stand 2 minutes. Cook on HIGH 1 minute. In large bowl, whisk egg yolks with ¼ cup sugar, the remaining ¼ cup milk, the lemon peel, lemon juice and 2 tablespoons brandy until blended. Cook on HIGH 5 to 6 minutes, stirring every 2 minutes, until slightly thickened. Stir in dissolved gelatine. Chill over larger bowl of ice water; stir occasionally, until consistency of unbeaten egg whites.

3. In small bowl of electric mixer, at high speed, beat egg whites until foamy. Gradually beat in remaining ¼ cup sugar until stiff peaks form. In another small bowl, whip cream until stiff peaks form. Fold egg whites, cream and chopped apricots into gelatine mixture. Spoon half into prepared loaf pan; place strawberries, point down, in 2 lengthwise rows. Top with remaining mixture. Refrigerate 3 hours, or until firm.

4. Puree remaining apricots with reserved syrup and 1 tablespoon brandy. Unmold Bavarian; if desired, garnish with apricots, strawberries and mint. Serve with sauce.

Makes 8 to 10 servings.

Three-Fruit Cream Tart

⅔ cup butter or margarine
1½ cups graham-cracker crumbs
½ cup finely chopped pecans
¼ cup granulated sugar
½ teaspoon ground cinnamon
1 package (8 ounces) cream cheese
½ cup confectioners' sugar
2 tablespoons heavy cream
2 tablespoons apple-flavored brandy
4 nectarines, pitted and cut in six wedges
1 kiwifruit, pared and thinly sliced crosswise
1 plum, pitted and cut into six wedges
⅓ cup apple jelly

1. In a medium glass bowl, melt butter on HIGH 1½ minutes. Stir in graham-cracker crumbs, pecans, granulated sugar and cinnamon. With back of spoon, press mixture up side and on bottom of 10-inch microwave-safe quiche dish. Cook on HIGH 3 minutes, rotating once; refrigerate.

2. In medium bowl, beat cream cheese, confectioners' sugar, cream and brandy until mixture is light and fluffy. Evenly spread into prepared crust. Arrange nectarine wedges, kiwifruit slices and plum wedges on top of tart.

3. Place apple jelly in custard cup; melt on HIGH 2 minutes, stirring once. Cool slightly; brush melted jelly over fruit. Refrigerate tart until serving.

Makes 8 servings.

Peach Melba en Croûte

1¾ cups milk
¾ cup sugar
4 teaspoons cornstarch
3 large egg yolks
½ teaspoon vanilla extract
4 medium peaches (1½ pounds)
1 cup dry white wine
½ cup almond-flavored liqueur
1 teaspoon lemon juice
1 package (11 ounces) pie-crust mix
¼ cup finely chopped almonds
⅓ cup seedless raspberry jam

1. In 2-cup glass measure, heat milk on HIGH 3 minutes; set aside. In medium glass bowl, combine ¼ cup sugar and the cornstarch; whisk in yolks and vanilla until blended. Stir in milk; cook on HIGH 3 minutes, stirring occasionally, until thickened. Cover; refrigerate.

2. Halve and pit peaches. In 3-quart glass casserole, combine wine, remaining ½ cup sugar, ¼ cup liqueur and the lemon juice. Add peaches; cover. Cook on HIGH 12 minutes, rotating after 6 minutes, until tender. Refrigerate until cool.

3. In medium bowl, combine pie-crust mix, nuts and remaining ¼ cup liqueur; mix with fork just until combined. Between 2 sheets waxed paper, roll each half dough to about ⅛-inch thickness. Remove top sheets of paper. From each half, cut out 4 peach-shape rounds about ½ inch larger than peach halves. Slide one sheet waxed paper and pastry onto microwave-safe baking sheet. Cook on HIGH 4 to 6 minutes, rotating every minute. Carefully slide waxed paper onto wire rack to cool; repeat. Reroll trimmings; cut 16 leaves and 8 stems; cook as above.

4. Carefully remove waxed paper from pastry. Spread each round with 2 teaspoons jam. Place peach half, cut side down, on top; place on dessert plate. Arrange 2 leaves and 1 stem on each; spoon some sauce over peach; pass remaining sauce.

Makes 8 servings.

Raspberry Bread Pudding

1 quart milk
¾ cup firmly packed
  light-brown sugar
¼ cup cornstarch
6 large eggs
1 teaspoon vanilla extract
½ teaspoon ground cinnamon
8 slices white bread, toasted
2 medium pears
1 cup raspberries

1. In 1-quart glass measure, heat milk on HIGH 5 minutes, or until scalded. In large bowl, combine light-brown sugar and cornstarch. With whisk, gradually beat in eggs, vanilla and cinnamon; gradually whisk in hot milk.

2. Slice toast diagonally in half. Core pears; cut into ¼-inch-thick slices. Cut pear slices crosswise in half. Grease shallow microwave-safe, 2-quart baking dish. Arrange half of pears and raspberries on bottom of dish; place bread on top. Carefully pour custard over bread and fruit. Arrange remaining fruit on top. Cook on HIGH 5 minutes; rotate dish after 2 minutes. Cook on MEDIUM 20 minutes, or until center is just firm, rotating dish every 4 minutes. Remove and let stand 10 minutes. Serve pudding warm or cold.

Makes 8 to 10 servings.

■ When you need an easy dish to take to a get-together, make this favorite cocktail appetizer treat: Coat seedless grapes with spreadable, cold-pack cheese or a mixture of equal parts cream cheese and blue cheese; then roll in finely chopped, toasted walnuts. Freeze on tray. When grapes are frozen, put your delicious creation into a sturdy container or prechilled wide-mouthed thermos container.

August

We crossed the country to bring you this mouth-watering collection of state-fair favorites, straight from the judges' tables. Every recipe is a winner—and you'll be one too when you choose from this tempting assortment.

Homemade Breads

Specialty Rolls

Assortment of Condiments

Doughnuts and Buns

Batches of Cookies

Cakes and Filled Cakes

Creams, Truffles and Toffee

KENTUCKY
STATE
FAIR
LOUISVILLE

FREE
TRY·ONE

2nd PRIZE

State-Fair Cookbook

All of the recipes in our August chapter are blue-ribbon winners from state-fair competitions and cookbooks.

Cocktail Rye Rounds

(pictured, page 131)
Starr Scherf, Iowa

8 to 9 cups unsifted all-purpose flour
3 cups unsifted rye flour
1 package fast-rising or regular dry yeast
½ cup firmly packed light-brown sugar
1 tablespoon salt
2 cups water
¾ cup mashed potatoes
⅔ cup evaporated milk
¼ cup (½ stick) butter or margarine
¾ cup molasses
1 large egg white
Caraway seeds
Rolled oats

1. In large bowl of electric mixer, combine 2 cups all-purpose flour,

---

Page 131: Breads, rolls and condiments. See page 137 for identification sketch.

Pages 132 and 133: More condiments and breads, along with doughnuts, buns and cookies. See page 140 for identification sketch.

Pages 134 and 135: Cakes and confections. See page 143 for identification sketch.

the rye flour, yeast, sugar and salt; mix well. In medium saucepan, heat water, mashed potatoes, milk, butter and molasses until very hot (120° to 130°F).

2. With mixer on low speed, pour hot potato mixture into flour mixture. Beat at medium speed 3 minutes, scraping bowl with rubber spatula. With wooden spoon, gradually add enough remaining flour until dough leaves side of bowl.

3. On lightly floured surface, knead dough 5 minutes, or until smooth and elastic. Place in lightly greased bowl; turn dough over to bring up greased side. Cover bowl with towel; let rise in warm place (85°F), free from drafts, 45 minutes, or until doubled.

4. Grease 2 large baking sheets. Punch dough down; turn out onto floured board. Divide in half; set one half aside, covered. From remaining half, pinch off a handful of dough. Roll out into 12-inch round; set aside. Roll out remainder into 12-inch round. Brush edge of thicker round with water. Place thinner round on top; press to seal. Place on baking sheet. Repeat with remaining dough half. Cover both rounds; let rise 30 minutes.

5. Preheat oven to 350°F. In small cup, beat egg white until foamy. Brush top of loaves with egg white; sprinkle with caraway seeds and oats. Bake 30 minutes, or until golden and loaves sound hollow when tapped.
Makes 2 large loaves.

Raisin Bread

(pictured, page 131)
Mary Ann Huber, Indiana (from *Kentucky State Fair Cookbook***)**

6½ to 7 cups unsifted all-purpose flour
2 packages fast-rising or regular dry yeast
1 cup granulated sugar
1 tablespoon salt
2 cups water
2 large eggs
¼ cup salad oil
1½ cups raisins
1 tablespoon ground cinnamon

Glaze
1½ cups confectioners' sugar
2 tablespoons butter or margarine, softened
1½ teaspoons vanilla extract
1 to 2 tablespoons water

1. In large bowl of electric mixer, combine 1½ cups flour, the yeast, ½ cup granulated sugar and the salt; mix well. With mixer at low speed, pour very warm water (120° to 130°F), eggs and oil into mixture. Beat at medium speed 3 minutes, scraping bowl with rubber spatula. With wooden spoon, gradually add enough remaining flour until dough leaves side of bowl.

2. On lightly floured surface, knead dough 5 minutes, or until smooth and elastic. Place in lightly greased bowl; turn dough over to bring up greased side. Cover bowl with towel; let dough rise in warm place (85°F), free from drafts, 45

minutes, or until doubled. Meanwhile, grease two 9-by-5-inch loaf pans; set aside.

3. Punch down dough; turn out onto board. Divide in half; knead ¾ cup raisins into each half. Roll each half into 18-by-9-inch rectangle; brush lightly with salad oil. In small cup, mix ½ cup granulated sugar with cinnamon; sprinkle half the mixture over each half dough.

4. Roll dough up, jelly-roll fashion, starting with short side. Fold ends under each loaf; place each, seam side down, in prepared pans. Brush with salad oil. Let rise 2 hours, or until doubled.

5. Preheat oven to 375°F. Bake loaves 30 to 35 minutes, until they are deep golden-brown and sound hollow when tapped on bottom. Remove from pans immediately; cool completely on wire racks.

6. Make Glaze: In small bowl, mix sugar, butter and vanilla until smooth. Stir in 1 to 2 tablespoons warm water, a teaspoonful at a time, until of pourable consistency. Drizzle over cooled loaves.

Makes 2 loaves.

Spicy Pineapple-Zucchini Bread

(pictured, page 131)
Elizabeth Anne Bridges, Texas

3 cups unsifted all-purpose flour
1 cup chopped walnuts
2 teaspoons baking soda
1½ teaspoons ground cinnamon
1 teaspoon salt
¾ teaspoon ground nutmeg
½ teaspoon baking powder
3 large eggs
1 cup salad oil
2 cups sugar
2 teaspoons vanilla extract
2 cups unpared, coarsely shredded zucchini
1 can (8¼ ounces) crushed pineapple, drained

1. Preheat oven to 350°F. Grease and flour two 8-by-4-inch loaf pans; set aside. In medium bowl, combine first 7 ingredients; set aside.

2. In large bowl of electric mixer, at high speed, beat eggs until frothy. Beat in salad oil, sugar and vanilla; beat until mixture is thick and foamy. Stir in zucchini, pineapple and flour mixture. Pour into prepared pans, dividing evenly. Bake 1 hour, or until cake tester inserted in center comes out clean.

3. Cool in pans 10 minutes. Turn out onto wire racks; cool.

Makes 2 loaves.

Bread and Butter Pickles

(pictured, page 131)
Robin Tarbell, Iowa

4 pounds small cucumbers, cut in ¼-inch-thick slices
3 onions, sliced
½ cup salt
3 cups vinegar
1 cup water
3 cups firmly packed brown sugar
2 tablespoons mustard seed
1½ teaspoons celery seed
1 teaspoon ground cinnamon
1 teaspoon turmeric
½ teaspoon ground ginger
1 pod hot-red pepper
1 teaspoon prepared horseradish
2 red peppers, seeded and coarsely chopped
2 green peppers, seeded and coarsely chopped

1. In large bowl, mix cucumbers with onions and salt. Let stand 5 hours; drain.

2. In large non-aluminum saucepan, combine vinegar, water, sugar and seasonings. Bring to boiling; simmer 3 minutes. Add cucumber-onion mixture and peppers; simmer 10 to 20 minutes. Spoon into clean pint jars; seal according to jar manufacturer's instructions.

Makes 6 pints.

Pictured on page 131.
1 Cocktail Rye Rounds
2 Raisin Bread
3 Spicy Pineapple-Zucchini Bread
4 Cranberry Vinegar
5 Bread and Butter Pickles
6 Corn Relish
7 Chicken Fajita Rolls
8 Honey Wheat Rolls
9 "Souper" Potato Bread
10 Nut Bread

Cranberry Vinegar

(pictured, page 131)
Rita Cunningham, New York

1 package (12 ounces)
    cranberries, rinsed and
    drained
¾ cup sugar
¾ cup vinegar
1 (3-inch) cinnamon stick
2 teaspoons dried basil leaves
¾ cup water

1. In large saucepan, combine all ingredients; stir until sugar dissolves. Bring to boiling; simmer 5 minutes, or until cranberries burst.

2. Cool; strain through fine sieve into bottles or jars. Cover; store in cool place.

Makes about 1 pint.

Honey Wheat Rolls

(pictured, page 131)
Mary Miller, Ohio

4 cups whole-wheat flour
4 cups unsifted all-purpose
    flour
2 packages fast-rising or
    regular dry yeast
1 teaspoon sugar
½ teaspoon baking soda
2 teaspoons salt
2 cups milk
½ cup (1 stick) butter or
    margarine
½ cup honey
¼ cup water
2 large eggs, at room
    temperature

1. In large bowl of electric mixer, combine 1½ cups each whole-wheat and all-purpose flour, the yeast, sugar, baking soda and salt; mix well. In small saucepan, heat milk, butter, honey and water until butter melts and mixture is 120° to 130°F. With mixer at low speed, pour milk mixture and eggs into flour mixture. Beat at medium speed 3 minutes, scraping bowl with rubber spatula. With wooden spoon, gradually add enough of remaining flours until dough leaves side of bowl. On a lightly floured surface, knead dough 5 minutes, or until smooth and elastic. Place dough in lightly greased bowl; turn dough over to bring up greased side. Cover bowl with a kitchen towel; let dough rise in warm place (85°F), free from drafts, 45 minutes or until doubled. Meanwhile, grease several large baking sheets; set aside.

2. Punch down dough; break into 3 dozen pieces. Shape each piece into a twist, knot, braid or ball; place on prepared baking sheets. Cover with towel; let rise 30 minutes, or until doubled.

3. Preheat oven to 350°F. Bake rolls 30 to 40 minutes; cover loosely with sheet of aluminum foil during last 10 minutes if rolls brown too quickly.

Makes 3 dozen.

Corn Relish

(pictured, page 131)
Lois Mullin, Iowa

2 quarts fresh corn
    kernels
3 cups cider vinegar
1½ cups sugar
1 cup chopped onion
1 cup chopped green
    pepper
1 cup chopped red pepper
1 cup chopped celery
1 tablespoon pickling salt
1 tablespoon mustard seed
2 teaspoons celery seed
1 teaspoon turmeric
1 clove garlic, minced

In large saucepan, cover corn with water. Bring to boiling; simmer 5 minutes. Drain; stir in remaining ingredients. Simmer 20 minutes; spoon mixture into clean pint jars. Seal according to jar manufacturer's instructions.

Makes 6 pints.

Chicken Fajita Rolls

(pictured, page 131)
Stephanie Martin, Texas

1 pound boneless chicken
    breasts, skinned
1 jar (8 ounces) fajita marinade
6 to 7 cups unsifted all-purpose
    flour
2 packages fast-rising or
    regular dry yeast
¼ cup sugar
1 tablespoon salt
2¼ cups milk, heated (120° to
    130°F)
1 large egg
¼ cup (½ stick) butter or
    margarine
1 medium onion, thinly sliced
1 green pepper, seeded and
    thinly sliced
1 red pepper, seeded and
    thinly sliced
1 can (16 ounces) refried
    beans
1 pound Monterey Jack cheese,
    shredded

1. In shallow bowl, combine chicken with marinade. Cover; refrigerate overnight.

2. Make rolls: In large bowl of electric mixer, combine 1½ cups flour, the yeast, sugar and salt; mix well. With mixer at low speed, pour warm milk and the egg into flour mixture. Beat at medium speed 3 minutes, scraping bowl with rubber spatula. With wooden spoon, gradually add enough remaining flour until dough leaves side of bowl.

3. On lightly floured surface, knead dough 5 minutes, or until smooth and elastic. Place in lightly greased bowl; turn dough over to bring up greased side. Cover bowl with towel; let dough rise in warm place (85°F), free from drafts, 45 minutes or until doubled.

4. Meanwhile, in large skillet, over medium-high heat, melt butter. Sauté onion and peppers 5 minutes, or until tender. Remove from pan; set aside. In same fat, cook chicken 12 minutes, or until tender. Slice

into thin pieces; toss with onion mixture. Grease 2 large baking sheets; set aside.

5. Punch down dough; turn out on floured board. Divide into 16 pieces. Roll or pat out into flat rounds about 6 inches in diameter. Spread center of each round of dough with about 1½ tablespoons refried beans; top each round with 2 tablespoons chicken mixture and 1 tablespoon cheese. Pinch each round into a ball; place, pinched side down, on prepared baking sheets. Pat ball to flatten slightly.

6. Let rolls rise 30 minutes. Preheat oven to 350°F. Bake rolls 15 minutes; sprinkle with remaining cheese. Bake 10 to 15 minutes longer, until golden.

Makes 16 rolls.

Nut Bread
(pictured, page 131)
Robbie Johnson, Alaska

2½ cups unsifted all-purpose
　flour
½ cup granulated sugar
½ cup firmly packed brown
　sugar
1¼ cups buttermilk
¼ cup shortening
2 large eggs
1 tablespoon baking powder
½ teaspoon baking soda
1 cup chopped nuts

1. Preheat oven to 350°F. Grease and flour 11-by-5-inch loaf pan; set pan aside.

2. In large bowl of electric mixer, at low speed, beat together all ingredients except nuts 15 seconds. At medium speed, beat 30 seconds; beat in nuts. Pour mixture into prepared loaf pan; bake 60 to 65 minutes, until cake tester inserted in center comes out clean. Remove bread from pan; cool completely on wire rack. Store bread at least 8 hours before slicing.

Makes 1 loaf.

"Souper" Potato Bread
(pictured, page 131)
Mrs. Harold Sauter, North Dakota

9 cups unsifted all-purpose
　flour
2 packages fast-rising or
　regular dry yeast
⅓ cup sugar
1 tablespoon salt
1 can (10¾ ounces) condensed
　cream-of-potato soup
2 cups milk
1 cup plus 1 tablespoon water
¼ cup shortening
1 large egg white
Sesame seeds

1. In large bowl of electric mixer, combine 3 cups flour, the yeast, sugar and salt; mix well. In blender or food processor, puree soup and 1 cup milk; transfer to medium saucepan. Add remaining 1 cup milk, 1 cup water and shortening. Heat soup mixture until very hot (120° to 130°F). With mixer at low speed, pour hot soup mixture into flour mixture. Beat at medium speed 3 minutes, scraping bowl with rubber spatula. With wooden spoon, gradually add enough remaining flour until dough leaves side of bowl.

2. On lightly floured surface, knead dough 5 minutes, or until smooth and elastic. Place in lightly greased bowl; turn dough over to bring up greased side. Cover bowl with towel; let dough rise in warm place (85°F), free from drafts, 45 minutes, or until doubled.

3. Grease three 8-by-4-by-2-inch loaf pans. Punch down dough; turn out onto floured board. Divide into six equal pieces. Roll each piece into 15-inch-long strands. Twist two strands together; pinch ends together. Tuck ends under; place loaf in a prepared pan. Repeat with remaining strands. Cover; let rise 30 minutes, or until doubled in bulk.

4. Preheat oven to 400°F. In small cup, beat egg white with remaining 1 tablespoon water; brush tops of

loaves; sprinkle generously with sesame seeds. Bake 10 minutes; reduce to 350°F, and bake 35 minutes longer, or until they are golden and sound hollow when tapped. Remove from pans; cool on wire racks.

Makes 3 loaves.

Chocolate Madeleines
(pictured, page 132)
Suzanne Kopf, Ohio

Nonstick cooking spray
10 tablespoons (1¼ sticks)
　unsalted butter
5 squares (1 ounce each)
　semisweet chocolate
1¼ cups unsifted all-purpose
　flour
¾ cup sugar
2 tablespoons unsweetened
　cocoa powder
⅛ teaspoon salt
3 large eggs, at room
　temperature
2 large egg yolks
1 teaspoon vanilla extract
1 tablespoon shortening

1. Preheat oven to 350°F. Grease small (1½-inch) madeleine pans with nonstick cooking spray.

2. In saucepan, over low heat, melt butter with 3 squares chocolate, stirring to blend. In large bowl, combine next 4 ingredients.

3. In medium bowl, with electric mixer at high speed, beat eggs, egg yolks and vanilla until light and fluffy. Pour into flour mixture; add chocolate mixture, and stir until blended. Fill prepared molds halfway with batter (cakes should be flat, not rounded on top); bake 5 minutes, or until wooden pick inserted in center comes out clean. Repeat with remaining batter, greasing pans between batches.

4. In small saucepan, over low heat, melt shortening with remaining chocolate. Drizzle over patterned side of madeleines.

Makes 42 madeleines.

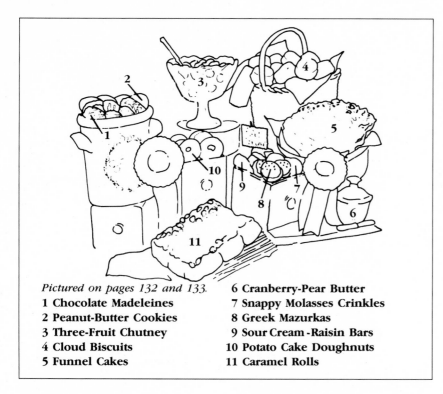

Pictured on pages 132 and 133.
1 Chocolate Madeleines
2 Peanut-Butter Cookies
3 Three-Fruit Chutney
4 Cloud Biscuits
5 Funnel Cakes
6 Cranberry-Pear Butter
7 Snappy Molasses Crinkles
8 Greek Mazurkas
9 Sour Cream-Raisin Bars
10 Potato Cake Doughnuts
11 Caramel Rolls

Three-Fruit Chutney
(pictured, page 132)
**Mary Kay Callaghan (Editor,
Oregon State Fair Cookbook)**

**2 pounds firm ripe nectarines
1 pound firm ripe plums
1 pound firm ripe peaches
3 cups diced onions
1½ cups light corn syrup
1½ cups cider vinegar
1 cup firmly packed brown
    sugar
1 cup raisins
2 teaspoons grated lemon peel
3 tablespoons lemon juice
1 teaspoon uniodized salt
1 teaspoon ground ginger
1 teaspoon ground allspice**

Halve, pit and dice nectarines, plums and peaches; place in large non-aluminum saucepan with remaining ingredients. Bring to boiling; simmer, uncovered, 50 to 60 minutes, or until mixture is thickened. Place mixture in clean half-pint jars; seal according to jar manufacturer's instructions.

Makes 10 cups.

Peanut-Butter Cookies
(pictured, page 132)
Georgia L. Crawford, Illinois

**½ cup granulated sugar
½ cup firmly packed
    light-brown sugar
½ cup (1 stick) margarine
½ cup chunky peanut butter
1 large egg
½ teaspoon vanilla extract
1¼ cups unsifted all-purpose
    flour
½ teaspoon baking powder
¾ teaspoon baking soda
¼ teaspoon salt
Additional flour or granulated
    sugar**

1. In large bowl, combine sugars, margarine, peanut butter, egg and vanilla; mix well. In medium bowl, mix flour, baking powder, baking soda and salt; stir into peanut-butter mixture, mixing until blended. Cover dough; refrigerate 3 hours.

2. Preheat oven to 375°F. Lightly grease several large baking sheets. With hands, roll level tablespoonfuls dough in 1¼-inch balls. Place balls 3 inches apart on prepared baking sheets. Dip tines of fork into flour or granulated sugar; flatten dough criss-cross style. Bake 10 to 12 minutes, or until slightly brown.

Makes 3 dozen cookies.

Cranberry-Pear Butter
(pictured, page 133)
Karla Dellner, California

**5 pounds firm, ripe pears
4 cups cranberries
Grated peel of 1 lemon
Juice of 1 lemon
3 cups cranberry juice
3 cups sugar
1½ teaspoons ground cinnamon
¾ teaspoon ground allspice
¼ teaspoon ground nutmeg**

1. Pare and core pears; cut into chunks. Place in non-aluminum saucepan with next 4 ingredients. Bring to boiling; simmer, covered, 30 minutes, or until soft.

2. Puree mixture through food mill or sieve. Place in clean large saucepan with remaining ingredients. Simmer, uncovered, 1½ hours, or until the consistency of thick applesauce.

3. Place mixture in clean half-pint jars; seal according to jar manufacturer's instructions.

Makes 5 cups.

Cloud Biscuits
(pictured, page 133)
**Nancy Grider, Indiana
(from Kentucky State Fair
Cookbook)**

**2 cups unsifted all-purpose
    flour
1 tablespoon sugar
4 teaspoons baking powder
½ teaspoon salt
½ cup shortening
1 large egg, beaten
⅔ cup milk**

1. Preheat oven to 450°F. Lightly grease large baking sheet. In medium bowl, combine flour, sugar, baking powder and salt. With a pastry blender or two knives, cut in shortening until mixture resembles coarse crumbs.

2. Make a well in center; with fork, stir in egg and milk all at once; stir until dough leaves side of bowl. Turn out dough onto a lightly floured surface; knead, lifting one side of dough over the other and pressing out lightly with palm of hand. Repeat 20 times. With floured rolling pin, gently roll out dough to ½-to-¾-inch thickness. Cut biscuits with floured 2½-inch cutter, being careful not to twist cutter. Place biscuits on baking sheet; bake 12 to 15 minutes.

Makes 8 biscuits.

Funnel Cakes
(pictured, page 133)
Leona Wilsonoff, Alaska

Salad oil
1 large egg
¾ cup milk
1 cup unsifted all-purpose flour
1 teaspoon baking powder
¼ teaspoon salt
⅛ teaspoon ground cinnamon
Confectioners' sugar

1. In electric skillet or heavy, wide saucepan, heat 1½ to 2 inches salad oil to 360°F on deep-fat thermometer.

2. In bowl, beat egg with milk; stir in next 4 ingredients. Mix until smooth. Holding finger under funnel with a ⅓-inch-wide opening, pour ¼ cup batter into funnel.

3. Starting in center of skillet, drop batter into hot oil; move funnel in circle to make snail-like coil of rings, each ring about 6 inches in diameter.

4. Fry cake, turning once with slotted spatula or chopsticks, 2 minutes on each side, or until cake is golden-brown. With spatula, lift cake from hot oil, holding over skillet to drain slightly. Place on paper-towel-lined wire rack in warm oven while frying remaining cakes. If batter thickens upon standing, add a little more milk so batter will flow freely through funnel. Sprinkle confectioners' sugar over cakes.

Makes 6 cakes.

Potato Cake Doughnuts
(pictured, page 132)
Arlene Thorp, Oregon

2¾ cups unsifted all-purpose flour
4 teaspoons baking powder
1 teaspoon ground mace
¼ teaspoon ground nutmeg
1 teaspoon salt
3 large eggs
¾ cup sugar
3 tablespoons shortening
1 cup plain mashed potatoes
Salad oil

1. In medium bowl, combine flour, baking powder, mace, nutmeg and salt; set aside. In large bowl, with electric mixer at high speed, beat eggs with sugar and shortening 2 minutes, until light and fluffy. At low speed, add potatoes; mix until blended. Add flour mixture gradually; beat at low speed until just combined. Cover bowl with plastic wrap; refrigerate 2 hours.

2. Place dough on well-floured pastry cloth; roll dough to ⅓-inch thickness; cut with floured 3-inch doughnut cutter, dipping cutter in flour between cutting.

3. Meanwhile, in electric skillet or heavy, wide saucepan, heat 1½ to 2 inches salad oil to 375°F on deep-fat thermometer. Gently drop three or four doughnuts and several "holes" into hot oil (adding too many doughnuts at a time reduces the temperature of the fat and causes greasy doughnuts); as doughnuts rise to the surface, turn with slotted spoon. Fry 3 minutes, or until browned on both sides. With slotted spoon, remove doughnuts and holes; drain over pan of oil. Place on paper-towel-lined wire rack. Repeat with remaining dough.

4. If desired, shake doughnuts in bag with confectioners' sugar or cinnamon-sugar.

Makes 18 doughnuts.

Sour Cream-Raisin Bars
(pictured, page 133)
Connie Jo Bierig, Oklahoma

2 cups raisins
1½ cups water
1 cup (2 sticks) butter or margarine, softened
1 cup brown sugar
1¾ cups uncooked rolled oats
1¾ cups unsifted all-purpose flour
1 teaspoon baking soda
3 large egg yolks
1½ cups sour cream
1 cup granulated sugar
2½ tablespoons cornstarch
1 teaspoon vanilla extract

1. In medium saucepan, cook raisins in water 10 minutes. Drain; set aside. In medium bowl, with electric mixer at high speed, beat butter with brown sugar until light and fluffy. At low speed, add oats, flour and baking soda; mix until blended. Press half of mixture into 13-by-9-by-2-inch baking pan; set aside.

2. Preheat oven to 350°F. In another medium saucepan, combine egg yolks, sour cream, granulated sugar and cornstarch. Over medium heat, cook, stirring constantly, until mixture thickens. Stir in raisins and vanilla; pour over oat mixture in pan. Sprinkle with remaining oat mixture; bake 30 minutes. When cool, cut into small bars.

Makes about 2 dozen bars.

Greek Mazurkas

(pictured, page 133)
Sunny Hickey, Ohio

1 can (12 ounces) poppy-seed filling
4 teaspoons lemon juice
1 cup (2 sticks) unsalted butter or margarine
1½ cups granulated sugar
3 large egg yolks
1 tablespoon grated lemon peel
2 teaspoons lemon extract
1 teaspoon vanilla extract
¾ cup buttermilk
1¼ teaspoons baking soda
3½ cups unsifted all-purpose flour
2 teaspoons baking powder

Icing

3 cups confectioners' sugar
2 tablespoons unsalted butter or margarine
1 teaspoon grated lemon peel
2 tablespoons milk
2 teaspoons lemon extract

1. In small bowl, combine poppy-seed filling with lemon juice; set mixture aside.

2. In large bowl, with electric mixer at high speed, beat 1 cup butter with granulated sugar, egg yolks, 1 tablespoon lemon peel, 2 teaspoons lemon extract and the vanilla until well mixed. In small glass measure, combine buttermilk and baking soda; beat into butter mixture. On sheet of waxed paper, mix flour with baking powder; beat into butter mixture.

3. Preheat oven to 350°F. Grease a large baking sheet. Place level tablespoon cookie batter on prepared baking sheet; with thumb, make a large indentation in center. Place one teaspoonful poppy-seed-filling mixture in indentation. Place one teaspoonful batter over filling; with small knife, carefully spread batter to cover filling. Repeat with remaining batter and filling. Bake 14 to 16 minutes; cool on wire rack.

4. Make Icing: In medium bowl, mix confectioners' sugar with 2 tablespoons butter until blended. Stir in remaining icing ingredients. Spread mazurka tops with icing; if desired, sprinkle with poppy seeds. Makes 3½ dozen.

Caramel Rolls

(pictured, pages 132 and 133)
Mrs. Harold Sauter, North Dakota

¾ cup granulated sugar
3 cups water
1 tablespoon salt
2 packages fast-rising or regular dry yeast
8½ cups unsifted all-purpose flour
3 large eggs, beaten
¾ cup melted shortening
½ cup (1 stick) butter, melted
1½ cups brown sugar
1½ cups raisins
1 teaspoon ground cinnamon

Caramel Topping

2 cups brown sugar
½ cup (1 stick) butter
¼ cup light corn syrup
1 tablespoon vinegar
1 teaspoon vanilla extract
1 cup pecan halves

1. In large saucepan, dissolve granulated sugar in water. Bring to boiling; simmer 5 minutes. Cool syrup to lukewarm; stir in salt and yeast until dissolved. Stir in 4¼ cups flour until blended. Stir in eggs and shortening; when blended, stir in remaining flour. Turn out onto floured board; let rest 5 minutes.

2. Knead dough 10 minutes, or until elastic. Place dough in large greased bowl; turn to bring up greased side. Cover dough with plastic wrap; place bowl in warm place 1 hour, or until dough has doubled in bulk. Punch dough down and let rise again.

3. Divide dough in half; roll each half into an 18-by-10-inch rectangle. Spread each with ¼ cup melted butter; sprinkle each with ¾ cup brown sugar, ¾ cup raisins and ½ teaspoon cinnamon. Roll up each rectangle from long side, jelly-roll fashion. With string, cut dough crosswise into 12 pieces.

4. In medium saucepan, combine Caramel Topping ingredients; bring to boiling. Simmer one minute; remove from heat. Grease two 13-by-9-by-2-inch baking pans or three 9-inch square cake pans; pour in Caramel Topping, dividing evenly.

5. Place rolls, cut side down, over topping in each pan, dividing evenly. Cover; let rise 30 minutes, or until doubled.

6. Preheat oven to 375°F. Bake rolls 25 minutes, until golden-brown. Let stand on wire rack 5 minutes; loosen edges with knife. Invert onto serving dish.

Makes 2 dozen.

Snappy Molasses Crinkles

(pictured, page 133)
Lena Forbis, Kentucky

2¼ cups unsifted all-purpose flour
1 teaspoon baking soda
1 teaspoon ground cinnamon
1 teaspoon ground ginger
½ teaspoon ground cloves
⅛ teaspoon salt
1 cup firmly packed brown sugar
¾ cup shortening
¼ cup molasses
1 large egg
Granulated sugar

1. On sheet of waxed paper, combine flour, baking soda, cinnamon, ginger, cloves and salt; set aside. In large bowl, with spoon, beat brown sugar with shortening, molasses and egg until well blended. Stir in flour mixture. Cover; refrigerate 1 hour.

2. Preheat oven to 375°F. Shape

dough into balls about 1 inch in diameter; roll in granulated sugar. Place 3 inches apart on ungreased baking sheets. Bake 10 to 12 minutes, or until tops have cracked.

Makes 4 dozen.

Piña Colada Creams
(pictured, page 134)
Lue Young, New Mexico

2 cups sugar
½ cup milk
2 tablespoons light corn syrup
2 tablespoons (¼ stick) butter
½ teaspoon coconut extract
½ teaspoon pineapple extract
¼ cup chopped candied pineapple
¼ cup chopped candied cherries
½ cup flaked coconut
2 packages (10 ounces each) semisweet-chocolate pieces, melted

1. In 3-quart heavy saucepan, over low heat, combine sugar with milk and syrup, stirring until sugar dissolves. Bring to boiling; simmer until mixture registers 228°F on candy thermometer, melting crystals as they form at edge of mixture with wet pastry brush.

2. Remove pan from heat. Add butter, without stirring; cool mixture to 110°F.

3. Grease an 8-inch square baking pan; set aside. Pour cooled candy mixture into large bowl of electric mixer. Add coconut and pineapple extracts; at medium speed, beat until candy loses its gloss. With spoon, stir in remaining ingredients except chocolate; pour mixture into prepared pan.

4. Refrigerate candy until set. With hands, roll about 1 teaspoonful mixture into balls. Dip balls into chocolate; place on waxed-paper-lined baking sheet until set.

Makes about 7 dozen creams.

Almond Cheesecake
(pictured, pages 134 and 135)
Joan Paal, Alaska

1½ cups vanilla-wafer crumbs
1¼ cups sugar
½ cup chopped pecans
½ teaspoon grated lemon peel
¼ cup (½ stick) butter or margarine, melted
3 packages (8 ounces each) cream cheese
3 large eggs
¾ teaspoon almond extract
1 cup sour cream
3 squares (1 ounce each) semisweet-chocolate pieces
1 teaspoon shortening
6 large strawberries, halved

1. In medium bowl, combine vanilla-wafer crumbs, 2 tablespoons sugar, the pecans, lemon peel and melted butter. Grease an 8-inch springform pan; with back of spoon, press crumb mixture into bottom and sides of pan. Refrigerate until crust is firm.

2. Preheat oven to 375°F. In large bowl of electric mixer, at high speed, beat cream cheese with 1 cup sugar until light and fluffy. Add eggs, one at a time, beating well after each addition. Beat in ½ teaspoon almond extract. Pour mixture into prepared crust; bake 45 minutes. Remove from oven; cool 10 minutes.

3. Meanwhile, in small bowl, blend sour cream with 2 tablespoons sugar and ¼ teaspoon almond extract. Spread sour-cream mixture over cooled cake; bake 10 minutes. Let cake cool completely; refrigerate overnight.

4. Before serving: In small saucepan, over low heat, melt chocolate with shortening; stir to blend. With tip of knife, outline an 8-inch circle on sheet of waxed paper; spread melted chocolate mixture within outline. Place on baking sheet; refrigerate until set. Remove from refrigerator; when slightly softened, with sharp knife, cut round into 12 wedges. Refrigerate until firm.

5. Remove cheesecake from pan; place on serving dish. Place strawberry halves around top edge of cheesecake. Using strawberries as support, place chocolate wedges on cake top so that long edge of chocolate wedge is on cake and wide end is at an angle.

Makes 12 servings.

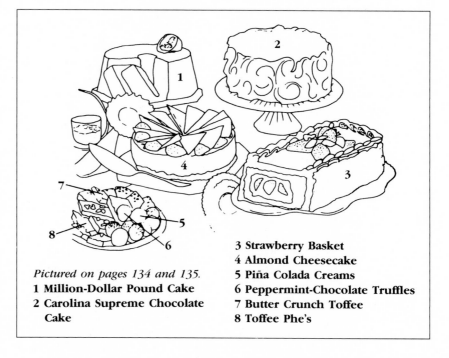

Pictured on pages 134 and 135.
1 Million-Dollar Pound Cake
2 Carolina Supreme Chocolate Cake
3 Strawberry Basket
4 Almond Cheesecake
5 Piña Colada Creams
6 Peppermint-Chocolate Truffles
7 Butter Crunch Toffee
8 Toffee Phe's

Carolina Supreme Chocolate Cake

(pictured, page 135)
Wendy Hamby, North Carolina

1 cup unsweetened cocoa
  powder
2 cups boiling water
2¾ cups unsifted all-purpose
  flour
2 teaspoons baking soda
½ teaspoon baking powder
½ teaspoon salt
1 cup (2 sticks) butter,
  softened
2½ cups granulated sugar
4 large eggs
1½ teaspoons vanilla extract

Filling
1 cup heavy cream
¼ cup confectioners' sugar
1 teaspoon vanilla extract

Frosting
1 package (12 ounces)
  semisweet-chocolate pieces
½ cup half-and-half
1 cup (2 sticks) butter,
  softened
1 box (1 pound) confectioners'
  sugar

1. Preheat oven to 350°F. Grease and flour three 9-inch round cake pans; set aside. Place cocoa in medium bowl; gradually stir in boiling water. Set aside to cool completely.

2. On sheet of waxed paper, combine flour, baking soda, baking powder and salt; set aside. In large bowl of electric mixer, at high speed, beat butter with granulated sugar until light and fluffy. Add eggs, one at a time, beating well after each addition. Beat in vanilla. Alternately add one-fourth flour mixture with one-third cocoa mixture; place in prepared pans, dividing evenly. Bake 25 minutes. Cool layers in pans 10 minutes; remove and cool on wire racks.

3. Make Filling: In large bowl, with electric mixer at high speed, beat filling ingredients together

until stiff. Place between cooled cake layers, dividing evenly.

4. Make Frosting: In medium saucepan, over medium heat, combine chocolate pieces, half-and-half and butter; cook, stirring until smooth. Transfer to large bowl; with portable electric mixer, at high speed, beat in confectioners' sugar. Place bowl in larger bowl of ice and water; at high speed, beat until firm enough to spread.

5. Cover cake with frosting; refrigerate until serving.

Makes 12 servings.

Million-Dollar Pound Cake

(pictured, page 134)
Bartee Worthington, Alabama

¾ cup milk
1 teaspoon almond extract
1 teaspoon vanilla extract
1 pound (4 sticks) butter,
  softened
3 cups sugar
6 large eggs, at room
  temperature
4 cups unsifted all-purpose
  flour

1. Preheat oven to 300°F. Grease and flour 10-inch tube pan; set aside. In small glass measure, combine milk with almond and vanilla extracts; set aside.

2. In large bowl of electric mixer, at high speed, cream butter with sugar until light and fluffy. Add eggs, one at a time, beating well after each addition. Alternately add one-fourth flour with one-third milk mixture; place in prepared pan.

3. Bake 1 hour and 40 minutes, or until cake tester inserted in center comes out clean. Cool cake in pan on wire rack 15 minutes; remove from pan. Cool thoroughly on wire rack. Serve plain or sprinkled with confectioners' sugar.

Makes 20 servings.

Strawberry Basket

(pictured, page 135)
Diane Johnson, Texas

Cake
2 cups unsifted all-purpose
  flour
1½ cups sugar
2 teaspoons baking powder
½ teaspoon salt
1½ cups heavy cream
3 large eggs
1½ teaspoons vanilla
  extract

**Strawberry Mousse (recipe
  follows)**
Frosting (recipe follows)
½ pint strawberries, halved
Mint leaves

1. Preheat oven to 350°F. Grease and flour 11-by-5-inch loaf pan; set pan aside.

2. On sheet of waxed paper, combine flour, sugar, baking powder and salt; set aside. In large bowl of electric mixer, at high speed, beat cream until stiff; set aside. In medium bowl of electric mixer, at high speed, beat eggs and vanilla until thick and lemon colored; fold into whipped cream. With rubber spatula, fold in flour mixture; pour into prepared pan. Bake 45 to 50 minutes, until cake tester inserted in center comes out clean. Remove from pan; cool on wire rack.

3. Cut and remove a 1-inch-thick horizontal slice from top of cake; set aside. With knife with serrated edge and fork, remove cake pieces to make a shell with 1-inch-thick walls; reserve cake pieces for another use.

4. Fill cake shell with Strawberry Mousse; place reserved cake top over all. Cover cake with Frosting; garnish top with halved strawberries and mint leaves. Place remaining frosting in pastry bag fitted with basket-weave tip; decorate side of cake with basket pattern. With star tip, use remaining cream to decorate top edges of cake.

Makes 12 servings.

Strawberry Mousse

1 envelope unflavored gelatine
¼ cup amaretto
1 cup heavy cream
1 pint strawberries, hulled and
sliced
½ cup sugar

1. In small glass measure, sprinkle gelatine over amaretto; set aside 5 minutes, or until gelatine softens. Meanwhile, in small bowl of electric mixer, at high speed, beat cream until stiff; refrigerate.

2. In large skillet, over low heat, toss strawberries with sugar until sugar dissolves—about 3 minutes. Remove from heat; stir in gelatine mixture until blended. Cool to room temperature; fold in whipped cream.

Makes about 4 cups.

Frosting

2 cups heavy cream
¼ cup confectioners' sugar
2 teaspoons vanilla extract

In large bowl of electric mixer, at high speed, beat ingredients until mixture is stiff. Frost cake.

Makes about 4 cups.

Toffee Phe's
(pictured, page 134)
Ken Phelan, Ohio

1 cup (2 sticks) butter,
softened
1 cup brown sugar
1 large egg yolk
1 teaspoon vanilla extract
1½ cups unsifted all-purpose
flour
1 package (8.7 ounces)
milk-chocolate candy (6 bars)
1 cup peanut-butter-flavored
pieces

1. Preheat oven to 350°F. Grease a 15½-by-10½-by-1-inch jelly-roll pan; set aside.

2. In large bowl of electric mixer, at high speed, beat butter with sugar until light and fluffy. Add egg yolk and vanilla; beat until blended. At low speed, beat in flour. With spatula, spread mixture in prepared pan. Bake 12 to 15 minutes.

3. Remove pan from oven; immediately cover with chocolate candy. Spread melted chocolate over dough; sprinkle peanut-butter pieces over chocolate. Swirl peanut-butter pieces lightly into chocolate. Cut into bars while warm.

Makes 70 bars.

Peppermint-Chocolate Truffles
(pictured, page 134)
Ken Leckler, Florida

¾ cup (1½ sticks) butter
3 cups sugar
1 can (5 ounces) evaporated
milk
1 package (10 ounces)
mint-flavored-chocolate
pieces
2 ounces semisweet-chocolate
pieces
1 jar (7 ounces) marshmallow
creme
1 teaspoon vanilla extract
2 packages (10 ounces each)
white candy melting wafers
6 tablespoons shortening

1. In large saucepan, over medium heat, melt butter with sugar and evaporated milk. Bring to boiling; cook, stirring constantly, until mixture registers 234°F on candy thermometer.

2. Remove pan from heat; stir in mint-flavored-chocolate pieces and semisweet-chocolate pieces until blended. Add marshmallow creme and vanilla; stir until blended.

3. Grease a 15½-by-10½-by-1-inch jelly-roll pan; spread candy mixture evenly in pan. Refrigerate 1 hour. Cut candy into 96 squares; with hands, roll into balls.

4. In medium saucepan, over low heat, melt white candy wafers with shortening, stirring to blend. With fork, dip candy balls into white-candy coating; place on waxed-paper-lined baking sheet. While coating is soft, sprinkle with chocolate candy sprinkles or, when coating hardens, drizzle with additional melted white candy coating, if desired. Let candy set until coating hardens.

Makes 96 truffles.

Butter Crunch Toffee
(pictured, page 134)
Helen McCauley, New Mexico

1 cup chopped almonds
1 cup (2 sticks) butter
1 cup sugar
1 tablespoon water
1 tablespoon light corn syrup
1 package (10 ounces)
milk-chocolate pieces

1. Preheat oven to 300°F. Grease a 15½-by-10½-by-1-inch jelly-roll pan; set aside. Place almonds on baking sheet; bake until lightly browned; keep warm.

2. In 1-quart heavy saucepan, over low heat, melt butter. Remove saucepan from heat; stir in sugar. Over low heat, cook sugar mixture, stirring, until boiling. Stir in water and corn syrup. Cook, stirring, until mixture registers 280°F on candy thermometer.

3. Remove from heat; stir in ¾ cup almonds. Spread mixture in prepared pan. While candy is warm, cut into 1½-inch squares. Cool until hardened.

4. In small saucepan, over low heat, melt chocolate pieces. Spread over candy; sprinkle with remaining ¼ cup nuts.

Makes 6 dozen pieces.

Lite Eating: State-Fair Salads

TOMATO AND CHINESE PEA-POD VINAIGRETTE
SOUTHERN-STYLE TOSSED SALAD
MUSHROOM-BEAN SALAD

Tomato and Chinese Pea-Pod Vinaigrette
Jill Baker, Texas

4 large tomatoes
2 cups pea pods, trimmed and cut in half on diagonal
1 green onion, thinly sliced

Dressing
¼ cup vinegar
1 tablespoon chopped parsley
1 teaspoon dried basil leaves
1 teaspoon sugar
¾ teaspoon dry mustard
½ teaspoon paprika
½ cup salad oil
¼ teaspoon salt
⅛ teaspoon pepper

1. Cut and discard ¼-inch slice from stem end of each tomato, pushing blade of paring knife halfway into tomato and alternating angle of blade while cutting to make a zigzag edge. Scoop out and discard seeds; cut out, chop and reserve pulp. Invert tomatoes onto a paper-towel-lined plate; refrigerate.

Left: (Clockwise from top) Southern-Style Tossed Salad, Mushroom-Bean Salad, Tomato and Chinese Pea-Pod Vinaigrette.

2. In a medium bowl, combine tomato pulp, pea pods and onion. In jar with tight-fitting lid, combine dressing ingredients; shake to blend. Pour dressing over tomato mixture; toss. Spoon into tomato shells, dividing mixture evenly.

Makes 4 servings; 298 calories each serving.

Southern-Style Tossed Salad
Jean Graham, Texas

3 cups each torn spinach, leaf lettuce and iceberg lettuce leaves
1 grapefruit, peeled and sectioned
2 oranges, peeled and sectioned
1 avocado, peeled, pitted and sliced
½ cup sliced celery
½ cup sliced green pepper
¼ cup slivered almonds, toasted

Dressing
1 package (.7 ounce) Italian salad-dressing mix
2 teaspoons grated grapefruit peel
½ cup grapefruit juice
⅔ cup salad oil

In large bowl, toss greens with grapefruit and orange sections, avocado, celery, green pepper and almonds. In jar with tight-fitting lid, combine dressing ingredients; shake. Toss with salad ingredients.

Makes 12 servings; 175 calories each serving.

Mushroom-Bean Salad
Mary Kay Callaghan (Editor, *Oregon State Fair Cookbook*)

1 pound green beans, cooked tender-crisp
1 can (8 ounces) garbanzos, drained
1 cup sliced mushrooms
¼ cup red-onion rings

Dressing
3 tablespoons garlic-flavored red-wine vinegar
1 teaspoon prepared horseradish
¼ teaspoon dried Italian herbs
3 tablespoons salad oil
1¼ teaspoons salt
⅛ teaspoon pepper

In large bowl, combine green beans, garbanzos, mushrooms and onion rings. In jar with tight-fitting lid, combine dressing ingredients; shake to blend. Pour over bean mixture; toss to combine. Garnish with tomato wedges, if desired.

Makes 4 servings; 171 calories each serving.

We would like to thank the following state-fair commissions for their cooperation in the production of State-Fair Cookbook: Alabama, Alaska, California, Florida, Illinois, Indiana, Iowa, Kentucky, New Mexico, New York, North Carolina, North Dakota, Ohio, Oklahoma, Oregon and Texas. In addition, Blue Ribbon Winners: America's Best State Fair Recipes by Catherine Hanley, HP Books.

Quick & Easy: State-Fair Snacks

Cheese Pizza
Marc Veigl, Kentucky

2½ cups unsifted all-purpose
  flour
1 package fast-rising or regular
  dry yeast
1 teaspoon salt
1 cup water
2 tablespoons salad oil
Pizza Sauce (recipe follows)
1 pound shredded mozzarella
  cheese
1 pound pork sausage, cooked
  and crumbled
¼ pound sliced mushrooms
1 small green pepper, diced

1. In large bowl, combine flour,
yeast and salt. Stir in very warm
water and salad oil. Turn out dough
onto floured surface; cover with
bowl. Let rest 10 minutes.
2. Preheat oven to 425°F. On
floured surface, roll dough into a
12-inch round; place on baking
sheet. Spread sauce over top of
dough; sprinkle with remaining ingredients. Bake 10 to 15 minutes, or
until crust is done and cheese is
melted.
Makes 4 servings.

Pizza Sauce

1 can (about 15 ounces) peeled
  whole tomatoes
1 can (6 ounces) tomato paste
1 medium onion, diced
1 tablespoon each minced
  basil, oregano and parsley
  leaves
1 teaspoon sugar
¼ teaspoon garlic powder
½ teaspoon salt
¼ teaspoon pepper

In large saucepan, combine all ingredients. Bring to boiling; simmer
10 to 15 minutes. Spread sauce over
top of pizza dough.
Makes enough sauce for a 12-inch
pizza.

Jalapeño Cornbread
Teresa Buchholz, New Mexico

1 cup cornmeal
1 cup buttermilk
1 cup unsifted all-purpose
  flour
1 tablespoon sugar
1 teaspoon salt
1 teaspoon baking powder
1 teaspoon baking soda
1 large egg
¼ cup salad oil
1 can (8¾ ounces)
  whole-kernel corn,
  drained
1 can (4 ounces) chopped
  jalapeño peppers
1 can (4 ounces) chopped
  pimiento
2 cups (8 ounces) grated
  Cheddar cheese

1. Preheat oven to 375°F. Grease
and flour a 13-by-9-inch pan. Set
pan aside.
2. In small bowl, mix cornmeal
with buttermilk; set aside. In large
bowl, combine flour, sugar, salt, baking powder, baking soda, egg, salad
oil and cornmeal mixture; stir until
blended. Stir in corn, jalapeño peppers, pimiento and grated cheese.
Pour batter into prepared pan; bake
30 minutes.
Makes 12 squares.

Date-Nut Refrigerator Bran Muffins
Anna Marie Davis, California

2 cups boiling water
6 cups shreds-of-wheat bran
  cereal
2½ cups sugar
9 ounces salad oil
4 large eggs, beaten
4 cups buttermilk
5 cups unsifted all-purpose
  flour
5 teaspoons baking soda
1 teaspoon salt
2 cups chopped dates
2 cups chopped walnuts

1. In medium bowl, pour water
over 2 cups cereal; allow mixture to
cool. In large bowl, blend sugar with
salad oil, eggs and buttermilk; stir in
remaining dry cereal and the soaked
cereal.
2. On sheet of waxed paper, combine flour with baking soda and salt;
stir into cereal mixture; fold in dates
and walnuts. Batter can be baked
immediately or refrigerated in a
tightly covered container up to 1
month. To bake: Line muffin cups
with paper liners; spoon batter into
each cup. Allow batter to stand in
pans while oven heats to 375°F.
Bake muffins 40 minutes, or until
wooden pick inserted in muffin center comes out clean.
Makes about 60 muffins.

Right: (Clockwise from right)
Cheese Pizza, Date-Nut
Refrigerator Bran Muffins,
Jalapeño Cornbread.

Micro-Way: Blue-Ribbon Entrées

Fiesta Casserole
Joan Bryant, Oklahoma

1 pound lean ground beef
1 package (1¼ ounces)
   taco-seasoning mix
1 can (16 ounces) refried
   beans
1 can (11 ounces)
   nacho-cheese soup
1 cup (4 ounces) shredded
   Monterey Jack cheese
½ cup pitted black olives,
   sliced
1 cup sour cream
2 green onions, minced
Round corn tortilla chips

1. In microwave-safe, 2-quart casserole, cook meat on HIGH 5 minutes, stirring after 2 minutes. Drain off fat; place meat in bowl. Add taco seasoning mix; stir until combined.

2. In bottom of casserole, spread beans; cover with beef mixture. Pour soup over meat to within 1 inch of edge of dish. Sprinkle with cheese and then olives. Cook on HIGH 15 minutes, or until cheese melts and mixture is bubbly. Place sour cream over cheese at one side of casserole; sprinkle with green onion. Arrange tortilla chips around edge of dish.

Makes 6 servings.

■ As a substitute for sour cream, combine 6 ounces cottage cheese and 1 teaspoon lemon juice; process in blender or food processor until smooth.

Lamb Stew

Mary Kay Callaghan (Editor,
***Oregon State Fair Cookbook*)**

2 pounds boneless lamb
   shoulder, cut in 1-inch
   pieces
3 tablespoons cornstarch
1 cup water
2 medium carrots
1 medium turnip
1 medium potato
3 small onions, quartered
2 teaspoons salt
¼ teaspoon hot-red-pepper
   sauce
1 tablespoon chopped parsley
2 teaspoons instant beef-flavored
   bouillon granules
¼ teaspoon ground thyme
   leaves
1 bay leaf
1 package (10 ounces) frozen peas

1. Place lamb in microwave-safe,
3-quart casserole. Cover; cook on
HIGH 10 minutes, stirring after 5
minutes. In 1-cup glass measure,
blend cornstarch with water; set
aside. Pare and cube carrots, turnip
and potato; add to lamb with onions,
salt, the cornstarch mixture and remaining ingredients except peas.
Mix well.

2. Cover with plastic wrap; turn
back one corner to vent. Cook on
HIGH 10 minutes, or until boiling,
stirring once. Cook on MEDIUM 35
minutes, or until tender. Stir in peas;
cook 6 minutes. Stir; let stand, covered, 5 minutes. Discard bay leaf.
   Makes 6 servings.

■ Freeze seedless grapes or small
whole plums for a healthy, low-
calorie snack or dessert. Eat right
out of the bag while still frozen.

September

No matter how it's served, pasta is one of our all-time favorites! Our menu of recipes and their photographs are a feast for the senses. Here, hearty meatballs in a pork-flavored sauce top piping-hot fusilli. Magnifico!

Marianne's Favorite Spaghetti and Meatballs

Chicken and Tomato Sauce Robusto

Northern Italian Mafalde Pie

Pork and Pasta Stir-Fry

Smoked-Salmon-Filled Rigatoni

Fried Stuffed Pasta Shells With Sun-Dried-Tomato Pesto

Tricolor Tortellini Soup

Pasta Nests With Vegetables

Eggplant and Sausage Casserole

Chicken-Stuffed Lasagna Rolls With Saffron Sauce

Pasta Cookbook

Pasta comes in all shapes and sizes. An exotic pork stir-fry, for instance, is combined with bow-tie pasta; other recipes feature ruffle pasta, curly-edged lasagna, pasta shells and nests.

Smoked-Salmon-Filled Rigatoni

(pictured, page 154, inset)

40 rigatoni
1 cup ricotta cheese
6 ounces smoked salmon
1 tablespoon minced green onion
1 tablespoon minced parsley
1 teaspoon minced fresh dill or ¼ teaspoon dried dillweed
½ cup grated Parmesan cheese
1 cup heavy cream
Fresh dill sprigs

1. Cook rigatoni as package label directs; drain; cool slightly.

2. In food processor, puree ricotta with half the salmon; place in medium bowl. Finely chop remaining salmon; stir into ricotta mixture with green onion, parsley and dill. Spoon mixture into pastry bag fitted with ½-inch plain tip; pipe mixture into rigatoni.

3. Preheat oven to 400°F. In small bowl, mix Parmesan cheese with cream. Lightly grease four ramekins. Arrange stuffed rigatoni in ramekins, dividing evenly; top each with one-fourth of the sauce. Bake 15 minutes or until bubbly and lightly browned. Garnish with dill sprigs.

Makes 4 servings.

Page 153: Marianne's Favorite Spaghetti and Meatballs.

Pages 154 and 155: (Clockwise from top center) Chicken and Tomato Sauce Robusto, Northern Italian Mafalde Pie, Pork and Pasta Stir-Fry. (Inset) left, Smoked-Salmon-Filled Rigatoni; right, Fried Stuffed Pasta Shells With Sun-Dried-Tomato Pesto.

Pages 156 and 157: (Clockwise from top left) Tricolor Tortellini Soup, Pasta Nests With Vegetables, Eggplant and Sausage Casserole. (Inset) Chicken-Stuffed Lasagna Rolls With Saffron Sauce.

Chicken and Tomato Sauce Robusto

(pictured, pages 154 and 155)

2 tablespoons salad oil
½ pound boneless chicken breasts, skinned and cubed
¾ cup minced green onion
1 jar (7 ounces) roasted red peppers
2 medium cloves garlic, peeled
2 tablespoons cilantro (fresh coriander) leaves
1 can (16 ounces) whole tomatoes, undrained
¼ teaspoon crushed red-pepper flakes
1 large green pepper, coarsely chopped
1 pound hot, cooked rigatoni

1. In large skillet, heat oil over medium-high heat. Add chicken and ½ cup green onion; cook 5 minutes, or until lightly browned.

2. Meanwhile, in food processor, puree red peppers and their juices, garlic and cilantro. Add puree, tomatoes and their juices and pepper flakes to chicken. Bring to boiling; simmer, uncovered, 5 minutes or until thickened. Add green pepper; simmer 3 minutes, or until tender-crisp. Toss with rigatoni. Top with remaining ¼ cup onion.

Makes 4 servings.

Fried Stuffed Pasta Shells With Sun-Dried-Tomato Pesto

(pictured, page 154, inset)

24 jumbo pasta shells
1 cup ricotta cheese
1 cup (4 ounces) shredded Swiss cheese
¼ pound smoked turkey breast, cut in ¼-inch cubes
½ cup chopped green onion
¼ cup chopped fresh basil leaves
2 large eggs, separated
1 tablespoon water
½ cup grated Parmesan cheese
½ cup fine seasoned dry bread crumbs
Sun-Dried-Tomato Pesto (recipe follows)

1. In large saucepan of boiling, salted water, cook shells 8 minutes; drain and cool.

2. In bowl, mix ricotta and Swiss cheese with turkey, green onion, basil and egg yolks. Spoon about 1 tablespoon mixture into each shell; press edges together.

3. In small bowl, lightly beat egg whites with water. On waxed paper, combine Parmesan and bread crumbs. Dip stuffed shells into egg white; coat in bread-crumb mixture. (Shells may be refrigerated overnight at this point.)

4. In deep-fat fryer, heat 2 inches salad oil to 375°F. Fry shells, a few at a time, 1 minute or until golden. Drain on paper towels. Serve hot with Sun-Dried-Tomato Pesto.

Makes 6 servings.

Sun-Dried-Tomato Pesto

¾ cup sun-dried tomatoes, packed in oil
¼ cup pine nuts
¼ cup packed parsley leaves
1 medium clove garlic, peeled
¾ cup chicken broth
¼ cup olive oil
⅛ teaspoon crushed red-pepper flakes

In food processor, puree tomatoes with nuts, parsley and garlic. With motor running, add broth and oil; process until blended. Stir in pepper.

Makes 1½ cups.

■ Cooking meatballs for spaghetti sauce on top of the range requires constant attention. Instead, bake them in a greased shallow baking pan at 375°F for 10 minutes—no turning needed; then add them to your sauce.

Marianne's Favorite Spaghetti and Meatballs

(pictured, page 153)

2 tablespoons olive oil
4 pork chops (about 1 pound)
1 large onion, chopped
1 large clove garlic, crushed
1 can (28 ounces) crushed tomatoes
1 jar (26 ounces) marinara sauce
1 teaspoon sugar
1 teaspoon dried basil leaves, crushed
1 pound ground chuck
½ pound lean ground pork
½ pound ground veal
⅓ cup fine dry bread crumbs
¼ cup chopped parsley
1 large egg
1 teaspoon salt
⅛ teaspoon pepper
1 package (1 pound) fusilli or spaghetti
Grated Parmesan cheese

1. In 5-quart saucepan, heat oil over medium heat. Add chops; brown on both sides. Remove to plate. Add onion and garlic to pan; sauté 3 minutes. Add tomatoes, marinara sauce, sugar and ½ teaspoon basil; bring to boiling. Reduce heat; return chops and juices to pan. Simmer, covered, 45 minutes.

2. Preheat oven to 350°F. In large bowl, combine ground chuck, pork, veal, bread crumbs, parsley, egg, salt, remaining ½ teaspoon basil and the pepper; mix well. Roll rounded tablespoonfuls into 1½-inch balls. Place in shallow roasting pan; bake 20 minutes, turning after 10 minutes. Add meatballs to sauce; simmer, covered, 15 minutes longer.

3. Meanwhile, cook fusilli as package label directs; drain. Serve with meatballs, pork chops, sauce and Parmesan cheese.

Makes 6 to 8 servings.

Pork and Pasta Stir-Fry

(pictured, page 154)

1 pound boneless pork loin, cut in ½-inch-wide strips
1 large egg white
5 teaspoons cornstarch
3 tablespoons salad oil
1 medium red pepper, cut in 1-inch triangles
1 medium yellow pepper, cut in 1-inch triangles
1 small zucchini, thinly sliced
2 tablespoons Chinese salted black beans, rinsed, or 2 tablespoons soy sauce
1 tablespoon shredded, pared ginger root
2 medium cloves garlic, crushed
1 cup chicken broth
2 tablespoons chopped cilantro (fresh coriander) leaves
1 teaspoon chili paste (optional)
2 cups hot, cooked large bow-tie pasta (4 ounces uncooked)

1. In medium bowl, mix pork with egg white and 3 teaspoons cornstarch until well coated. In wok or large skillet, heat 2 tablespoons salad oil. Over medium-high heat, stir-fry pork in a single layer, in batches, 5 minutes, or until golden-brown. Remove pork to a platter; keep warm.

2. Add remaining 1 tablespoon salad oil to wok; add peppers, zucchini, black beans or soy sauce, the ginger and garlic. Stir-fry 1 minute or until vegetables are tender-crisp.

3. In small bowl, blend broth with remaining cornstarch. Return pork to wok; add broth mixture, cilantro and chili paste. Bring to boiling, stirring, until slightly thickened. Toss with pasta.

Makes 4 servings.

Northern Italian Mafalde Pie

(pictured, page 155)

3 tablespoons olive or salad oil
2 celery stalks, chopped
1 carrot, chopped
1 small red onion, chopped
¼ cup chopped parsley
1 tablespoon grated lemon peel
1 large clove garlic, crushed
½ pound ground veal
½ pound ground beef
1 can (28 ounces) Italian plum
   tomatoes
⅓ cup dry red wine
2 tablespoons tomato paste
1 teaspoon salt
⅛ teaspoon pepper
1 package (1.8 ounces)
   white-sauce mix
2¼ cups milk
1 pound mafalde or
   curly-edged lasagna
1 package (8 ounces)
   mozzarella cheese, shredded

1. In large saucepan, heat oil over medium-high heat. Add next 6 ingredients; cook 3 minutes, or until tender. Add veal and beef; cook 3 minutes, or until lightly browned. Stir in tomatoes and their juices, wine, tomato paste, salt and pepper; bring to boiling, stirring to break up tomatoes. Simmer, uncovered, and stirring occasionally, 45 minutes or until slightly thickened.

2. Prepare white sauce with milk as package label directs; set aside. Cook mafalde as package label directs; drain.

3. Preheat oven to 350°F. Grease 9-inch springform pan. Place one-fourth of mafalde, overlapping, to cover bottom. Top with half of white sauce; sprinkle with one-third of cheese. Top with one-fourth (of original amount) mafalde and half of meat sauce. Cover with one-fourth (of original amount) mafalde, remaining white sauce and half the cheese. Layer remaining mafalde, then remaining meat sauce. Sprinkle remaining cheese on edge.

4. Bake 30 minutes, or until heated through. Remove from oven; let stand 10 minutes.
Makes 12 servings.

Pasta Nests With Vegetables

(pictured, page 157)

3 tablespoons butter or
   margarine
1 medium onion, chopped
2 large carrots, cut diagonally
   into ⅛-inch slices
2 tablespoons all-purpose flour
1 teaspoon grated lemon peel
½ teaspoon salt
⅛ teaspoon pepper
¾ cup milk
1 cup sour cream
1 package (10 ounces) frozen
   chopped spinach, thawed and
   well-drained
½ package (1-pound size)
   linguine
1 large egg
¼ cup grated Parmesan cheese

1. In medium saucepan, over medium heat, melt butter. Add onion and carrots; sauté 3 minutes. Remove from heat; stir in flour and next 3 ingredients until blended. Gradually stir in milk; cook, stirring, 3 minutes or until thickened. Remove from heat; stir in sour cream and spinach; pour into 2-quart shallow baking dish.

2. Preheat oven to 350°F. Cook linguine as package label directs; drain. In medium bowl, beat egg with cheese; add linguine; toss until evenly coated. Using a long-tined fork, twirl several strands around the tines into "nests." Remove pasta from fork; stand upright in spinach mixture. Continue with remaining linguine, making 9 nests.

3. Cover with aluminum foil; bake 20 minutes. Remove foil; bake 10 minutes longer or until golden.
Makes 6 servings.

Chicken-Stuffed Lasagna Rolls With Saffron Sauce

(pictured, page 157, inset)

4 sheets (4 ounces) uncooked
   lasagna, each 8 to 9 inches
   square
6 tablespoons butter or
   margarine
¾ pound chicken cutlets, cut
   in ½-inch cubes
1 medium onion, chopped
3 medium cloves garlic,
   crushed
1 package (10 ounces) frozen
   chopped broccoli, thawed
1 container (15 ounces) ricotta
   cheese
2 large eggs
6 tablespoons all-purpose flour
¾ cup sliced pitted black olives
1 jar (4 ounces) chopped
   pimiento, drained
1 cup chopped parsley
1 teaspoon salt
⅓ cup grated Parmesan cheese
Saffron Sauce (recipe follows)

1. In large pot of boiling, salted water, cook lasagna sheets 3 minutes; drain. Stack sheets on oiled baking sheet, placing plastic wrap between each layer; set aside.

2. In large skillet, over medium heat, melt 2 tablespoons butter; cook chicken, onion and garlic 3 minutes, or until brown. In food processor, finely chop chicken mixture and broccoli. Transfer to bowl; stir in ricotta, eggs, flour, olives, pimiento, ⅓ cup parsley and salt; mix.

3. Preheat oven to 375°F. Grease a jelly-roll pan; set aside. Spread about 1¼ cups filling on each lasagna sheet to ½ inch from edges; roll up jelly-roll fashion. Place rolls, seam-side down, in prepared pan.

4. Melt remaining 4 tablespoons butter; generously brush some over each roll. On a sheet of waxed paper, combine remaining ⅔ cup parsley and the Parmesan cheese; evenly sprinkle some over each roll.

Bake, uncovered, 45 minutes, or until crisp and golden. Slice on the diagonal. Serve with Saffron Sauce and, if desired, steamed broccoli.

Makes 6 servings.

Saffron Sauce

3 tablespoons butter or margarine
3 tablespoons all-purpose flour
1 cup milk
½ cup chicken broth
¼ cup dry white wine
2 tablespoons tomato paste
Generous dash ground saffron threads
¼ teaspoon salt
Generous dash ground red pepper

In large saucepan, over medium heat, melt butter; blend in flour, stirring until smooth and bubbly. Remove from heat; gradually stir in milk, broth and wine. Cook, stirring, until boiling; simmer 1 minute or until thickened. Stir in remaining ingredients. Cook 1 minute.

Makes about 2 cups.

Tricolor Tortellini Soup

(pictured, page 156)

1 package (8 ounces) tricolor tortellini
¼ pound bacon, cut in strips
2 medium cloves garlic, peeled and thinly sliced
4 cups washed and coarsely chopped escarole or chicory
4 cups chicken broth
1 can (1 pound) small white beans
1 can (28 ounces) Italian plum tomatoes
1 medium yellow pepper, cut in ¼-inch cubes
¼ teaspoon pepper

1. Cook tortellini as package label directs; drain and set aside. In 4-quart saucepan or Dutch oven, cook bacon and garlic 3 minutes or until bacon is browned; remove with slotted spoon.

2. In drippings, cook escarole 2 minutes or until wilted. Stir in broth, beans and their liquid, tomatoes and their liquid, yellow pepper cubes and pepper. Bring to boiling. Stir in cooked pasta, bacon and garlic; heat through.

Makes 10 to 12 servings.

Eggplant and Sausage Casserole

(pictured, pages 156 and 157)

2 tablespoons olive or salad oil
2 pounds sweet Italian sausage, cut in 1-inch diagonal pieces
1 medium eggplant (1½ pounds), cut in ½-inch cubes
1 large Spanish onion, chopped
1 large clove garlic, chopped
2 teaspoons paprika
1 can (28 ounces) crushed tomatoes
1 can (6 ounces) tomato paste
1 tablespoon chopped fresh basil or 1 teaspoon dried basil leaves
1 teaspoon salt
1 box (1 pound) penne
1 container (15 ounces) ricotta cheese
1 package (1 pound) mozzarella cheese, shredded

1. In large skillet or saucepan, heat oil over medium heat. Add sausage; sauté 8 minutes. Add eggplant, onion and garlic; cook 5 minutes, or until tender. Stir in paprika; cook 1 minute. Add tomatoes, tomato paste, basil and salt; bring to boiling. Simmer, partially covered and stirring occasionally, 35 minutes, or until sauce is slightly thickened.

2. Preheat oven to 350°F. Cook penne as package label directs;

drain. Stir into eggplant sauce.

3. In 2½-quart shallow baking dish or large roasting pan, arrange half of eggplant mixture; top with ricotta and half of mozzarella. Top with remaining pasta mixture; sprinkle with remaining mozzarella.

4. Bake 40 minutes or until heated through. Remove from oven; let stand 10 minutes before serving.

Makes 12 servings.

Four-Cheese Ruffles

2 tablespoons butter or margarine
1 large tomato, peeled, seeded and chopped
1 medium clove garlic, crushed
1 cup heavy cream
1 cup (4 ounces) shredded mozzarella cheese
1 cup (4 ounces) shredded provolone cheese
1 cup (4 ounces) cubed Italian fontina cheese
¼ cup chopped fresh basil
¼ cup chopped Italian parsley
¼ teaspoon salt
¼ teaspoon pepper
1 package (14 ounces) tricolor ruffle pasta, cooked and drained
¼ cup shredded Parmesan cheese

1. In large skillet, over medium heat, melt butter; cook tomato and garlic 3 minutes. Add cream and all cheeses except Parmesan. Cook, stirring, until cheeses melt and mixture is bubbly. Stir in basil, parsley, salt and pepper.

2. In bowl, toss pasta with sauce; sprinkle with Parmesan cheese.

Makes 4 to 6 servings.

■ Substitution for 1 cup heavy cream: ¾ cup milk plus ⅓ cup butter or margarine.

Quick & Easy: Pasta Main Dishes

Rotelle Aioli With Walnuts

½ cup olive oil
8 medium cloves garlic, slivered
1 cup walnut halves or pieces
¼ pound sliced ham, cut in 2-by-½-inch strips
1 package (14 ounces) tricolor rotelle pasta
1 teaspoon salt
¼ teaspoon pepper

1. In medium skillet, heat oil over medium heat. Add garlic and walnuts; sauté 2 minutes. Add ham; cook 1 minute longer.

2. Cook rotelle as package label directs; drain. Toss pasta with garlic mixture, salt and pepper; mix well. Serve immediately.

Makes 4 servings.

Crispy Pasta Pancake With Creamed Broccoli

2 packages (9 ounces each) refrigerated angel-hair pasta
6 large eggs
¾ cup grated Parmesan cheese
¼ cup olive oil
1 can (10¾ ounces) condensed cream-of-chicken soup
½ cup milk
1 package (10 ounces) frozen chopped broccoli, thawed
½ cup sour cream

1. Cook pasta as package label directs; drain. In large bowl, beat eggs with cheese. Add pasta; toss until evenly coated.

2. In 8-inch nonstick skillet, heat oil over medium-high heat; add pasta-egg mixture. Cook 8 minutes, shaking pan occasionally.

3. Meanwhile, in medium saucepan, combine soup, milk and broccoli; cook 5 minutes, or until heated through. Gradually stir in sour cream; simmer 1 minute.

4. Cover handle of skillet with aluminum foil; broil pancake, 6 inches from heat, 5 minutes, or until puffed and lightly golden. With spatula, carefully loosen pancake from skillet; place serving platter over pancake. Invert skillet; remove pan from pancake. Arrange some of the sauce around pancake; serve remainder with pancake. Garnish with tomato and fresh herbs, if desired.

Makes 6 to 8 servings.

■ A convenient way to store small amounts of leftover tomato paste is to spoon level tablespoonfuls of the extra paste onto a waxed-paper-lined baking sheet, and freeze. Then simply remove the spoonfuls from the sheet, place in a plastic bag and return the frozen tomato paste to the freezer. Use the individual portions of tomato paste in recipes as needed.

Quick & Easy

Agnolotti With Chicken Piccata

½ cup (1 stick) butter or
  margarine
2 tablespoons olive oil
3 whole boneless chicken
  breasts, skinned and split
  (2¼ pounds)
1 medium clove garlic, crushed
2 packages (9 ounces each)
  refrigerated agnolotti pasta
1 package (10 ounces) frozen
  peas
¼ cup grated Parmesan cheese
¼ teaspoon salt
⅛ teaspoon pepper
2 tablespoons lemon juice
1 tablespoon Dijon-style
  mustard

1. In large skillet, over medium heat, melt 2 tablespoons butter in the oil. Add chicken and garlic; sauté 8 minutes, or until golden.

2. Meanwhile, cook agnolotti as package label directs, adding peas the last 3 minutes. Drain; toss with remaining butter, the cheese, salt and pepper. Place pasta on large serving platter; top with chicken. Whisk lemon juice and mustard into drippings in skillet; simmer 1 minute. Pour over chicken.

Makes 6 servings.

*Left: (Clockwise from right)
Crispy Pasta Pancake With
Creamed Broccoli, Rotelle Aioli
With Walnuts, Agnolotti With
Chicken Piccata.*

Special Microwave Section: 4 Dinners to Fix in a Jiffy

Here, imaginative menus, perfect for family and friends, are all prepared in minutes.

SHRIMP-TOPPED MUSHROOMS
STUFFED VEAL MARINARA
GRAPEFRUIT CREAM TART
WITH ALMOND PASTRY
CREAM

Shrimp-Topped Mushrooms
(pictured, right)

**12 large mushrooms
(1 pound), cleaned
1 cup (4 ounces) frozen
cooked small shrimp, thawed
and well drained
½ cup (3 ounces) herb-cheese
spread
½ cup French-fried onions**

1. Remove stems from mushrooms; reserve for another use. Place, open-side down, on paper-towel-lined microwave-safe platter. Cover with plastic wrap. Cook on HIGH 5 minutes, turning once. Discard plastic and paper towel.

2. Place a few shrimp in each mushroom cap. Spoon 1½ teaspoons cheese in each. Sprinkle with onions. Cook, uncovered, on MEDIUM 4 minutes, until heated through.

Makes 4 to 6 servings.

Stuffed Veal Marinara
(pictured, right)

**8 slices (¼ pound) prosciutto
8 slices (6 ounces) provolone
cheese
4 large veal cutlets (6 ounces
each), pounded ¼-inch thick
(9-by-6-inch rectangle)
1 jar (30¾ ounces) marinara
sauce
Cooked pasta**

1. Place 2 slices prosciutto and 2 slices cheese on each veal cutlet. Roll up and secure with wooden picks. Arrange rolls inside shallow 2-quart microwave-safe baking dish. Pour sauce over veal. Cover casserole with plastic wrap. Cook on HIGH 8 to 10 minutes, turning over rolls once during cooking.

2. Let rolls stand 5 minutes before serving. Cut each roll in ½-inch slices. Serve with marinara sauce and cooked pasta.

Makes 4 to 6 servings.

Right: (Clockwise from top)
Shrimp-Topped Mushrooms,
Stuffed Veal Marinara, Grapefruit
Cream Tart With Almond Pastry
Cream.

Note: Recipes were tested in 600- to 700-watt microwave ovens.

Grapefruit Cream Tart With Almond Pastry Cream

(pictured, page 165)

Crust (See *Note*)
5 tablespoons butter or margarine
1 cup graham-cracker crumbs
⅓ cup finely ground almonds
2 tablespoons sugar

Filling
1 cup milk
½ cup heavy cream
4 large egg yolks
½ cup sugar
¼ cup unsifted all-purpose flour
1 teaspoon vanilla extract
½ teaspoon almond extract
3 cups pink-grapefruit sections, well drained
¼ cup raspberry jam

1. Make Crust: In 1-quart glass measure, melt butter on HIGH 30 seconds; stir in cracker crumbs, almonds and sugar. Press mixture into bottom and up 1 inch of sides of greased 10-inch microwave-safe quiche dish or 9-inch ceramic quiche dish with removable bottom. Cook on HIGH 90 seconds. Press crumbs again if necessary. Cool.

2. Make Filling: In 1-quart glass measure, heat milk and cream on HIGH 3 minutes. Meanwhile, in small bowl, mix egg yolks, sugar and flour. Whisk in some of the hot milk mixture. Return all to measuring cup, whisking constantly. Cook on HIGH 3 minutes, stirring every 30 seconds. Stir in vanilla and almond extracts. Pour into prepared shell. Cover with plastic wrap. Chill several hours or overnight.

3. Just before serving, arrange grapefruit sections on top of custard. Heat jam on HIGH 1 minute or until bubbly. Drizzle over grapefruit.
   Makes 6 to 8 servings.
   Note: A 9-inch prepared graham-cracker crust may be substituted.

HOT AND SOUR SOUP
SZECHWAN STIR-FRY
MANDARIN ICE CREAM SAUCE
OVER ICE CREAM

Hot and Sour Soup

1 package (2.1 ounces) mushroom-and-pork flavor soup mix
4 cups hot water
1 boneless pork loin, finely shredded (4 ounces)
½ cup thinly sliced carrots
1 tablespoon salad oil
½ cup thinly sliced cucumber
¼ cup rice vinegar
½ teaspoon ground white pepper

1. In bowl, blend soup mix with 1 cup water; set aside. In 2-quart glass measure, combine next 3 ingredients. Cook, covered, on HIGH 1½ minutes; stir after 1 minute.

2. Add soup mixture and remaining 3 cups water. Cook, covered, on HIGH 8 minutes, stirring once. Stir in cucumber, vinegar and pepper. Cook, covered, on HIGH 2 minutes.
   Makes 4 to 6 servings.

Szechwan Stir-Fry

1 package (3.5 ounces) Japanese-style quick-cooking noodles-and-soup mix
3 cups hot water
1 pound boneless chicken breasts, skinned and cut in ½-inch-wide strips
2 tablespoons salad oil
1 package (1 pound) frozen broccoli-and-carrot combination vegetables, thawed
1 can (15 ounces) baby corn, drained
½ cup prepared Chinese stir-fry sauce
1½ teaspoons chili oil or hot-red-pepper sauce to taste

1. In 1-quart glass measure, combine noodles and hot water. Reserve seasoning packet from noodles. Cook, covered, on HIGH 3 minutes. Drain; set aside.

2. In 13-by-9-by-2-inch microwave-safe baking dish, combine chicken with salad oil. Cook, covered, on HIGH 3 minutes. Add vegetables, stir-fry sauce, noodles and seasoning packet from noodles; mix well. Cook, covered, on HIGH 6 minutes, stirring and rotating dish once. Toss with chili oil.
   Makes 4 servings.

Mandarin Ice Cream Sauce

1 can (11 ounces) mandarin orange sections
1 can (8 ounces) crushed pineapple in heavy syrup
1 tablespoon cornstarch
½ cup shredded coconut

In 1-quart glass measure, combine oranges and their juices, pineapple and cornstarch; mix gently. Cook, covered, on HIGH 5 minutes, stirring once. Stir in coconut. Serve over ice cream.
   Makes 2 cups.

CHILI CON QUESO
LAYERED ENCHILADA CASSEROLE
LEMON-CARAMEL FLANS

Chili con Queso

2 cups (8 ounces) cubed process American cheese
1 jar (12 ounces) artichoke hearts, drained and quartered
1 can (4 ounces) chopped green chiles

Combine all ingredients in 1-quart glass bowl. Cover with plastic wrap; cook on MEDIUM 6 minutes, or until melted, stirring once. If desired, garnish with chopped tomatoes and green onions. Serve with taco chips or crudités.

Makes 2 cups.

Layered Enchilada Casserole

1 pound ground beef
1 can (16 ounces) refried beans
1 package (1⅜ ounces) chili
**   seasoning mix**
1 cup water
1 can (15 ounces) tomato sauce
1 package (10 ounces) flour
**   tortillas**
2 cups (8 ounces) shredded
**   Cheddar cheese**

1. Place beef in 2-quart glass measure or bowl; cover with plastic wrap. Cook on HIGH 3 minutes. Stir in beans, mix and water. Cook on HIGH 5 minutes, stirring once.

2. Pour tomato sauce into pie plate. Dip both sides of tortillas in sauce. Layer beef mixture and tortillas in 13-by-9-by-2-inch microwave-safe baking dish, cutting tortillas to fit. Top with cheese. Cover tightly with plastic wrap. Cook on MEDIUM-HIGH 10 minutes, turning once. Let stand 10 minutes. If desired, garnish with shredded lettuce, chopped tomato and sliced black olives.

Makes 4 to 6 servings.

Lemon-Caramel Flans

½ cup firmly packed
**   light-brown sugar**
4 teaspoons water
¾ cup milk
¼ cup heavy cream
3 large eggs
¼ cup granulated sugar
2 teaspoons vanilla extract
1 teaspoon grated lemon peel
⅛ teaspoon salt

1. In 2-cup glass measure, combine brown sugar and water. Cook on HIGH 2 minutes, or until bubbly and sugar is dissolved, stirring once. Divide evenly among four 6-ounce glass custard cups.

2. In 1-quart glass measure, combine milk and cream. Cook on HIGH 2 minutes, or until hot. Meanwhile, in medium bowl, beat eggs, granulated sugar, vanilla, lemon peel and salt. Slowly beat in hot milk mixture; pour into custard cups, dividing mixture evenly. Arrange cups 1 inch apart in a circle in microwave. Cook on MEDIUM 8 to 10 minutes or until firm, rotating cups every 2 minutes.

3. Serve warm or cold. To unmold: Run a knife around edge of cup; invert custard onto dish.

Makes 4 servings.

FILLET OF SOLE WITH RICE
STUFFING
HOT CABBAGE SLAW
CHOCOLATE-CHEESE MOUSSE

Fillet of Sole With Rice Stuffing

1 package (8 ounces) rice,
**   vegetable and**
**   Cajun-seasoning mix**
3 cups boiling water
3 tablespoons salad oil
8 ounces surimi (fish and crab
**   blend), shredded**
6 fillets (about 6 ounces each)
**   sole or flounder**
Paprika
Chopped parsley

1. In 3-quart bowl, combine rice and seasoning mix, water and 2 tablespoons oil. Cook, covered, on HIGH 15 minutes, stirring every 5 minutes. Stir in surimi. Set aside.

2. On large microwave-safe platter, arrange fillets in spoke fashion. Spoon about ½ cup rice stuffing on

one-half of each fillet. Fold over remaining half to enclose stuffing. Brush outsides of fish with remaining 1 tablespoon oil. Sprinkle with paprika and parsley. Cover platter tightly with plastic wrap. Cook on MEDIUM 10 minutes, or until fish flakes with a fork, rotating dish a quarter turn every 2 minutes.

Makes 6 servings.

Hot Cabbage Slaw

½ cup mayonnaise
¼ cup Dijon-style mustard
2 tablespoons cider vinegar
1 teaspoon poppy seeds
4 cups firmly packed shredded
**   red or green cabbage**
1 cup thinly sliced celery
½ cup sliced green onion

In 3-quart glass bowl, combine first 4 ingredients. Cook on HIGH 1 minute, or until bubbly. Add vegetables; toss well. Cook, covered, on HIGH 2 minutes or until wilted. Stir.

Makes 6 servings.

Chocolate-Cheese Mousse

3 squares (3 ounces) semisweet
**   chocolate**
1 package (3 ounces) cream
**   cheese**
2 tablespoons milk
½ cup sifted confectioners' sugar
2 cups whipped cream

1. In 1-quart glass measure, combine chocolate, cream cheese and milk. Cook on HIGH 60 seconds, or until chocolate is melted; stir until smooth. Blend in sugar. Cool.

2. Stir about ½ cup of the whipped cream into chocolate mixture. Fold in remaining whipped cream. Spoon into dishes; refrigerate or freeze until serving time.

Makes 6 servings.

Special Microwave Section: Perfect Party Fare

Party foods prepared ahead of time and warmed just before guests arrive make entertaining easy.

Shrimp Creole

2 tablespoons olive oil
1 cup chopped onion
1 cup chopped celery
¾ cup chopped green
   pepper
1 teaspoon salt
1 teaspoon pepper
1 teaspoon dried thyme leaves,
   crushed
½ teaspoon dried basil leaves,
   crushed
1 small clove garlic, crushed
½ cup chicken broth
1 can (28 ounces) crushed
   tomatoes
1 can (8 ounces) tomato
   sauce
1 teaspoon sugar
2 pounds large shrimp, peeled
   and deveined

1. In glass bowl, combine oil and onion. Cook on HIGH 7 minutes, until onion is tender. Stir in celery and green pepper. Cover; cook on HIGH 5 minutes, until vegetables are tender. Stir in salt, pepper, thyme, basil, garlic and broth. Cover; cook on HIGH 5 minutes, stirring once. Stir in tomatoes, tomato sauce and sugar. Cover; cook on HIGH 5 minutes, stirring once, until boiling.
2. Stir shrimp into mixture. Cover; let stand 10 minutes, until shrimp are just firm.
Makes 6 servings.

Creamy Black Bean Dip

1 medium onion,
   chopped
1 medium clove garlic,
   crushed
1 tablespoon butter or
   margarine
1 can (1 pound) black beans
1 cup sour cream
Assorted fresh vegetables for
   dipping

1. In 1½-quart microwave-safe casserole, cook onion, garlic and butter on HIGH 3 minutes. Stir in beans and their liquid. Cook on HIGH 3 minutes. In food processor or blender, puree bean mixture; transfer mixture to bowl. Cover; refrigerate until mixture is thoroughly chilled.
2. Before serving, stir sour cream into chilled bean mixture. If desired, garnish with sliced green onion. Serve dip with assorted cut fresh vegetables.
Makes 2 cups dip.

■ To roast nuts, place in a microwave-safe bowl with a dollop of butter. Cook on HIGH 2 minutes; let stand for 1 minute. Stir mixture well; then cook 2 minutes more on HIGH.

Parmesan Crisps

1 package (17½ ounces) frozen
   puff pastry, thawed
1 large egg
1 tablespoon water
1 cup grated Parmesan cheese
½ teaspoon paprika

1. On cutting board, unfold one pastry sheet. In small cup, beat egg with water. Brush pastry with some egg mixture; sprinkle with ¼ cup cheese and ⅛ teaspoon paprika. With rolling pin, press lightly into pastry. Turn over; repeat. Cut pastry into eight 1-inch strips; cut strips crosswise in half.
2. Twist each strip several times. Arrange half of strips on waxed-paper-lined microwave-safe baking tray. Cook on HIGH 3 minutes; rotate tray, and cook 1 to 3 minutes longer, or until sticks are light golden on bottom. Remove from tray; cool. Repeat procedure with remaining pastry, egg mixture, cheese and paprika.
Makes 32 sticks.

Right: (Clockwise from top right) Creamy Black Bean Dip, Parmesan Crisps, Shrimp Creole, Stuffed Meatballs.

Note: Recipes were tested in 600- to 700-watt microwave ovens.

Stuffed Meatballs

1 pound ground beef
¾ cup soft bread crumbs
1 large egg
2 tablespoons prepared steak
** sauce**
28 cocktail onions
1 jar (18 ounces) grape jelly
⅓ cup prepared yellow
** mustard**

1. In medium bowl, combine beef, bread crumbs, egg and steak sauce; mix well. Shape 1 tablespoon beef mixture around an onion; roll into ball. Repeat with remaining beef mixture and onions. Arrange meatballs in 13-by-9-by-2-inch glass baking dish. Cover with waxed paper; cook on HIGH 3 minutes. Rearrange meatballs and cover.

Cook on HIGH 1 to 3 minutes, until firm. Let stand, covered, 3 minutes.

2. In large glass bowl, mix jelly with mustard. Cook on HIGH 1 to 3 minutes, stirring occasionally, until jelly is melted and mixture is blended. Add meatballs to sauce; cook on HIGH 2 minutes to heat through.

Makes 28 meatballs.

Special Microwave Section: Perk Up Packaged Foods

Convenience foods plus a little ingenuity add up to creative new dishes in a flash.

Broccoli Pizza Appetizers

1 package (10 ounces) frozen baby broccoli spears
4 packages (7.1 ounces each) microwave frozen deluxe cheese pizzas
¼ cup crumbled blue cheese
½ cup sliced pitted black olives

1. Prepare broccoli as package label directs; cut each spear crosswise into 4 pieces. Center pizza on silver side of tray in package; sprinkle with 1 tablespoon cheese and 2 tablespoons olives; top with one-fourth of the broccoli.
2. Cook on HIGH 5 minutes, rotating once after 2 minutes. Place on plate; let stand 1 to 2 minutes. Repeat with remaining ingredients. Cut each pizza into 8 wedges.
Makes 32 wedges.

Super Supper Burritos

4 packages (5 ounces each) frozen beef-bean burritos
1 cup bottled chunky salsa
1 cup (4 ounces) shredded Cheddar cheese
1 cup sour cream
1 green onion, chopped

Arrange burritos around edge of 2-quart microwave-safe baking dish.

Heat on HIGH 6 minutes, turning burritos over after 3 minutes. Spoon some salsa over each burrito; sprinkle with shredded cheese. Cover burritos loosely with waxed paper; heat on HIGH 6 minutes, rotating once, until cheese melts. Serve burritos with sour cream and chopped green onion. If desired, garnish with lettuce, sliced tomatoes and jalapeño pepper.
Makes 4 servings.

Fish Fillets With Shrimp Sauce

½ cup finely chopped celery
2 green onions, thinly sliced
1 tablespoon butter or margarine
1 package (4 ounces) frozen cooked small shrimp, thawed and drained
⅓ cup mayonnaise
⅓ cup plain yogurt
1 tablespoon lemon juice
1 tablespoon capers, well drained
¼ teaspoon salt
2 packages (7 ounces each) microwave frozen fish fillets

1. In 1-quart glass bowl, combine chopped celery, sliced onions and butter. Cook mixture on HIGH 4 minutes, stirring after 2 minutes. Stir

in shrimp, mayonnaise, yogurt, lemon juice, capers and salt. Cover and set mixture aside.
2. Prepare fish, one package at a time, as package label directs; keep warm. Cook sauce on MEDIUM 2 minutes, stirring twice. Place 2 fillets on each serving plate; spoon ⅓ cup sauce over fish. If desired, serve with steamed asparagus.
Makes 4 servings.

Eggs Verdi

½ cup butter or margarine
¼ cup water
1 tablespoon lemon juice
⅛ teaspoon ground red pepper
3 large egg yolks, beaten
1 package (12 ounces) frozen spinach soufflé, thawed
4 large eggs
2 English muffins, split and toasted

1. In 1-quart glass bowl, combine butter, water, lemon juice and pepper. Cook, uncovered, on HIGH 2½ minutes, or until boiling. With wire whisk, gradually beat in egg yolks. Cook, uncovered, on HIGH 15 seconds (sauce will be thin). Let stand 5 minutes or until thickened, stirring occasionally.
2. Meanwhile, place soufflé in 4 custard cups, dividing evenly. Cook

Note: Recipes were tested in 600- to 700-watt microwave ovens.

Left: (Clockwise from top) Banana-Walnut Cake, Fish Fillets With Shrimp Sauce, Super Supper Burritos, Eggs Verdi, Broccoli Pizza Appetizers.

on HIGH 4 minutes, stirring once. Crack 1 egg into each cup over soufflé mixture; with wooden pick, puncture yolk. Cover cups with waxed paper. Cook on HIGH 3 to 4 minutes, rearranging cups in oven after 2 minutes. Let stand, covered, 3 minutes.

3. Reheat sauce on HIGH 1 minute. Run spatula around edge of soufflé mixture in each cup; turn out each onto muffin half. Spoon some sauce over each; serve immediately. If desired, garnish with lemon wedge and parsley sprig.

Makes 4 servings.

Apple Dessert Pancakes

½ cup sliced almonds
1 package (12 ounces) frozen scalloped apples
¼ cup raisins
1 cup heavy cream
1 tablespoon confectioners' sugar
2 tablespoons almond-flavored liqueur
4 microwave frozen pancakes

1. In 9-inch glass pie plate, spread out almonds. Cook on HIGH 3 to 4 minutes, stirring twice; set aside.

2. Prepare scalloped apples as package label directs for microwave. Stir in raisins and all but 2 tablespoons sliced almonds.

3. In small bowl of electric mixer, at high speed, beat cream with sugar until stiff. Fold in liqueur; set aside.

4. Place pancakes on microwave-safe plate; top each with one-fourth apple mixture. Heat on HIGH 2 minutes, turning once; top each pancake with some of the whipped cream and reserved almonds.

Makes 4 servings.

Peanut-Butter Brownies

1 package (10.3 ounces) microwave brownie mix
2 tablespoons unsweetened cocoa powder
⅓ cup creamy peanut butter
2 bars (1.65 ounces each) milk-chocolate candy, broken into pieces
¼ cup dry-roasted peanuts, chopped

1. Prepare brownie mix as package label directs, except to add cocoa powder. Spread batter in pan

from mix; drop peanut butter by teaspoonfuls over batter. With knife, swirl peanut butter into batter.

2. Cook on HIGH 4 minutes, rotating a half turn after 2 minutes, until center loses shine. Remove from oven; sprinkle with chocolate candy. Let stand 2 minutes, until candy melts. Spread chocolate over brownie; sprinkle with nuts. When cool, cut into 12 pieces.

Makes 12 brownies.

Banana-Walnut Cake

1 package (12 ounces) microwave cinnamon-streusel-swirl cake mix
1 medium banana, sliced
⅔ cup walnuts, finely chopped

1. Prepare and bake cake mix as package label directs, except to place banana slices over bottom of pan before adding batter, and to sprinkle all but 2 tablespoons of the nuts over streusel mixture in batter.

2. Invert onto wire rack 10 minutes. Drizzle glaze and sprinkle nuts over cake. Serve warm or cool.

Makes 12 servings.

October

Nothing's nicer on a blustery fall day than soup and a sandwich. Make your own winning combinations from our robust recipes. The titles below are pictured on the next five pages, showing ways to pair soup with sandwich.

Shaker Bean Chowder

Caesar-Salad Sandwich

Garden Chowder With Fresh Dill

Ham and Cheese With Honey-Mustard Slaw

Spanish Soup With Little Meatballs

Potato Tortilla on a Roll

Quick Calzones

Smoky Split-Pea Soup

California Croissant-Wiches

Wild Rice Cream-of-Mushroom Soup

Prosciutto and Brie With Sweet-Onion Spread

Squash and Apple Bisque

Steak Heroes

Beef-Barley Soup

Grilled Apple and Pear Sandwich

Soup and Sandwich Cookbook

Enjoy our savory garden vegetable chowder, seasoned with bacon and dill. Serve it with all-American ham and Swiss on pumpernickel, topped with a mixed vegetable slaw in honey-mustard dressing.

Caesar-Salad Sandwich

(pictured, page 173)

2-pound round loaf Italian bread
¾ cup bottled Caesar-salad dressing
2 tablespoons drained capers
8 large leaves Romaine lettuce, washed, crisped and torn into large pieces
4 hard-cooked large eggs, peeled and sliced
1 can (2 ounces) flat anchovies, rinsed
4-ounce piece Parmesan cheese, at room temperature
½ pound sliced salami
¼ pound sliced provolone cheese

1. Cut bread horizontally in half; brush cut sides with ¼ cup salad dressing. Place bottom half of bread on serving board; sprinkle bread with capers. Top with lettuce pieces. Arrange egg slices and anchovies over all; brush with remaining ½ cup salad dressing.

2. With cheese plane or meat slicer, cut thin slices of Parmesan cheese; arrange Parmesan slices over layer of anchovies. Arrange a layer of salami slices and then a layer of provolone cheese over all layers. Top all with remaining half bread loaf; secure sandwich with long wooden skewers. To serve, cut sandwich with serrated knife into ½-inch-thick slices.

Makes 12 servings.

Shaker Bean Chowder

(pictured, page 173)

1 pound Great Northern beans, rinsed and sorted
½ pound salt pork, cut in ½-inch strips
1 large onion, chopped
3 celery stalks, sliced
2 carrots, sliced
3 medium leeks, white part only, washed and thinly sliced
3 small cloves garlic, crushed
8 cups water
1 can (28 ounces) tomatoes in puree
1 cup diced ham (6 ounces)
¼ cup firmly packed brown sugar
1 teaspoon dried thyme leaves
1 teaspoon salt
¼ teaspoon pepper
¼ pound fresh spinach leaves, coarsely chopped

1. In 3-quart saucepan, place beans and enough cold water to cover. Bring to boiling; simmer, covered, 2 minutes. Remove from heat; let stand 1 hour. Drain.

2. In 5-quart Dutch oven, over medium heat, cook salt pork until crisp and all fat is rendered. With slotted spoon, remove salt pork; set aside. Drain off all but 2 tablespoons fat. Add onion, celery, carrots, leeks

---

Page 173: Shaker Bean Chowder, Caesar-Salad Sandwich.

Pages 174 and 175: (Clockwise from top right) Spanish Soup With Little Meatballs, Ham and Cheese With Honey-Mustard Slaw, Potato Tortilla on a Roll, Quick Calzones, California Croissant-Wiches, Smoky Split-Pea Soup, Garden Chowder With Fresh Dill.

Pages 176 and 177: (Clockwise from top right) Squash and Apple Bisque, Prosciutto and Brie With Sweet-Onion Spread, Steak Heroes, Grilled Apple and Pear Sandwich, Beef-Barley Soup, Wild Rice Cream-of-Mushroom Soup.

and garlic; over medium-high heat, sauté 5 minutes. Add salt pork, beans and water. Bring to boiling; simmer, covered, 30 minutes, or until beans are just tender.

3. Add tomatoes, ham, sugar, thyme, salt and pepper. Return soup to boiling; simmer, partially covered, 15 minutes, or until beans are tender. In food processor, puree 2 cups cooked bean mixture; stir into soup mixture. Add chopped spinach; cook until heated through.

Makes 12 to 14 servings.

Spanish Soup With Little Meatballs

(pictured, page 175)

½ pound smoked ham, cut in
   1-inch pieces
½ cup packed parsley leaves
3 tablespoons fresh oregano or
   1 teaspoon dried oregano
   leaves
1 medium clove garlic, peeled
½ pound ground turkey
¼ cup fine dry bread crumbs
1 large egg
½ teaspoon salt
¼ teaspoon pepper
2 tablespoons salad oil
1 medium red onion, cut in
   ¼-inch-thick wedges
8 cups chicken broth
½ teaspoon saffron threads
½ cup acini di pepe pasta
   (small pasta balls)
1 medium green zucchini,
   sliced
1 medium yellow zucchini,
   sliced
½ pound plum tomatoes,
   chopped

1. Make meatballs: In food processor, process ham, parsley, oregano and garlic until ham is finely

chopped. Add turkey, bread crumbs, egg, salt and pepper; process just until mixed. Shape mixture into ¾-inch balls, using 1 level teaspoonful for each. In 5-quart Dutch oven, heat oil. Over medium-high heat, cook meatballs in batches until evenly browned. Add onion; sauté until tender. With slotted spoon, remove all to plate. Pour off drippings.

2. Make soup: Pour broth into pan; add saffron and bring to boiling. Add pasta; cook 8 minutes. Add meatballs, onion, zucchini and tomatoes; return to boiling. Simmer 5 minutes, or until vegetables are tender.

Makes 10 to 12 servings.

Ham and Cheese With Honey-Mustard Slaw

(pictured, page 175)

Honey-Mustard Slaw
¼ cup honey
¼ cup prepared mustard
¼ cup mayonnaise
2 tablespoons prepared
   horseradish
½ teaspoon salt
¼ teaspoon pepper
2 cups finely shredded green
   cabbage
1 carrot, shredded
1 small cucumber, seeded and
   shredded

Sandwich
¼ pound sliced mild Swiss
   cheese
8 slices pumpernickel or
   whole-wheat bread
½ pound sliced Virginia ham

1. Make slaw: In large bowl, blend honey with mustard, mayonnaise, horseradish, salt and pepper.

Add remaining slaw ingredients; toss well. Refrigerate until chilled.

2. Assemble sandwich: Arrange cheese over each of 4 slices bread, dividing evenly. Arrange one-fourth of ham over each; top with slaw, dividing evenly. Cover each with remaining slices of bread.

Makes 4 servings.

California Croissant-Wiches

(pictured, page 174)

6 large croissants, cut
   horizontally in half
2 large avocados
2 tablespoons lemon juice
1 package (1.25 ounces)
   cheese-sauce mix
1 cup milk
1 teaspoon Dijon-style mustard
2 beefsteak tomatoes
2 packages (3½ ounces each)
   enoki mushrooms, rinsed,
   ends trimmed
1 cup clover sprouts
2 tablespoons toasted sesame
   seeds

1. In warm oven, heat croissants until crisp. Place bottom half of each on a salad plate.

2. Peel, pit and slice avocados. Toss with lemon juice; set aside. Prepare cheese sauce with milk as package label directs; stir in mustard. Keep sauce warm.

3. Thinly slice tomatoes; cut slices crosswise in half. Arrange tomato and avocado slices, mushrooms and sprouts over each croissant bottom, dividing evenly. Spoon cheese sauce over each, dividing evenly; sprinkle with sesame seeds. Cover each with top half of croissant. Serve immediately.

Makes 6 servings.

Potato Tortilla on a Roll

(pictured, page 175)

4 onion rolls, cut horizontally
in half
¼ cup plus 1 tablespoon salad
oil
¼ pound chorizo sausage or
pepperoni
1 medium green pepper, cut in
strips
1 pound russet potatoes, pared
and thinly sliced
5 large eggs
¼ teaspoon salt
¼ teaspoon pepper

Olive-and-Garlic Spread
½ cup mayonnaise
½ cup slivered almonds
2 to 3 small cloves garlic,
peeled
¼ cup pitted oil-cured olives
1 tablespoon red-wine vinegar
¼ teaspoon salt

Lettuce leaves, washed and
crisped
1 jar (6 ounces) whole
pimientos, quartered

1. Remove excess bread from the inside of the rolls; set aside for another use.

2. Prepare tortilla: In 10-inch nonstick skillet, heat 1 tablespoon salad oil. Add sausage and pepper; sauté over medium-high heat, breaking up sausage with spoon, 5 minutes, or until pepper is tender. Remove from pan; set aside. In same pan, heat ¼ cup salad oil. Add potatoes; over medium-high heat, sauté 10 minutes, or until tender and golden. Spread potatoes in an even layer in pan. In medium bowl, beat eggs until well mixed; add sausage mixture, salt and pepper. Pour over potatoes. Cook until egg is set, pushing edges of tortilla toward center to let uncooked egg run underneath. Cook, covered, 3 to 5 minutes, or until set. Remove from pan; cut into quarters.

3. Prepare sandwich spread: In

food processor or blender, process mayonnaise, almonds and garlic until smooth. Add olives, vinegar and salt; process until olives are finely chopped. Spread about 3 tablespoons mixture over cut sides of bottom half of rolls; arrange lettuce leaves and pimientos over top, dividing evenly. Place one portion tortilla and then roll top on each.

Makes 4 servings.

Quick Calzones

(pictured, page 175)

1 package (15 ounces) ricotta
cheese
1 package (8 ounces)
mozzarella cheese, shredded
2 ounces sliced prosciutto,
coarsely chopped
2 tablespoons chopped basil
leaves
¼ teaspoon pepper
2 loaves (1 pound each) frozen
bread dough, thawed
1 large egg
1 tablespoon water
Salad oil

1. In large bowl, combine ricotta, mozzarella, prosciutto, basil and pepper; set aside. Preheat oven to 400°F. Brush 2 large baking sheets with salad oil; set aside.

2. Divide each loaf of bread dough into 3 equal pieces; on floured surface, roll each piece into a 7-inch round. On one half of each round, place ½ cup ricotta mixture; spread to within ½ inch of edge.

3. In small bowl, beat egg with water; brush over edges of dough rounds. Fold empty half of dough round over filling; form into a crescent shape. Press or decoratively pinch edges to seal.

4. Place 3 calzones on each prepared baking sheet; brush with oil. Bake 30 to 35 minutes, or until lightly browned. Serve immediately.

Makes 6 servings.

Garden Chowder With Fresh Dill

(pictured, page 174)

8 slices bacon, coarsely
chopped
1 medium onion, chopped
1 medium green pepper,
chopped
2 cans (10¾ ounces each)
condensed cream-of-potato
soup
1 can (about 14 ounces)
chicken broth
1 cup heavy cream
1 cup milk
1 package (10 ounces) frozen
chopped broccoli
1 package (10 ounces) frozen
chopped cauliflower
1 package (10 ounces) frozen
cut corn
½ teaspoon salt
⅛ teaspoon pepper
1 tablespoon snipped fresh dill

In 5-quart Dutch oven, over medium-high heat, sauté bacon 3 minutes, or until crisp. With slotted spoon, remove bacon; set aside. Remove all but 2 tablespoons fat from Dutch oven. Add onion and pepper; sauté 3 minutes longer. Stir in potato soup, broth, cream and milk; bring to boiling. Add broccoli, cauliflower and corn. Simmer, covered, 10 to 12 minutes, or until vegetables are tender. Add salt, pepper and dill. Garnish with bacon.

Makes 8 to 10 servings.

■ A paper bag lets fresh mushrooms "breathe" and stay fresh longer, so when you buy a plastic package of mushrooms or purchase them loose in a plastic bag, be sure to place them in a paper bag, twisted closed, in the refrigerator. When you're ready to use the mushrooms, simply wipe them with a damp paper towel—never soak them, or they'll become soggy.

Smoky Split-Pea Soup

(pictured, page 174)

1 package (2.4 ounces)
  leek-soup mix
6 cups water
1 cup dried green split peas
2 smoked ham hocks (1 pound
  each), skins removed
1 package (10 ounces) frozen
  peas
3 tablespoons chopped mint
  leaves
½ teaspoon salt (optional)
¼ teaspoon pepper (optional)

1. In 6-quart Dutch oven, blend soup mix with water. Add split peas and ham hocks; bring to boiling. Cover; simmer 1½ hours.

2. Remove ham to cutting board; cool slightly. Stir frozen peas and mint into soup. Bring to boiling; simmer, covered, 5 minutes longer.

3. Remove ham from bones; cut into strips. Add to soup; heat through. If desired, season soup with salt and pepper.

Makes 6 to 7 servings.

Squash and Apple Bisque

(pictured, page 177)

2 tablespoons butter or
  margarine
2 Granny Smith apples, pared,
  cored and sliced
1 large onion, sliced
2 carrots, thinly sliced
2 cans (about 14 ounces each)
  chicken broth
2 packages (11 ounces each)
  frozen butternut squash,
  thawed
1 cup heavy cream
¼ teaspoon crushed dried
  rosemary leaves
½ teaspoon salt
¼ teaspoon pepper
¼ cup dry white wine
Apple slices

1. In 6-quart Dutch oven, melt butter. Add apples, onions and carrots; over medium heat, cook 5 minutes. Add 1 cup broth. Cover; simmer 5 minutes.

2. In food processor, puree apple mixture; return to pan. Add remaining broth, the squash and next 4 ingredients. Bring to boiling; simmer, uncovered, 10 minutes. Stir in wine; simmer 2 minutes. Serve hot or cold, garnished with apple slices.

Makes 8 servings.

Prosciutto and Brie With Sweet-Onion Spread

(pictured, page 177)

¼ cup (½ stick) butter or
  margarine
2 large Bermuda onions, sliced
6 small cloves garlic, chopped
¼ cup cider vinegar
2 tablespoons coarse
  Dijon-style mustard
2 tablespoons light-brown
  sugar
½ teaspoon salt
¼ teaspoon pepper
1 oval loaf sourdough or
  pumpernickel bread
1 bunch watercress, rinsed and
  patted dry
½ pound Brie cheese, thinly
  sliced
½ pound sliced prosciutto

1. In large skillet, melt butter. Add onions and garlic; over medium-low heat, cook 30 minutes, stirring occasionally, until onions are tender and slightly golden. Add vinegar, mustard, sugar, salt and pepper. Cook, stirring, 15 minutes, or until mixture is very thick. Remove mixture from heat.

2. Cut loaf of bread horizontally in half. Spread onion mixture over cut side of bottom half. Arrange watercress over onion spread; top with layer of Brie and then layer of prosciutto. Place remaining half bread loaf over all. Serve immediately.

Makes 8 servings.

Wild Rice Cream-of-Mushroom Soup

(pictured, page 176)

1 ounce dried porcini
  mushrooms
1 ounce dried shiitake
  mushrooms
2 cups hot water
3 tablespoons butter or
  margarine
1 large onion, chopped
⅓ cup uncooked wild rice
6 cups beef broth
½ pound fresh mushrooms,
  sliced
1 cup heavy cream
¼ cup unsifted all-purpose flour
¼ cup sherry
Chopped parsley

1. In medium bowl, soak dried mushrooms in water 1 hour. Strain through double thickness cheesecloth; reserve liquid. Cut off and discard tough stems; cut caps into ¼-inch-wide strips.

2. In 3-quart saucepan, melt 1 tablespoon butter. Over medium-high heat, sauté onion 3 minutes, or until tender. Add rice, broth, reconstituted mushrooms and the mushroom liquid. Bring to boiling; simmer, covered, 35 minutes, or until rice is just tender.

3. Meanwhile, in skillet, melt remaining 2 tablespoons butter. Add fresh mushrooms; over medium-high heat, sauté 3 minutes, or until golden. In small bowl, gradually stir cream into flour until blended. Add sautéed mushrooms and cream mixture to soup. Heat, stirring, until boiling; simmer 10 minutes, or until thickened. Stir in sherry; simmer 2 minutes. Garnish with parsley.

Makes 8 servings.

Soup and Sandwich Cookbook

Beef-Barley Soup

(pictured, page 176)

2 tablespoons salad oil
1 pound boneless chuck, cut in
  ½-inch cubes
1 large onion, chopped
6 cups beef broth
1 bay leaf
2 teaspoons dried basil leaves,
  crushed
2 teaspoons dried Italian
  seasoning
½ teaspoon salt
¼ teaspoon pepper
½ cup uncooked barley, rinsed
1 can (28 ounces) crushed
  tomatoes
1 package (1 pound) frozen
  mixed vegetables

1. In 5-quart Dutch oven, heat oil. Over medium heat, sauté meat 5 minutes, or until browned. Add onion; cook 3 minutes. Drain off fat.

2. Add broth and next 5 ingredients. Bring to boiling; simmer, partially covered, 30 minutes. Add barley; simmer 30 minutes, or until tender. Skim off foam. Add tomatoes and vegetables. Return to boiling; simmer 5 minutes. Remove bay leaf.

Makes 8 to 10 servings.

Grilled Apple and Pear Sandwich

(pictured, page 176)

6 tablespoons butter or
  margarine
1 large apple, cored and thinly
  sliced
1 large pear, cored and thinly
  sliced
½ cup bottled chutney
½ cup chopped walnuts
½ pound white Cheddar
  cheese, thinly sliced
8 thick slices white or egg
  bread
¼ pound blue cheese,
  crumbled

1. In large skillet, melt 4 tablespoons butter; add apple and pear. Over high heat, cook, stirring, 5 minutes, or until fruit is tender and most juices evaporate. Stir in chutney and walnuts; remove from heat.

2. Arrange Cheddar slices on 4 slices bread, dividing evenly. Spread about ½ cup fruit mixture over cheese on each slice. Sprinkle blue cheese over fruit mixture, dividing evenly. Cover each with a slice of bread.

3. In large skillet, over low heat, melt remaining butter. Carefully place sandwiches in skillet; cook until golden brown on bottom. Turn sandwiches over; brown on other side. Serve warm.

Makes 4 servings.

Steak Heroes

(pictured, page 177)

¼ cup olive oil
⅓ cup red-wine vinegar
1 large clove garlic, crushed
1 tablespoon dried oregano
  leaves, crushed
1 can (4 ounces) chopped
  green chiles
2 packages (14 ounces each)
  frozen chopped, shaped and
  thinly sliced sandwich steaks,
  thawed
⅓ cup mayonnaise
1 tablespoon Dijon-style
  mustard
4 long hard rolls, cut
  horizontally in half
1 medium red onion, thinly
  sliced
1 small bunch radishes,
  trimmed and thinly sliced
½ pound sliced American
  cheese

1. In medium bowl, mix oil with vinegar, garlic, oregano and chiles; set aside. Keeping 2 steak slices together as packaged, arrange steaks on racks of broiler pans. Brush steaks generously with half of oil mixture; broil, 4 inches from heat, 5 minutes.

2. In small bowl, blend mayonnaise with mustard; spread over cut sides of rolls, dividing evenly. Top with onion and radish slices, dividing evenly. Arrange 3 steak slices and then 3 cheese slices over each sandwich. Place on baking sheet; broil 1 to 2 minutes, or until cheese melts. Brush cut sides of tops of rolls with remaining oil mixture; place each on top of sandwich.

Makes 4 servings.

Hearty Minestrone With Pesto Sauce

½ pound ground beef
1 medium onion, chopped
2 large cloves garlic,
  crushed
3 cans (10½ ounces each)
  condensed beef broth
Water
1 can (28 ounces) whole
  tomatoes
½ teaspoon salt
¼ teaspoon pepper
1 cup small egg-pasta bows
1 package (16 ounces) frozen
  vegetable combination:
  broccoli, green beans, pearl
  onions and red peppers
1 medium zucchini, sliced
Pesto Sauce (recipe follows)

In 6-quart Dutch oven, over medium-high heat, brown beef 5 minutes. Add onion and garlic; sauté 3 minutes longer. Add broth, 3 soup cans water, the tomatoes and their juices, salt and pepper. With wooden spoon, break up tomatoes. Bring to boiling; add pasta. Simmer, partially covered, 8 minutes, or until pasta is al dente. Stir in frozen vegetables and zucchini; cook 5 minutes longer. Serve minestrone with Pesto Sauce.

Makes 8 to 10 servings.

Pesto Sauce

2 cups fresh basil
½ cup olive oil
1 jar (3 ounces) pine nuts
  (½ cup)
2 large cloves garlic
½ cup freshly grated Parmesan
  cheese
2 tablespoons grated Romano
  cheese
¼ cup (½ stick) unsalted
  butter, softened

In food processor, process basil with olive oil, pine nuts and garlic until smooth. Add cheeses and butter; process until blended.
Makes 1 cup.

Sherry-Carrot Bisque

¼ cup (½ stick) butter or
  margarine
2 pounds carrots, sliced
1 medium onion, chopped
1 cup chopped celeriac
  (optional)
1 small clove garlic, crushed
5 cups chicken broth
2 cups half-and-half
2 tablespoons dry sherry
1 teaspoon grated orange peel
½ teaspoon salt
¼ teaspoon white pepper
¼ cup chopped pistachios

1. In 5-quart Dutch oven, melt butter. Add carrots, onion, celeriac and garlic; over medium-high heat, sauté 10 minutes, stirring occasionally. Add chicken broth; simmer, covered, 45 minutes.
2. Drain carrots over large bowl, reserving liquid. In food processor or blender, puree carrot mixture. Return puree and reserved liquid to pan; stir in half-and-half, sherry, orange peel, salt and white pepper. Over low heat, simmer 5 minutes. Garnish each serving with chopped pistachios.
Makes 6 to 8 servings.

Open-Face Tuna Melt

1 can (12½ ounces) tuna,
  drained and flaked
⅓ cup bottled garlic-vinaigrette
  dressing
2 medium celery stalks,
  chopped
½ large green pepper, chopped
4 thick slices rye bread, toasted
1 package (4 ounces) clover
  sprouts
½ small red onion, thinly
  sliced
1 avocado, peeled, pitted and
  cut in ½-inch-thick slices
1½ cups (6 ounces) shredded
  Edam or Monterey Jack
  cheese

1. In medium bowl, mix tuna with dressing, celery and pepper. Arrange in layers, in order, over bread slices, dividing evenly: sprouts, tuna mixture, red-onion and avocado slices and cheese.
2. Place sandwiches on baking sheet. Broil, 5 inches from heat, 1 minute, or until cheese melts.
Makes 4 sandwiches.

Avocado-Cucumber Soup

2 medium cucumbers, pared,
  seeded and coarsely chopped
1 large avocado, peeled, pitted
  and chopped
1 small onion, quartered
1 can (about 14 ounces)
  chicken broth
1 cup plain yogurt
1 cup half-and-half
¾ teaspoon salt
¼ teaspoon pepper
1 small Kirby cucumber,
  diced
1 medium tomato, seeded
  and diced
½ cup croutons

1. In blender or food processor, process chopped cucumber, avocado, onion and broth until smooth.

Add yogurt, half-and-half, salt and pepper; process until mixture is blended. Chill thoroughly.
2. Serve in glass bowls set over crushed ice. Sprinkle each serving with diced cucumber and tomato and croutons.
Makes 6 to 8 servings.

Vegetable Burritos

1 tablespoon salad oil
1 medium red pepper, cut in
  1½-inch strips
1 medium green pepper, cut in
  1½-inch strips
1 small jalapeño pepper,
  chopped
1 medium zucchini, thinly
  sliced
2 medium cloves garlic, crushed
1½ teaspoons chili powder
1 medium tomato, chopped
4 (10-inch) flour tortillas,
  warmed
1½ cups (6 ounces) shredded
  Monterey Jack cheese

1. In 10-inch skillet, over medium heat, heat salad oil. Add peppers, zucchini, garlic and chili powder; cook 3 minutes, or until vegetables are tender. Stir in tomato; heat through.
2. Spread one-fourth of vegetable mixture across center of each tortilla; sprinkle with one-fourth of cheese. Fold sides over filling; roll up to make burrito.
Makes 4 servings.

■ Cast-iron skillets are wonderful for cooking because they distribute heat evenly, but rusting can be a problem. To prevent this, wash the skillet in warm, soapy water, dry it with paper towels and place it on a low-heat burner or in a warm oven for a few minutes until completely dry.

Lite Eating: Delicious Veal Dinner

EASY VEAL PAPRIKA
DILL CUCUMBERS
LOW-CALORIE BEER
STRAWBERRY-PEACH TRIFLE

Easy Veal Paprika

1 tablespoon salad oil
¾ pound veal stew meat,
   cut in ¾-inch cubes
1 large onion, sliced
2 teaspoons paprika
2 tablespoons all-purpose flour
⅛ teaspoon pepper
1 cup beef broth
½ teaspoon Worcestershire
   sauce
1 large carrot, cut in ½-inch
   pieces
1 green pepper, chopped
2 cups hot cooked rice
2 tablespoons chopped parsley

1. Over medium-high heat, in 5-quart Dutch oven, heat oil; brown veal on all sides. Remove and drain on paper-towel-lined tray.

2. Reduce heat to medium. Add onion and paprika; sauté 5 minutes. Stir in flour and pepper; add broth, Worcestershire, carrot and veal. Bring to boiling; simmer 30 minutes, or until veal and carrot are tender.

3. Stir in green pepper; simmer 5 minutes, or until tender. Toss rice with parsley; serve with veal.

Makes 4 servings; 275 calories each serving.

Left: Dill Cucumbers, Easy Veal Paprika, Strawberry-Peach Trifle.

Dill Cucumbers

2 tablespoons white-wine
   vinegar
½ teaspoon dry mustard
½ teaspoon salt
¼ teaspoon dried dillweed,
   crushed
3 unpared medium Kirby
   cucumbers, thinly sliced (2
   cups)
Red cabbage or radicchio
   leaves

1. In medium bowl, combine vinegar, mustard, salt and dillweed. Add cucumbers; mix well. Cover and chill several hours.

2. Serve on a bed of red cabbage or radicchio leaves.

Makes 4 servings; 10 calories each serving.

Strawberry-Peach Trifle

¼ cup reduced-calorie
   strawberry jam
8-inch spongecake layer
1 package (3 ounces)
   reduced-calorie instant
   vanilla-flavored-pudding mix
2½ cups skim milk
¼ teaspoon almond extract
1 can (1 pound) peach slices
   in light syrup, drained
1 cup nondairy whipped
   topping
Mint leaves

1. Spread jam over cake layer; cut cake in 1-inch cubes. In large bowl, combine pudding mix, milk and almond extract; whisk until consistency of a thin pudding.

2. In 1½-quart bowl, fit half of cake cubes, jam side up. Top with half of peach slices. Spoon half of pudding on top. Repeat layering, ending with pudding. Garnish with whipped topping and mint.

Makes 8 servings; 180 calories each serving.

■ With just a few tricks, you can turn nutritional, low-calorie vegetables into eye-catching garnishes. To make Turnip-and-Carrot Flowers, you'll need turnips, carrots and capers. First, wash a medium turnip; pare. Cut crosswise into ⅛-inch-thick slices. With tip of paring knife, divide each slice into eighths by cutting out thin slivers from center section to edge. Be careful not to cut through center of turnip. Trim each eighth to a point; place in a bowl of ice water to which a little lemon juice has been added. Refrigerate, covered. Next, repeat procedure, using a large carrot. When ready to use, drain all flowers well on paper towel. Secure carrot flower to center of turnip flower with part of a wooden pick. Last, place a caper in center. Now you're ready to garnish a platter or cheese board.

Quick & Easy: Soup 'n' Sandwich in a Snap

Clam Marinara Soup

1 tablespoon olive oil
1 cup sliced mushrooms
½ cup chopped green
  pepper
¼ cup dry white wine
1 can (11 ounces) condensed
  zesty tomato soup
1 cup chicken broth
½ cup water
12 little-neck clams, well
  scrubbed
⅛ teaspoon pepper

In 3-quart saucepan, heat oil over medium heat. Add mushrooms and green pepper; cook until tender. Stir in wine; simmer 1 minute. Stir in soup, broth, water, clams and pepper; simmer 15 minutes, or until clams are open, stirring occasionally. Discard any unopened clams.
Makes 4 servings.

Roast Beef Pitas

2 tablespoons mayonnaise
1 tablespoon prepared
  horseradish
1 tablespoon sour cream
2 (6-inch) pita breads, cut
  crosswise in half
8 ounces thinly sliced cooked
  roast beef
Lettuce leaves, washed and
  crisped
8 slices tomato

In small bowl, blend mayonnaise, horseradish and sour cream. Spread mixture in pita halves, dividing evenly. Arrange roast beef slices, lettuce leaves and tomato slices in each pita half.
Makes 4 servings.

Asparagus Frittata on a Roll

8 large eggs
¼ cup crumbled feta or goat
  cheese
3 tablespoons water
¼ teaspoon salt
⅛ teaspoon pepper
2 tablespoons butter or
  margarine
1 small onion, chopped
1 package (10 ounces) frozen
  cut asparagus, thawed and
  drained
¼ cup sliced pitted black
  olives
Romaine lettuce leaves, washed
  and crisped
4 Kaiser rolls, split and toasted

1. Preheat oven to 425°F. In large bowl, beat eggs until foamy. Stir in cheese, water, salt and pepper.
2. In 10-inch oven-safe skillet, over medium heat, melt butter. Add onion; cook until tender. Add asparagus; cook 1 minute.
3. Pour egg mixture into skillet; sprinkle with olives. Cook 2 minutes, or until edges are set. Place skillet in oven; bake 10 minutes, or until eggs are set.
4. Cut frittata into 4 portions; place each on lettuce leaf on bottom half of each roll.
Makes 4 servings.

Confetti Chicken Soup

1 tablespoon butter or
  margarine
½ cup julienned red pepper
½ cup julienned parsnip
⅛ teaspoon pepper
2 cans (10¾ ounces each)
  condensed chicken-vegetable
  soup with long-grain and
  wild rice
Water
1 tablespoon chopped parsley

In 2½-quart saucepan, over medium heat, melt butter. Add red pepper, parsnip and pepper; cook until vegetables are tender, stirring often. Add soup, 2 soup cans water and the parsley; bring to boiling. Cover; simmer 10 minutes.
Makes 4 servings.

Right: (Clockwise from top left) Clam Marinara Soup, Confetti Chicken Soup, Asparagus Frittata on a Roll, Roast Beef Pitas.

Micro-Way: Souped-Up Soups and Sandwiches

Gyros

1 pound ground lamb
1 large egg
1 small onion, finely chopped
⅓ cup fine dry bread crumbs
2 tablespoons chopped parsley
1 teaspoon dried oregano
  leaves, crushed
1 teaspoon salt
⅛ teaspoon pepper
1 cup plain yogurt
1 medium clove garlic, crushed
2 tablespoons chopped green
  onion
6 (6-inch) pita breads
Lettuce leaves, washed and
  crisped
Tomato slices

1. In medium bowl, combine lamb, egg, onion, bread crumbs, parsley, oregano, ½ teaspoon salt and the pepper; mix well. Roll rounded tablespoonfuls of mixture into 1½-inch meatballs. Place in shallow 2-quart microwave-safe baking dish; cover with waxed paper. Cook on HIGH 8 minutes, rotating dish and rearranging meatballs after 4 minutes.

2. In small bowl, combine yogurt, garlic, green onion and ½ teaspoon salt; cover and refrigerate. Dampen a microwave-safe paper towel; wrap around 2 or 3 pita breads. Cook on HIGH 1 minute; repeat with remaining breads.

3. Place each pita bread on a 10-inch round parchment or waxed paper or aluminum foil. Place lettuce leaves, tomato slices and 4 meatballs on each bread. Using the paper, roll up to form a loose cone.

Drizzle some of the chilled yogurt sauce over pita breads; pass the remaining sauce.

Makes 6 servings.

Greek Lemon Soup

4 cups chicken broth
⅓ cup orzo (rice-shape pasta)
¾ pound boneless chicken
  breasts, skinned and cut in
  thin strips
2 large eggs
3 tablespoons lemon juice
1 tablespoon chopped fresh dill
1 tablespoon chopped parsley

1. In 2-quart microwave-safe casserole, place broth. Cover with plastic wrap; vent. Cook on HIGH 8 to 10 minutes, or until boiling. Add orzo; cook, covered, on HIGH 7 minutes. Add chicken; cook, covered, on HIGH 5 minutes longer, until orzo and chicken are tender.

2. In medium bowl, beat eggs with lemon juice. Whisk in some of the hot broth; return to casserole. Cook, covered, on MEDIUM 3 minutes; stir in dill and parsley. Garnish with lemon slices, if desired.

Makes 4 to 6 servings.

■ To give new crunch to stale pretzels, crackers or chips, just heat in a 325° oven for five to ten minutes, and cool—they'll taste as crisp as when they were fresh!

Egg Salad on Rye

6 large eggs
¼ cup mayonnaise
2 teaspoons white vinegar
2 teaspoons Dijon-style
  mustard
½ teaspoon Worcestershire
  sauce
¼ teaspoon salt
⅛ teaspoon pepper
1 small red onion, chopped
2 medium celery stalks,
  chopped
Sliced rye bread
¼ pound sliced Virginia ham
Lettuce leaves, washed and
  crisped

1. Crack an egg into each cup of 6-cup microwave-safe muffin pan. With wooden pick, puncture yolks. Cover with waxed paper; cook on MEDIUM 6 minutes, rotating dish after 3 minutes. Let stand 2 minutes.

2. In medium bowl, blend mayonnaise and next 5 ingredients. Coarsely chop eggs and add to mayonnaise mixture; stir in onion and celery.

3. For each sandwich, on 1 slice bread, place about ½ cup egg salad; top with 2 slices ham, some lettuce and 1 slice bread.

Makes 4 to 6 sandwiches.

Cream of Broccoli and Carrot Soup

¼ cup (½ stick) butter or
  margarine
1 medium onion, chopped
¼ cup unsifted all-purpose
  flour
¼ teaspoon salt
⅛ teaspoon pepper
2 cups milk
1 can (about 14 ounces)
  chicken broth
1 package (10 ounces) frozen
  chopped broccoli, thawed
⅛ teaspoon ground nutmeg
1 package (10 ounces) frozen
  baby carrots, thawed
2 teaspoons grated orange peel
Parsley sprigs
Julienne orange peel

1. In 1-quart microwave-safe casserole, cook butter and onion on HIGH 2 minutes. Stir in flour, salt and pepper. Blend in milk. Cover with plastic wrap; vent. Cook on HIGH 4 to 5 minutes, stirring occasionally, until mixture is thickened. Pour half of sauce into another microwave-safe casserole.

2. In 2-cup glass measure, combine chicken broth and enough water to make 2 cups. Blend 1 cup broth mixture into sauce in each casserole.

3. To one casserole, add broccoli and nutmeg. Cover and vent; cook on HIGH 6 minutes. Pour into blender; puree. Return to casserole. Cover. To second casserole, add carrot and orange peel. Cover and vent; cook on HIGH 6 minutes. Pour into blender; puree.

4. For each serving, at the same time, ladle equal amounts of broccoli and carrot soups into same soup bowl. Gently rotate bowl to make swirl. Garnish with parsley sprigs and julienne orange peel.

Makes 4 to 6 servings.

November

You are cordially invited to share our staff's very favorite holiday recipes. To start things off—a glorious turkey, served with sweet, tangy cranberries. Next, a lavish spread from soup to eggnog stars a crown roast of lamb, and ends with a dazzling array of sweets.

Herb-Basted Turkey With Vegetable and Sausage Stuffing

Cranberry-Rhubarb Sauce

Marinated Shrimp Appetizer

Wild Rice and Turkey Bisque

Crown Roast of Lamb With Biscuit Stuffing

Spinach Cheese Pie

Brussels Sprouts With Garlic Hollandaise

Smooth and Creamy Eggnog

Easy Apple Strudel   Classic Apple Tart

Carmen's Walnut Kuchen

Traditional Mincemeat Tarts

Boone Family Holiday Nuggets

Quick Cranberry Pie   Alice's Fruitcake Supreme

Our Family Thanksgiving Cookbook

From our McCall's family to yours—a treasury of Thanksgiving recipes, along with our best wishes for a memorable holiday feast.

Cranberry-Rhubarb Sauce

(pictured, page 191)
Janet Andreas

Janet's flair with food extends from the test kitchen to the behind-the-scenes styling for the photographs on our food pages, so it follows that her recipe is both delicious and beautiful!

1½ cups sugar
½ cup water
1 package (12 ounces) cranberries
1 package (16 ounces) frozen sliced rhubarb, thawed (4 cups)
2 cups kumquats, thinly sliced and seeded, or 2 oranges, chopped
¼ cup chopped candied ginger
1 cup coarsely chopped walnuts

In large saucepan, combine sugar and water. Bring to boiling; cook, stirring, until sugar dissolves. Add cranberries, rhubarb, kumquats and ginger. Return to boiling; simmer, stirring, 5 minutes, or until thickened. Stir in walnuts.

Makes 6 cups.

Herb-Basted Turkey With Vegetable and Sausage Stuffing

(pictured, page 191)
Dale Lang

These tasty turkey and stuffing recipes are based on our publisher's remembrance of his grandmother Hannah's turkey. She came to America from Norway and raised 13 children in what was then the wilds of Wisconsin. No doubt she baked her own bread—we've taken the liberty of modernizing her recipes.

16- to 18-pound turkey, thawed if frozen
Vegetable and Sausage Stuffing (recipe follows)
2 large onions, cut in wedges
Herb-Butter-and-Wine Basting Sauce (recipe follows)
¼ teaspoon salt
⅛ teaspoon pepper
3 cups chicken broth
¼ cup unsifted all-purpose flour
Oregano sprigs
Frosted grapes (instructions, see *Note*, page 120)

1. Remove turkey giblets and neck; set aside. Remove and discard excess fat. Wash turkey; pat dry.

2. Preheat oven to 325°F. Lightly spoon stuffing into neck cavity. Bring neck skin over stuffing; secure with poultry pins. Spoon remaining stuffing into body cavity—do not pack. (Place extra stuffing in greased baking dish; cover and bake last 45 minutes turkey is in oven.) Close body cavity with poultry pins; lace with string. Tie legs together. Pin wings to breast.

3. Place turkey, breast side up, on rack in large roasting pan. Place onions, giblets and neck in pan around turkey. Brush turkey with

---

Page 191: Herb-Basted Turkey With Vegetable and Sausage Stuffing, Cranberry-Rhubarb Sauce.

Pages 192 and 193: (Clockwise from top right) Wild Rice and Turkey Bisque, Smooth and Creamy Eggnog, Spinach Cheese Pie, Brussels Sprouts With Garlic Hollandaise, Marinated Shrimp Appetizer, Crown Roast of Lamb With Biscuit Stuffing.

Pages 194 and 195: (Clockwise from top right) Easy Apple Strudel, Classic Apple Tart, Carmen's Walnut Kuchen, Traditional Mincemeat Tarts, Boone Family Holiday Nuggets, Quick Cranberry Pie, Alice's Fruitcake Supreme.

some of basting sauce; sprinkle with salt and pepper. Insert meat thermometer into thickest portion of thigh, away from bone. Roast, uncovered, 5½ hours, basting every 30 minutes, until meat thermometer registers 170°F. After 1 hour, add 1 cup chicken broth to pan. When skin turns golden, cover turkey loosely with foil tent.

4. Place turkey on warm serving platter. Remove poultry pins and string. Let stand 15 minutes for easier carving. Skim off and discard all fat from pan juices. Blend flour with remaining 2 cups broth; add to pan juices. Place pan over medium heat; bring gravy to boiling, stirring constantly to loosen any browned bits. Reduce heat and simmer 5 minutes, stirring, until thickened; strain. Garnish platter with oregano sprigs and frosted grapes.

Makes 16 to 18 servings.

Vegetable and Sausage Stuffing

1 loaf braided egg bread (challah), cut in ½-inch cubes
2 pounds country sausage
½ cup butter or margarine
6 carrots, pared and thinly sliced (3 cups)
1 head celery, thinly sliced (4 cups)
5 medium leeks, white portion only, washed and thinly sliced
½ pound mushrooms, sliced
2 cups coarsely chopped pecans
4 large eggs
1 can (about 14 ounces) chicken broth
1 tablespoon poultry seasoning
½ teaspoon pepper

1. Preheat oven to 325°F. Arrange bread cubes in large roasting pan. Bake 15 minutes, until lightly toasted. Transfer to 6-quart bowl.

2. In 12-inch skillet, crumble sausage. Over medium-high heat, cook sausage, stirring, until evenly browned. With slotted spoon, remove sausage from pan; place in bowl with bread.

3. In drippings in skillet, melt butter; add carrots, celery, leeks and mushrooms. Over medium-high heat, sauté mixture 10 minutes, or until vegetables are tender. Add contents of skillet to bowl with bread; stir in pecans.

4. In medium bowl, with whisk, beat eggs with broth, poultry seasoning and pepper. Pour over bread mixture; toss well to coat evenly.

Makes about 20 cups.

Herb-Butter-and-Wine Basting Sauce

1½ cups unsalted butter
½ cup dry white wine
2 tablespoons salt-free herb blend
¼ cup chopped parsley
¼ cup minced chives
2 tablespoons chopped fresh thyme or marjoram or 1 teaspoon dried thyme or marjoram leaves
½ teaspoon salt

1. Clarify butter: In small saucepan, over low heat, melt butter. Let stand 5 minutes, until milk solids settle. With basting bulb or gravy separator, remove clear liquid (clarified butter) on top (there should be about 1 cup). Discard milky residue.

2. In clean, small saucepan, combine clarified butter, wine and herb blend. Bring to boiling. Remove mixture from heat; stir in fresh herbs and salt.

Makes about 1½ cups.

Wild Rice and Turkey Bisque
(pictured, page 193)
Karen Sethre White

A native of Minnesota, the land of wild rice, Karen contributed this special soup recipe. It's a perfect first course for any meal during the holiday season.

¼ cup butter or margarine
1 large onion, diced
2 carrots, finely diced
2 celery stalks, finely diced
2 cups diced cooked turkey
¼ cup unsifted all-purpose flour
8 cups chicken broth
4 cups cooked wild rice (1½ cups uncooked)
½ teaspoon salt
¼ teaspoon pepper
2 cups half-and-half

1. In large saucepan, over medium-high heat, melt butter. Add onion, carrots, celery and turkey; sauté 3 minutes, or until vegetables have just softened. Gradually stir in flour until mixture is blended; cook 1 minute.

2. Gradually stir in broth, until blended. Bring to boiling; simmer, partially covered, 10 minutes, until vegetables are tender.

3. Stir in rice, salt and pepper. Add half-and-half; heat mixture over low heat, until hot but not boiling.

Makes 14 servings.

Spinach Cheese Pie

(pictured, page 193)
Donna Meadow

Donna's mother was inspired by her Neapolitan ancestors when she started making this recipe for family gatherings. It was one of our favorites too.

Pastry
2 packages (10 or 11 ounces each) piecrust mix
½ cup grated Parmesan cheese
5 to 9 tablespoons cold water
1 large egg yolk
1 tablespoon water

Filling
2 packages (10 ounces each) frozen chopped spinach, thawed and drained
1 pound ricotta cheese
1 pound cottage cheese
¾ cup grated Parmesan cheese
3 large eggs, beaten
1 large egg white
¼ teaspoon grated nutmeg

1. Grease 9-inch springform pan; set aside. Preheat oven to 375°F.
2. In large bowl, combine piecrust mix with ½ cup grated cheese. Quickly sprinkle 5 to 9 tablespoons water, 1 tablespoon at a time, over piecrust mixture, tossing lightly with fork after each addition (pastry should be just moist enough to hold together, not sticky).
3. Shape two-thirds pastry into ball; roll out into 12-inch round. Carefully place in prepared pan, pressing gently to line bottom and side. Cut off extra pastry at top of pan. In small cup, beat egg yolk until smooth. Brush some of egg yolk over pastry on bottom; stir 1 tablespoon water into remaining egg yolk. Set aside.
4. In large bowl, combine filling ingredients; spoon into pastry shell.
5. Shape remaining pastry into ball; roll out to 9-inch round. Place over spinach mixture, pinching pastry top to pastry side to seal. Brush top with egg-yolk mixture. With tip of knife, make slashes in top for steam vents.
6. Bake 1½ hours. Let stand 10 minutes before serving, or cool completely and refrigerate. Serve hot or cold.
Makes 16 to 20 servings.

Smooth and Creamy Eggnog

(pictured, page 193)
Don Rash

When Don Rash, one of our salesmen in Chicago, got married, his mother-in-law, Rita, not only gained a son—she also gained his mother's recipe for eggnog. Now Rita serves it every holiday season.

6 large eggs, separated
1 cup sugar
1 cup rum
½ cup brandy
6 cups milk
3 cups heavy cream, whipped until soft peaks form
Ground nutmeg

1. In large bowl of electric mixer, at high speed, beat egg yolks until very thick and light. Gradually beat in sugar. At medium speed, beat in rum and brandy. Refrigerate 1 hour, stirring occasionally.
2. In another large bowl, beat egg whites until stiff; set aside. At medium speed, beat milk into egg-yolk mixture; transfer to large punch bowl. With rubber spatula, fold in whipped cream and egg whites.
3. If desired, store punch mixture in covered jars or bowl in refrigerator for a day or up to a month before serving. Pour into punch bowl; serve in punch glasses, sprinkled with dash of nutmeg.
Makes about 25 servings.

Marinated Shrimp Appetizer

(pictured, pages 192 and 193)
Bill McDermitt

This recipe came from McCall's national sales director. It was passed on to Bill's wife, Laurie, by her mother, who first used it for embassy entertaining when she and her husband were stationed in Mexico with the State Department.

3 ripe avocados
2 pounds cooked, peeled large shrimp
¼ teaspoon salt
¼ teaspoon pepper
6 tablespoons Cognac
¼ cup red-wine vinegar
1½ teaspoons dry mustard
3 large egg yolks
¼ cup chopped celery
2 tablespoons prepared horseradish
2 tablespoons chopped chives
2 tablespoons minced parsley
¼ cup chopped shallots
1 cup olive oil
6 tablespoons prepared chili sauce
1 tablespoon lemon juice
Lettuce leaves, washed and crisped

1. Halve and pit avocados; remove peel. Cut into 1-inch pieces; place in large bowl with shrimp.
2. In small bowl, mix salt, pepper and all remaining ingredients except lettuce until blended. Pour into bowl with avocados; toss to coat.
3. Line platter with lettuce. Spoon avocado mixture over lettuce. If desired, garnish with chives.
Makes 8 servings.

■ Remember, if you purchase a frozen turkey you'll need to thaw it for a minimum of three days in the refrigerator before it's ready to go into the oven.

Coquilles Saint Jacques
Mary Johnson

This was a great first course at one of many Thanksgiving family reunions/dinners made by Mary's sister-in-law, Mrs. George M. Johnson.

1 cup dry white wine
½ cup water
½ teaspoon salt
1 small bay leaf
Dash pepper
1 pound sea scallops, washed and drained
5 tablespoons butter or margarine
½ pound sliced mushrooms
2 large shallots, minced
¼ cup unsifted all-purpose flour
¾ cup milk
2 large egg yolks
½ cup heavy cream
½ cup grated Swiss or Gruyère cheese

1. In medium saucepan, combine wine with water, salt, the bay leaf and pepper. Bring to boiling; simmer 5 minutes. Add scallops; cover and simmer 5 minutes. Drain scallops on paper towels; boil liquid to reduce to 1¼ cups. Set aside.

2. In skillet, over medium-high heat, melt 3 tablespoons butter. Add next 2 ingredients; sauté until tender, 5 minutes. Stir in flour until blended. Off heat, stir in 1 cup reserved cooking liquid and the milk. Bring to boiling, stirring. Simmer 4 minutes, stirring frequently.

3. In small bowl, blend egg yolks with cream. Stir in a little of the hot-milk mixture; pour into sauce in skillet. Simmer 1 minute, stirring; add a little more cooking liquid from scallops if necessary.

4. With 2 teaspoons butter, grease 8 scallop shells. In medium bowl, place scallops, cut crosswise into pieces ⅛-inch thick. Stir in two-thirds of sauce mixture. Spoon into prepared shells, dividing evenly. Cover with remaining sauce. Sprinkle with cheese; dot with remaining butter. Arrange shells on broiling pan. (Cover and refrigerate, if desired; remove and uncover about 15 minutes before serving.) Broil 8 inches from heat 6 minutes, or until heated through and golden brown.
Makes 8 servings.

Crown Roast of Lamb With Biscuit Stuffing
(pictured, page 192)
Marianne Langan

Life as a food editor means being exposed to the untraditional at holidays—as well as all year long. This is a favorite for a main course at small gatherings.

6-pound crown roast of lamb (21 ribs)
1 teaspoon salt
¼ teaspoon pepper
Biscuit Stuffing (recipe follows)

Spiced Raisin Sauce
2 tablespoons salad oil
¾ cup chopped shallots
1 large clove garlic, crushed
⅓ cup Benedictine liqueur
1¼ cups beef broth
¾ cup orange juice
¼ cup lime juice
1 medium bay leaf
2 whole cloves
½ cup raisins
1 tablespoon slivered orange peel
¼ teaspoon salt
⅛ teaspoon pepper
2 tablespoons cornstarch

1. Preheat oven to 300°F. Rub lamb well with 1 teaspoon salt and ¼ teaspoon pepper. Place in shallow roasting pan. Cover bone ends with strips of aluminum foil to prevent scorching. Roast, uncovered, 2 hours, or until meat thermometer registers 140°F for rare and 160°F for medium; spoon stuffing in center of roast after 30 minutes.

2. Meanwhile, prepare sauce: In small saucepan, heat salad oil. Add shallots and garlic; over medium heat, sauté 3 minutes, stirring occasionally. Add Benedictine; heat 1 minute. Add 1 cup broth, the fruit juices, bay leaf and cloves; bring to boiling. Simmer, covered, 20 minutes. Add raisins, orange peel, ¼ teaspoon salt and ⅛ teaspoon pepper. Dissolve cornstarch in remaining broth; add to sauce. Cook, stirring, until thickened and smooth. Set aside.

3. When lamb is done, remove to serving platter. Cover loosely with foil. Let stand 10 minutes. Reheat sauce before serving. If desired, garnish with herbs and kumquats.
Makes about 10 servings.

Biscuit Stuffing

5 day-old flaky biscuits
7 day-old corn muffins
½ cup butter or margarine
10 celery stalks, thinly sliced
1 large Spanish onion, diced
½ teaspoon freshly ground pepper
1 teaspoon poultry seasoning
½ teaspoon paprika
¼ cup chopped parsley
½ cup chicken broth
2 large eggs, beaten

1. Preheat oven to 350°F. Coarsely crumble biscuits and muffins onto jelly-roll pan. Dot with 2 tablespoons butter. Bake 25 minutes, until lightly toasted.

2. In 8-quart Dutch oven, over medium-high heat, melt remaining butter. Add celery, onion, pepper, poultry seasoning and paprika; sauté until vegetables are soft.

3. Remove pan from heat; gently stir in parsley and crumbled bread until well mixed, keeping bread pieces as large as possible. Add broth and eggs; toss to coat.
Makes 11 cups.

Brussels Sprouts With Garlic Hollandaise
(pictured, page 193)
Karen Sethre White

Karen has developed recipes for McCall's for more than 14 years. A graduate of the Paris Cordon Bleu, she adds a French touch to this recipe for brussels sprouts, a traditional seasonal vegetable.

2 pints brussels sprouts (1¼ pounds)
1 tablespoon salad oil
1 small clove garlic, crushed
1 package (1.25 ounces) hollandaise-sauce mix
¾ cup water
1 tablespoon capers
1 tablespoon chopped pimiento

1. Trim stems and remove any wilted leaves from sprouts. With tip of knife, cut an *X* in base of each sprout. In large skillet, bring ½ inch salted water to boiling. Add sprouts; simmer 10 minutes, or until tender-crisp. Drain; keep warm.

2. Meanwhile, in 1-quart saucepan, heat oil over medium heat. Cook garlic until golden. Remove pan from heat; stir in sauce mix. Gradually add water, stirring until blended. Cook, stirring, until sauce is thickened.

3. Place sprouts in serving dish. Pour sauce over sprouts; sprinkle with capers and pimiento.
Makes 6 to 8 servings.

Easy Apple Strudel
(pictured, page 195)
Mara Rosenberg

Mara credits her mother with this creation, and we think its use extends to year-round entertaining!

Dough
1 cup butter or margarine
2½ cups unsifted all-purpose flour
1 cup sour cream

Filling
½ cup golden raisins
1 tablespoon Grand Marnier or orange juice
1 can (21 ounces) apple-pie filling
1 teaspoon grated lemon peel
¾ cup sugar
2 teaspoons ground cinnamon
½ cup currant jelly
½ cup pecan pieces
½ cup cornflake crumbs
Salad oil

1. Make dough: In large bowl, with pastry blender or two knives, using a short, cutting motion, or in food processor, cut butter into flour until mixture resembles coarse crumbs. With fork, stir in sour cream until blended (dough will be sticky). Divide evenly into fourths; roll into balls. Wrap each ball in plastic wrap; refrigerate 2 hours or overnight.

2. Make filling: In small bowl, mix raisins with Grand Marnier. Cover; soak overnight.

3. Next day, cut apples in pie filling into small pieces. Place in medium bowl; mix with lemon peel. Set aside. In small cup, mix sugar with cinnamon; set aside.

4. On heavily floured surface, with floured rolling pin, roll dough balls into 16-inch rounds, occasionally turning and sprinkling dough and rolling pin with flour.

5. In small saucepan, melt jelly; let cool. Brush each round of dough with jelly to within 1 inch of edges. Sprinkle apple mixture over jelly, dividing evenly; sprinkle, in order, raisins, pecans, ½ cup sugar mixture and cornflake crumbs over apple mixture, dividing evenly.

6. Roll up each round, jelly-roll fashion; pinch ends and bottom seam to seal. Fold ends under; shape roll into crescent. Freeze several hours, or overnight.

7. Preheat oven to 400°F. Grease two baking sheets. Place 2 frozen strudels on each baking sheet. Brush each with salad oil; sprinkle with

remaining sugar mixture, dividing evenly. Bake 50 minutes, brushing tops of strudels with salad oil after 25 minutes.

8. To serve: Cut strudels crosswise into 1-inch-thick slices.
Makes about 16 servings.

Classic Apple Tart
(pictured, page 195)
Lydia Moss

This sensational tart has been a family favorite ever since Lydia, McCall's travel editor, tasted it in a Manhattan restaurant. No wonder the recipe quickly found its way into her cookbook!

Sweet Pastry Crust (recipe follows)
3½ pounds medium Golden Delicious apples (about 9)
¾ cup butter or margarine
1-inch piece vanilla bean
¼ cup confectioners' sugar
½ cup marmalade
2 tablespoons water
2 tablespoons Cointreau or other orange-flavored liqueur
¼ cup toasted slivered almonds

1. On cold surface, roll out pastry to 9-by-12-inch rectangle. Carefully fit into 8-by-11-inch fluted tart pan with removable bottom, or place in a 10-inch pie plate. Refrigerate.

2. Set aside 5 apples. Pare, core and thinly slice remainder. In large skillet, over medium heat, melt ½ cup butter. Add sliced apples and vanilla bean. Cook, stirring, 30 minutes, until apples are dry and browned. Stir in remaining butter. Pour mixture into the tart pan.

3. Preheat oven to 400°F. Pare, core and thinly slice remaining apples. Arrange, overlapping in neat pattern, over apples in pan. With sieve, sprinkle confectioners' sugar over apples. Bake 1 hour; place on wire rack to cool.

4. In small saucepan, combine

marmalade with water. Over medium heat, cook, stirring, until marmalade melts. Cool slightly; stir in Cointreau. With pastry brush, spread mixture over tart; sprinkle with almonds.

Makes 10 to 12 servings.

Sweet Pastry Crust

½ cup butter or margarine, cut in small pieces and chilled
½ cup confectioners' sugar
2 large egg yolks
Dash salt
1¼ cups unsifted all-purpose flour
1½ to 3 teaspoons ice water

1. In large bowl of electric mixer, at low speed, beat butter with sugar, egg yolks and salt until mixture is blended. Sift one-fourth flour into bowl; beat at low speed until blended. When mixed in, add 1 teaspoon ice water.

2. Repeat with remaining flour and ½ to 2 teaspoons more water—only enough to hold pastry together.

Form into a ball; pat into ½-inch thickness. Wrap in plastic wrap; refrigerate at least one hour before rolling out.

Alice's Fruitcake Supreme
(pictured, page 194)
Don Rash

Alice Rash, Don's mother, is renowned for this recipe. She is expected to serve it to all her guests and to bring it to all family celebrations.

1 pound mixed candied fruit
½ pound candied cherries
½ pound candied pineapple
1 box (15 ounces) golden raisins
1 cup wine (any kind)
2 cups butter or margarine
3 cups confectioners' sugar
7 large eggs, separated
3½ cups pecan halves or pieces
4 cups unsifted all-purpose flour
1 teaspoon baking powder
2 teaspoons ground cinnamon
½ teaspoon salt

1. Set aside 4 cherries and 8 pecan halves. In large bowl, mix remaining fruits with wine. Cover; set aside overnight.

2. Next day, in large bowl of electric mixer, at high speed, beat butter until fluffy. Gradually add sugar, beating until mixture is light and fluffy. Add egg yolks, one at a time, beating well after each addition. With wooden spoon, mix in fruit mixture and nuts.

3. On sheet of waxed paper, combine flour, baking powder, cinnamon and salt; gradually add to butter mixture, stirring just until blended.

4. Preheat oven to 250°F. Grease 10-inch tube pan; set aside. In another large bowl, with electric mixer at high speed, beat egg whites until stiff. With rubber spatula, fold into batter, mixing lightly only until no white streaks remain. Pour batter into prepared pan. Cut reserved cherries in half; decorate top of batter with cherries and reserved pecans. Bake 3½ to 4 hours. Cool in pan 1 hour; remove onto wire rack to cool completely.

Makes one 7½-pound cake, or about 24 servings.

Party Planning

■ Planning a party may begin with a guest list, but after that, food will probably be your focus. What to serve can amount to assembling tried-and-true family favorites, or you may want to introduce some new foods or attach a theme to the cuisine.

But even the most adventurous party givers will want to keep the menu manageable, scaled to room size or kitchen space, time or budget. Whatever your menu, there are some built-in time-and-energy-saving steps to lessen preparation and cleanup time. Here are a few helpful hints.

■ Clear shelf space in the freezer and refrigerator before you go grocery shopping—and take inventory before you head out to the market. Set aside areas for chilling bowls and platters. Keep in mind that you or your bartender will need access to the ice cubes, chilled wines, juices and soda. When you get home, organize your ingredients, placing those that will be used first at the front of the refrigerator. Allow ample room for easily crushed and bruised lettuces and berries.

■ Of course, do as much as you can ahead of party time. Wash and polish special serving pieces.

Make place cards, butter curls and an ice ring or two for the punch bowl. Set the table well in advance, too (but beware of pets and small children). Arranging your table in advance also gives you a chance to take inventory, allowing you some extra time to borrow a chair or another steak knife, or remove a stubborn stain from a napkin.

■ Position the punch bowl on a table with plastic place mats under the tablecloth. Drips, spills and sticky punch-cup bottoms will be confined to the fabric, leaving the surface of your wood furniture spot-free.

Carmen's Walnut Kuchen
(pictured, page 195)
Carmen Miguel

Carmen is from southern Chile, where there is a strong German influence in the food. The candied walnut topping on this dessert treat is fantastic!

1 cup unsifted all-purpose flour
1 teaspoon baking powder
½ cup butter or margarine, at room temperature
¾ cup sugar
3 large eggs, separated
Topping (recipe follows)

1. Preheat oven to 350°F. Grease 9-inch springform pan or tart pan with removable bottom; set aside. On sheet waxed paper, combine flour with baking powder; set aside.
2. In large bowl of electric mixer, at high speed, beat butter, sugar and egg yolks until light and fluffy. At low speed, beat in flour mixture just until blended. With clean beaters, in small bowl of electric mixer, at high speed, beat egg whites until stiff. With rubber spatula, fold whites into butter mixture; pour batter into prepared pan, spreading evenly. Bake 20 minutes, or until top of cake is golden.
3. Immediately pour topping over cake; bake 5 minutes longer. Cool cake in pan on wire rack. When completely cooled, remove cake from pan. Store, covered, but do not refrigerate or topping will become too hard.
   Makes 8 servings.

Topping

1 cup sugar
½ cup butter or margarine, cut in ½-inch pieces
2 tablespoons milk
2 cups chopped walnuts

In large skillet, over medium heat, cook sugar, stirring constantly, until it is a pale brown syrup. Add butter; stir until melted and blended. Stir in milk. Add walnuts; stir to coat.

Traditional Mincemeat Tarts
(pictured, page 194)
Debbie Garmhausen

Debbie tells us this family recipe was created by her grandmother, Elizabeth Garmhausen. It's an authentic mincemeat and well worth the effort. Use it as a filling for pies and tarts or as a topping on cakes and ice cream.

½ cup butter or margarine, softened
1 package (3 ounces) cream cheese, softened
1 cup unsifted all-purpose flour
1 cup Mincemeat (recipe follows)
½ cup sweetened whipped cream

1. In medium bowl, blend butter with cream cheese. Stir in flour until combined.
2. Roll pastry into 24 balls, dividing evenly; place on baking sheet. Cover with plastic wrap; refrigerate 20 minutes.
3. Grease and lightly flour twenty-four 1-inch tart pans. Place a pastry ball on heavily floured surface; with rolling pin, roll out slightly. Fit into tart pan, patting evenly over bottom and side of pan. Repeat with remaining pastry and tart pans. Refrigerate 1 hour.
4. Preheat oven to 400°F. Fill each prepared tart pan with rounded teaspoon mincemeat. Bake 15 minutes. Remove tart from pan; serve warm. (If tarts are to be transported or given as gifts, freeze them first as they are very fragile.) Pipe whipped-cream rosette onto top of each tart before serving.
   Makes 24.

Mincemeat

1 pound top round or sirloin, coarsely chopped
2 pounds medium tart apples, pared, cored and finely chopped (4 cups)
3 pounds medium green tomatoes, seeded and finely chopped (4 cups)
1 package (15 ounces) raisins, finely chopped
1 package (10 ounces) dried currants
1 cup chopped citron
1 cup chopped suet
2 cups sugar
1 cup apple cider
1 tablespoon ground cloves
1 tablespoon ground cinnamon
1 tablespoon ground nutmeg
1 can (10½ ounces) beef broth

1. In 2-quart saucepan, cover beef with about 2 cups water. Simmer, covered, 1 hour, or until tender. Cool meat in cooking liquid; coarsely shred by hand or in food processor.
2. In 6-quart Dutch oven, combine shredded meat, cooking liquid and remaining ingredients. Cover; bring to boiling; simmer 1 hour. Cool. Store in refrigerator.
   Makes 14 cups.

Quick Cranberry Pie
(pictured, page 194)
Elizabeth Sloan

From McCall's *editor in chief comes this delicious dessert. It's ideal for everyone who has a busy work and entertaining schedule.*

4 cups cranberries
2 cups sugar
1 cup chopped pecans
2 large eggs
1 cup unsifted all-purpose flour
¼ cup melted shortening
½ cup butter or margarine, melted

1. Grease 10-inch quiche dish or pie plate. Preheat oven to 325°F. Spread cranberries over bottom of dish; sprinkle with 1 cup sugar and the pecans.

2. In small bowl of electric mixer, at high speed, beat eggs until frothy. Add remaining sugar; beat until well combined. At low speed, beat in flour, shortening and butter; at medium speed, beat until batter is blended. Pour batter over cranberries and nuts; bake 1 hour, or until pie is golden. Serve hot or cold, with sweetened whipped cream or ice cream, if desired.

Makes 8 to 10 servings.

Boone Family Holiday Nuggets

(pictured, page 194)
Sharon Boone

These tasty holiday cookies were developed by Sharon's great-aunt Helen Boone Thompson some years ago when she was putting together a family Thanksgiving dinner. Colorful and festive, they were the hit of the party!

¾ cup butter or margarine, softened
¾ cup sugar
1 large egg
1 teaspoon grated lemon peel
1 teaspoon vanilla extract
2 cups unsifted all-purpose flour
½ teaspoon salt
1 cup flaked coconut
¾ cup raisins
¼ cup candied cherries, chopped

1. Preheat oven to 350°F. Grease large baking sheet; set aside.

2. In large bowl of electric mixer, at high speed, beat butter until fluffy. Gradually add sugar; beat until light and fluffy. Beat in egg, lemon peel and vanilla.

3. On sheet waxed paper, combine flour with salt; at medium speed, beat into sugar mixture, just until blended. With wooden spoon, stir in coconut, raisins and cherries.

4. Drop dough by teaspoonfuls, 2 inches apart, onto prepared sheet; bake 15 minutes, or until golden. Remove to wire rack. If desired, make a thin icing by blending a few tablespoons confectioners' sugar with just enough syrup from a jar of maraschino cherries to make a pourable consistency; with tip of spoon, drizzle icing over cooled cookies.

Makes about 3 dozen.

Nerina's Walnut Cake
Bruno Blazina

We thank Bruno's wife, Nerina, for sharing this Yugoslavian specialty with us.

9 large eggs, separated
1½ cups granulated sugar
2 teaspoons rum
1½ cups finely ground walnuts
½ cup finely crushed unsalted saltines
¼ teaspoon cream of tartar
3 cups heavy cream
¼ cup confectioners' sugar
12 walnut halves

1. Grease three 9-inch round cake pans. Line each with a 9-inch round of waxed paper; grease and flour paper. Set aside. Preheat oven to 350°F.

2. In large bowl of electric mixer, at high speed, beat egg yolks with granulated sugar and the rum 10 minutes, until thick and pale. With rubber spatula, fold in walnuts and crushed saltines until well mixed; set aside.

3. In another large bowl, with clean beaters, beat egg whites with cream of tartar until frothy. At high speed, beat until stiff peaks form. With rubber spatula, gently fold whites into egg-yolk mixture until no white streaks remain.

4. Pour batter into prepared pans, dividing evenly and spreading tops smoothly. Bake 30 minutes, or until tops spring back when lightly touched. Cool cakes in pans on wire rack 20 minutes. (Cakes will shrink.) Invert layers on cloth-covered rack; peel off waxed paper. Carefully invert again; cool.

5. In small bowl of electric mixer, at high speed, beat cream with confectioners' sugar until stiff. Place one cake layer, top side down, on serving plate; spread with ¾ cup whipped cream. Place another cake layer, top side up, over cream; spread top with ¾ cup whipped cream. Top with remaining cake layer, top side up; with remaining whipped cream, cover top and side. Garnish with walnuts. Refrigerate.

Makes 10 to 12 servings.

How to Brew a Perfect Cup of Coffee

■ Start with the right blend for your brewing equipment—a coarse grind for a percolator, a fine one for a drip pot.

■ Use fresh, cold water. (Hot tap water tastes flat and stale.)

■ Measure one to two level tablespoons of coffee for each six-ounce cup.

■ When brewing is over, remove grounds to prevent a bitter taste.

■ Serve coffee immediately—it stays fresh for only a half hour.

■ Never reheat coffee—that spoils its taste. Instead, keep it warm in a thermal carafe.

Quick & Easy: Fruit-and-Vegetable Salads

Mexican Holiday Salad

¼ cup white vinegar
2 tablespoons sugar
¼ teaspoon chili powder
¼ teaspoon salt
2 medium oranges
2 large red apples
1 medium banana
2 tablespoons lime juice
1 can (8 ounces) sliced beets, drained
½ cup sliced celery
Romaine lettuce leaves
2 tablespoons unsalted peanuts

1. In small bowl, combine vinegar, sugar, chili powder and salt; stir until sugar dissolves.
2. Cut off and discard peel and pith from oranges; cut crosswise in ¼-inch-thick slices. Cut apples in ¼-inch wedges; cut banana in 1-inch chunks. Dip apples and banana into lime juice to prevent browning.

3. Arrange oranges, apples, banana, beets and celery on lettuce-lined platter. Pour dressing over salad; sprinkle with peanuts.
Makes 6 servings.

Pea Pod and Pineapple Medley

2 tablespoons salad oil
½ pound snow pea pods, trimmed
1 large red pepper, cut in 1-inch pieces
3 green onions, sliced
1 can (8 ounces) pineapple chunks in juice
¾ cup chicken broth
⅓ cup prepared sweet-and-sour sauce
1 tablespoon cornstarch
1 can (8 ounces) sliced water chestnuts, drained

In large skillet, heat oil. Add pea pods, pepper and green onions; sauté, stirring, 2 minutes. Drain pineapple chunks, reserving ¼ cup juice. In small bowl, combine broth, sweet-and-sour sauce, reserved pineapple juice and cornstarch until blended. Pour into skillet; cook, stirring, 1 minute, or until thickened. Stir in pineapple chunks and water chestnuts.
Makes 4 to 6 servings.

Zesty Avocado Dip for Vegetables

1 medium ripe avocado
1 cup sour cream
1 package (.56 ounce) green-onion-dip mix
1 tablespoon lemon juice
1 cherry tomato, cut in wedges
Cooked broccoli flowerets, cauliflowerets, julienne zucchini, artichoke hearts and sliced carrots

In food processor, blend avocado, sour cream, green-onion-dip mix and lemon juice until smooth. Transfer to small serving bowl. Garnish with tomato; cover and let stand until serving time. Serve with prepared vegetables.
Makes 8 servings.

Above: (Clockwise from top) Pea Pod and Pineapple Medley, Mexican Holiday Salad, Zesty Avocado Dip for Vegetables.

Micro-Way: Hurry-Up Entrées

Kielbasa-and-Potato Salad

1½ pounds medium new
  potatoes, quartered
1 cup water
½ pound kielbasa, cut in
  ¼-inch diagonal slices
1 medium onion, cut in
  ¼-inch wedges
1 medium green pepper,
  chopped
½ cup cider vinegar
½ cup water
1 teaspoon instant beef-flavored
  bouillon granules
1 teaspoon sugar
1 large egg yolk
1 tablespoon cornstarch
¼ cup chopped parsley
Lettuce leaves, rinsed

1. Place potatoes and ½ cup water in 3-quart glass baking dish. Cover with plastic wrap, turning back one corner to vent. Cook on HIGH 8 minutes, or until potatoes are just tender, stirring once. Let stand on counter.

2. In large glass bowl, place kielbasa, onion and green pepper; cover and vent. Cook on HIGH 4 minutes. In 2-cup glass measure, combine vinegar, water, bouillon granules, sugar, egg yolk and cornstarch; mix well. Add to kielbasa mixture; cover and vent. Cook on HIGH 4 minutes, stirring once, or until thickened. Drain potatoes; add potatoes and parsley to kielbasa mixture, and mix well. Arrange salad in lettuce-lined serving bowl.

Makes 8 servings.

Turkey Lo Mein

2½ cups hot water
2 packages (3 ounces each)
  instant Oriental noodle
  soup (also called Ramen
  noodles)
⅓ cup creamy peanut butter
¼ teaspoon crushed
  red-pepper flakes
2 tablespoons soy sauce
1 tablespoon dark sesame
  oil
1 package (16 ounces) mixed
  frozen broccoli, carrot,
  water chestnut and red
  pepper
1 can (15 ounces) straw
  mushrooms, drained
½ pound cooked turkey,
  cut in ¼-inch strips

1. In 3-quart glass casserole, heat 2 cups hot water on HIGH 3 minutes. Discard seasoning packets from noodle-soup packages; separate layers of noodles. Arrange in casserole so that all noodles are in water. Cover with plastic wrap; turn back one corner to vent. Cook on HIGH 5 minutes, stirring once to separate noodles.

2. In small bowl, whisk together ½ cup hot water, the peanut butter, red-pepper flakes, soy sauce and sesame oil until mixture is blended. Add peanut butter mixture to noodles with frozen vegetables, mushrooms and turkey strips; mix well. Cover and vent. Cook on HIGH 5 minutes, or until vegetables are tender-crisp, stirring once.

Makes 4 servings.

Special Breakfast Section: Terrific 10-Minute Breakfasts

It's easier than you think to prepare quick-fix dishes that are worth getting up for!

Apricot Nog

1 can (12 ounces) chilled apricot nectar
¾ cup chilled buttermilk
2 large eggs
¼ teaspoon vanilla extract
2 sprigs fresh mint

In blender, combine apricot nectar, buttermilk, eggs and vanilla; at high speed, blend 1 minute. Pour into two 16-ounce glasses. Garnish each drink with mint sprig; serve immediately.

Makes 2 servings.

Tropical Smoothie

1 cup low-fat strawberry yogurt
1 can (8 ounces) crushed pineapple, drained
1 small orange, peeled, seeded and chopped
1 cup ice cubes
Ground cinnamon
2 strawberries with hulls

In blender, combine yogurt, crushed pineapple, orange and ice; at high speed, blend 1 minute. Pour mixture into two 16-ounce glasses. Sprinkle top of each drink with cinnamon; garnish with strawberry. Serve immediately.

Makes 2 servings.

Brie-Topped Belgian Waffles

1 tablespoon sugar
2 teaspoons cornstarch
1 package (10 ounces) frozen strawberries in syrup, thawed
2 tablespoons orange juice
4 frozen prepared Belgian waffles
4 ounces Brie cheese

1. In saucepan, combine sugar and cornstarch. Stir in frozen strawberries; add orange juice and bring to boiling. Cook, stirring, until thickened. Keep warm.

2. Prepare waffles as package label directs; keep warm. Cut Brie into 4 wedges. Place one wedge on each waffle; spoon sauce on top. If desired, garnish with thin slices orange and a parsley sprig.

Makes 4 servings.

Quick Bacon-and-Egg Sandwich

4 slices bacon
2 large eggs
¹⁄₁₆ teaspoon seasoned pepper
4 slices American pasteurized process cheese food
2 Kaiser rolls
2 tablespoons softened butter or margarine
2 small tomatoes, sliced

1. In 10-inch skillet, over medium heat, cook bacon until almost crisp. Arrange two slices of bacon side by side on each half of skillet. Break one egg over each pair of bacon slices; sprinkle each egg with some seasoned pepper. Cover; cook eggs 1 to 2 minutes, or until set. Top each egg with 2 slices cheese. Cover; cook 1 more minute, or until cheese melts.

2. Cut rolls in half horizontally; spread each with half of butter. Arrange tomato slices on bottom halves of rolls, dividing evenly. Place an egg on top of tomatoes on each sandwich; cover with top halves of rolls. If desired, garnish sandwiches with fresh chives.

Makes 2 servings.

Right: (Clockwise from top) Apricot Nog, Quick Bacon-and-Egg Sandwich, Brie-Topped Belgian Waffles, California-Style Huevos Rancheros, Country-Style French Toast, Tropical Smoothie.

Special Breakfast Section

Country-Style French Toast

4 slices frozen prepared French toast
¼ cup apricot preserves
1 teaspoon lemon juice
½ cup ricotta cheese
1 large banana, cut crosswise in ¼-inch-thick slices
½ teaspoon ground cinnamon

1. Prepare French toast as package label directs; keep warm. In small saucepan, heat preserves with lemon juice, stirring frequently, until warm and smooth.

2. Spread ricotta over French toast; arrange banana slices on top. Spoon warm apricot sauce over cheese; sprinkle with cinnamon.

Makes 2 servings.

California-Style Huevos Rancheros

2 tablespoons butter or margarine
4 large eggs
¼ cup prepared salsa
¼ cup shredded extra sharp Cheddar cheese
4 slices ripe avocado
2 tablespoons sour cream
Parsley sprig (optional)

1. In large skillet, over medium heat, melt butter. Break eggs into skillet; cook 3 minutes, or until set.

2. On each of 2 heat-safe plates, spread salsa, dividing evenly. Top with 2 eggs. Sprinkle eggs with cheese, dividing evenly. Broil, 4 inches from heat, 1 minute, or until cheese melts.

3. Place avocado and sour cream next to eggs, dividing evenly. If desired, garnish with parsley sprig.

Makes 2 servings.

Special Breakfast Section: Microwave-Easy Breakfasts

Make your morning meal something special with a little help from your microwave oven.

Raisin and Honey Oatmeal

1⅓ cups uncooked rolled oats
½ cup golden raisins
⅓ cup honey
¾ teaspoon pumpkin-pie spice
2⅔ cups water
½ cup chopped walnuts
Heavy cream
Sliced bananas
Chopped apples

In 3-quart microwave-safe casserole, combine first 5 ingredients. Cook on HIGH 8 to 10 minutes, or until liquid is absorbed, stirring once. Top with nuts. Serve with cream and fruit.

Makes 4 servings.

Filled Puffy Herb Omelet

Nonstick cooking spray
4 large eggs, separated
1 container (4 ounces) garlic-and-herb semisoft cheese, at room temperature
¼ teaspoon cream of tartar
2 ounces thinly sliced smoked salmon
10 frozen asparagus spears, thawed (2 ounces)

1. Generously spray 9-inch glass pie plate. In bowl, mix yolks with cheese. In large bowl of electric mixer, beat whites and cream of tartar until foamy; at high speed, beat until stiff peaks form. With rubber spatula, fold in cheese mixture until no white streaks remain. Pour into pie plate; smooth top.

2. Cook on MEDIUM 2½ minutes. Push cooked outer edges to center, let uncooked portion flow to outside. Cook 3 to 4 minutes, or until set. Loosen edges; place salmon and asparagus on half. Fold top half over filling. Slide onto plate.

Makes 2 servings.

Bacon-and-Egg Casserole

¼ pound bacon, cut in 1½-inch pieces
½ cup chopped green pepper
1 can (3 ounces) sliced mushrooms, drained
6 large eggs
5 tablespoons water
½ cup canned Cheddar-cheese soup (undiluted)
2 tablespoons fine dry bread crumbs

1. Place bacon in 9-inch glass pie plate. Cover loosely with microwave-safe paper towel. Cook on HIGH 3 minutes. Drain off fat, reserving 1 tablespoon; set aside. Stir pepper and mushrooms into bacon; cover and cook on HIGH 2 minutes.

2. In small bowl, beat eggs with 3 tablespoons water. Pour over bacon mixture. Cook, uncovered, on HIGH 2 minutes. Stir; cook 1 minute longer, or until just set.

3. In bowl, blend soup with 2 tablespoons water; pour over eggs. Add crumbs to fat; sprinkle over soup. Cook on HIGH 30 seconds.

Makes 4 servings.

Bread Pudding Bake With Cran-Raspberry Sauce

8 (½-inch) slices braided egg bread (challah), toasted
2½ cups milk
½ cup maple syrup
½ cup sugar
3 tablespoons cornstarch
6 large eggs
¾ teaspoon pumpkin-pie spice
¼ teaspoon salt
Cran-Raspberry Sauce (recipe follows)

1. In greased 2-quart microwave-safe dish, arrange bread, lengthwise and overlapping, in 2 rows; set aside. In 1-quart glass measure, heat milk with syrup on HIGH 5 minutes. In large bowl, combine sugar with cornstarch. Beat in eggs, spice and salt. Gradually whisk in milk.

2. Pour over bread. Cook on HIGH 5 minutes. Cook on MEDIUM 10 minutes, turning once, until center is just set. Serve with sauce.

Makes 6 to 8 servings.

Above: (Clockwise from top) Carrot Timbales With Mornay Sauce, Bread Pudding Bake With Cran-Raspberry Sauce, Bacon-and-Egg Casserole, Raisin and Honey Oatmeal, Filled Puffy Herb Omelet, Berry Muffins.

Cran-Raspberry Sauce

1½ cups cranberries
1 package (10 ounces) frozen
  raspberries in syrup, thawed
⅓ cup sugar
1 tablespoon cornstarch
1 tablespoon water
1 teaspoon grated lemon peel

In 2-quart glass measure, combine first 3 ingredients. Cover loosely with waxed paper; cook on HIGH 8 minutes, stirring once. In bowl, combine cornstarch with water; stir into mixture. Add lemon peel; mix well. Cook on HIGH 2 minutes, or until thickened.

Makes 2 cups.

Carrot Timbales With Mornay Sauce

Nonstick cooking spray
2 tablespoons grated Parmesan
  cheese
1½ cups finely shredded
  carrots
2 tablespoons minced green
  onion
2 tablespoons butter or
  margarine
2 tablespoons water
3 large eggs, beaten
2 cups milk
2 tablespoons chopped fresh
  basil or 1 teaspoon dried
  basil leaves
¼ teaspoon salt
⅛ teaspoon pepper
1 package (1 ounce)
  white-sauce mix
½ cup (2 ounces) shredded
  Gruyère cheese

1. Grease four 6-ounce custard cups with nonstick cooking spray. Sprinkle with Parmesan cheese, dividing evenly; set aside.

2. In 2-quart glass measure, combine carrots, green onion, butter and water. Cover tightly with plastic wrap; cook on HIGH 5 minutes, stirring once. Stir in eggs, ¾ cup milk, the basil, salt and pepper. Spoon evenly into custard cups. Cook on MEDIUM 8 minutes, rotating each cup once, until knife inserted in center of each comes out clean. Let stand 5 minutes.

3. Make sauce: In 1-quart glass measure, heat remaining milk on HIGH 2 minutes. Stir in sauce mix. Cook on HIGH 2 minutes, or until thickened. Add Gruyère cheese; stir until melted.

4. With knife, loosen edges of timbales; invert to remove from cup. Serve with sauce.

Makes 4 servings.

Berry Muffins

½ cup sour cream
1 large egg
½ cup firmly packed brown
  sugar
½ teaspoon vanilla extract
½ teaspoon grated orange
  peel
3 tablespoons salad oil
1¼ cups unsifted all-purpose
  flour
1½ teaspoons baking powder
¼ teaspoon salt
¾ cup coarsely chopped
  cranberries or frozen
  blueberries
1 tablespoon granulated
  sugar
¼ teaspoon ground
  cinnamon
2 tablespoons chopped pecans

1. Line each of six 6-ounce custard cups with 2 paper muffin-cup liners. In medium bowl, beat sour cream with egg, brown sugar, vanilla, orange peel and oil until combined; set aside. In small bowl, mix flour, baking powder and salt; stir in chopped cranberries. Add sour-cream mixture; mix just until flour is moistened.

2. Spoon ⅓ cup batter into each muffin cup. In small bowl, mix granulated sugar with cinnamon; sprinkle muffin batter with some of the sugar mixture and the pecans, dividing evenly.

3. Arrange cups, 1 inch apart, in a ring in oven. Cook on HIGH 4½ minutes, rotating each cup after 2 minutes, until cake tester inserted in center of each comes out clean. (Tops of muffins may appear wet.) Remove muffins from custard cups; cool on wire rack 1 minute.

Makes 6 muffins.

Note: Recipe may be doubled; cook 6 muffins at a time.

December

Enjoy our glorious cookbook of holiday recipes. Here, old favorites take on new twists. The collection starts with a marvelous herb-crusted fresh ham, pictured at right. You'll find most of these festive dishes—those listed below—pictured on the following pages.

Marinated Fresh Ham

Acorn Squash With Glazed Fruit

Orange-Mincemeat Cheesecake

Scallop and Clam Bisque

Deluxe Creamed Peas

Herbed Wild Rice

Cornish Hens With Brandied Shiitake Sauce

Champagne Oysters Florentine

Herbed Popovers

Hazelnut-Cranberry-Cream Cake

Red-Hot Wassail

Restuffed Sweet Potatoes

Roast Tenderloin With Goat-Cheese Stuffing

Leek and Carrot au Gratin

Christmas Cookbook

Celebrate in style with all-American favorites or an English-style feast complete with an old-fashioned wassail.

Acorn Squash With Glazed Fruit
(pictured, page 211)

2 acorn squashes (1 pound each)
Salad oil
Salt and pepper
¼ cup butter or margarine
2 pears, cored and coarsely chopped
½ cup pecan halves
½ cup sugar
1½ cups cranberries
½ cup golden raisins
½ teaspoon ground cinnamon

1. Preheat oven to 400°F. Cut squashes lengthwise in half; scoop out and discard seeds. Place squashes, cut side up, in baking dish; add water to come ½ inch up sides.

Page 211: Marinated Fresh Ham, Acorn Squash With Glazed Fruit.

Pages 212 and 213: (clockwise from top right) Scallop and Clam Bisque, Deluxe Creamed Peas, Herbed Wild Rice, Cornish Hens With Brandied Shiitake Sauce, Champagne Oysters Florentine, Orange-Mincemeat Cheesecake.

Pages 214 and 215: (Clockwise from top right) Hazelnut-Cranberry-Cream Cake, Red-Hot Wassail, Restuffed Sweet Potatoes, Roast Tenderloin With Goat-Cheese Stuffing, Leek and Carrot au Gratin, Herbed Popovers.

Brush flesh with oil; sprinkle with salt and pepper. Cover dish with aluminum foil. Bake 30 minutes.

2. Meanwhile, in large skillet, over medium-high heat, melt butter. Add pears, pecans and sugar; cook, stirring, 8 minutes, until glazed and tender. Add last three ingredients; cook until slightly thickened.

3. Uncover squashes; fill with fruit mixture, dividing evenly. Bake, uncovered, 15 minutes, or until tender. Cut lengthwise in half.
    Makes 8 servings.

Marinated Fresh Ham
(pictured, page 211)

9-pound whole (bone-in) fresh ham
1 head (2 ounces) garlic, peeled and crushed
2 teaspoons salt
½ teaspoon pepper
2 tablespoons dried oregano leaves, crushed
2 teaspoons ground cumin
¾ cup lemon juice

1. With sharp knife, trim some of fat and rind from ham; score fat decoratively. Pierce ham in several places; insert one-third of garlic into holes. Place ham in roasting pan.

2. In small bowl, combine remaining garlic with the remaining ingredients. Generously brush ham with mixture. Cover; refrigerate overnight, brushing occasionally with marinade.

3. Next day: Let ham stand at room temperature 2 hours. Preheat oven to 325°F. Uncover ham; brush with marinade. Place skin side up on rack in roasting pan. Bake 25 minutes per pound, or to an internal temperature of 170°F, basting occasionally—3¾ hours.

4. Remove ham to platter; cover loosely with aluminum foil. Let stand 10 minutes for easier carving.
    Makes 8 to 10 servings.

Champagne Oysters Florentine
(pictured, page 212)

⅓ cup sliced shallots
¼ cup thinly sliced celery
2 cups champagne
2 tablespoons tarragon white-wine vinegar
1 teaspoon fennel seeds
2 cups heavy cream
½ teaspoon salt
⅛ teaspoon ground white pepper
½ teaspoon hot-red-pepper sauce
2 packages (10 ounces each) frozen chopped spinach, thawed and squeezed dry
¼ cup butter, at room temperature
3 dozen oysters, shucked and on half shell
2 tablespoons grated Parmesan cheese

1. In small saucepan, combine shallots, celery, champagne, vinegar and fennel seeds. Bring to boiling; boil until liquid is reduced to ½ cup. Strain; discard solids. Return liquid to saucepan. Add cream; bring to boiling. Boil until liquid is reduced to 1¼ cups. Stir in salt, pepper and hot-red-pepper sauce.

2. Preheat oven to 425°F. In medium bowl, combine spinach with ¼ cup sauce and the butter. Drain off liquid from oysters. Arrange oysters on baking sheet; spoon spinach mixture, then sauce and cheese over each. Bake 12 minutes. Transfer to platter; if desired, garnish with tomato and lemon roses and parsley.

Makes 12 servings.

Scallop and Clam Bisque

(pictured, page 213)

2 tablespoons salad oil
1 cup julienned leeks
1 cup julienned carrots
½ pound sea scallops, cut crosswise in thirds
1 can (16 ounces) crushed tomatoes
Dry white wine
1 tablespoon minced fresh thyme or 1 teaspoon dried thyme leaves
¼ teaspoon pepper
2 dozen littleneck clams, well scrubbed
4 cups water
2 extralarge fish bouillon cubes
1 cup heavy cream
¼ cup butter
⅓ cup unsifted all-purpose flour
¼ cup chopped parsley
2 tablespoons dry sherry

1. In large saucepan, heat oil until hot. Add leeks and carrots; sauté 3 minutes. Push vegetables to side of pan; add scallops. Sauté 2 minutes, or until scallops just turn white.

2. With slotted spoon, remove scallops to plate. Strain liquid from tomatoes into 1-cup measure; add enough wine to make 1 cup. Pour into pan; add thyme and pepper. Place clams in a single layer in pan; bring to boiling. Cover; simmer 4 minutes, or until clams open. (Discard clams not opened in this time.) With slotted spoon, remove clams and vegetables to deep dish.

3. Add water, bouillon and cream to pan. Bring to boiling, stirring.

4. In small bowl, with wooden spoon, beat butter until creamy; beat in flour. Add 1 cup hot bouillon liquid, whisking until smooth. Pour into liquid in pan, whisking to blend. Simmer 5 minutes.

5. Remove clams from shells; add to pan. Stir in reserved scallops, vegetables, the tomatoes, parsley and sherry. Simmer 2 minutes, or until heated through.

Makes 6 servings.

Cornish Hens With Brandied Shiitake Sauce

(pictured, pages 212 and 213)

3 Cornish game hens (1½ pounds each), livers removed
¼ pound butter, melted
¼ teaspoon dried rosemary leaves, crushed
¼ teaspoon dried tarragon leaves, crushed
⅛ teaspoon ground white pepper
1½ teaspoons lemon juice

Sauce
5 slices pancetta or bacon (2 ounces), diced
½ cup brandy
2 tablespoons butter
1 teaspoon olive oil
½ pound shiitake mushrooms, sliced
⅓ cup minced shallots
1 can (about 14 ounces) chicken broth

Herbed Wild Rice (page 218)
2 teaspoons cornstarch

1. Preheat oven to 425°F. With poultry shears, split hens lengthwise, removing backbone and neck. Rinse hens; with paper towels, pat dry. Arrange hens, skin side up, in roasting pan.

2. In bowl, combine ¼ pound butter with herbs, pepper and lemon juice; brush over hens. Bake 50 minutes, basting occasionally.

3. Make Sauce: In skillet, over medium heat, sauté pancetta until crisp. Drain on paper towel. Add brandy to drippings; reduce to ¼ cup. Remove and set aside. In same skillet, melt 2 tablespoons butter in oil. Add mushrooms; sauté until golden brown. Add shallots; sauté 2 minutes. Add 1 cup broth, the pancetta and reserved ¼ cup brandy.

4. Cut hens in half lengthwise along breastbone; place on platter with Herbed Wild Rice. Keep warm.

5. Spoon off and discard fat from drippings in roasting pan. Add sauce and reserved livers to pan; bring to boiling, stirring constantly to loosen browned bits. Cook 1 minute. In cup, blend cornstarch with remaining broth; stir into sauce. Bring to boiling, stirring; cook 1 minute. Spoon some sauce over hens; pass remainder. If desired, garnish with parsley and kumquats.

Makes 6 servings.

Roast Tenderloin With Goat-Cheese Stuffing

(pictured, pages 214 and 215)

1 ounce dried porcini
  mushrooms
½ cup hot water
4 tablespoons salad oil
1½ cups diced yellow peppers
1½ cups diced zucchini
3 medium cloves garlic,
  crushed
1½ cups fresh bread crumbs
  (see *Note*)
8 ounces goat cheese (chèvre),
  crumbled
½ cup coarsely chopped fresh
  basil, or 1 tablespoon dried
  basil leaves
1 teaspoon dried oregano
  leaves
¾ teaspoon salt
½ teaspoon pepper
4½- to 5-pound beef tenderloin
  (trimmed weight)
Additional salt and pepper

1. Place mushrooms in bowl; cover with hot water. Soak 30 minutes, until softened. Squeeze liquid from mushrooms; reserve for another use. Finely chop mushrooms.

2. In large skillet, heat 3 tablespoons oil. Add next 4 ingredients; sauté 4 minutes, or until tender. Stir in bread crumbs, cheese, basil, oregano, ¾ teaspoon salt and ½ teaspoon pepper; mix well.

3. Preheat oven to 500°F. Brush tenderloin with remaining 1 tablespoon oil; sprinkle with salt and pepper. Cut tenderloin about two-thirds through in thick slices about ¾ inch apart. Spoon stuffing between slices. Reshape roast; tie lengthwise with kitchen string. Place on rack in roasting pan. Bake 30 minutes, or 7 minutes per pound for rare. Let stand, loosely covered with aluminum foil, 15 minutes.

Makes 12 servings.

Note: Preferably made from semolina bread.

Deluxe Creamed Peas

(pictured, page 213)

3 tablespoons butter or
  margarine
1 package (10 ounces) frozen
  pearl onions, thawed
1 medium red onion, chopped
Dash pepper
2 tablespoons all-purpose flour
1½ cups half-and-half
2 packages (10 ounces each)
  frozen peas, thawed
¾ teaspoon salt
⅛ teaspoon pepper
⅛ teaspoon ground nutmeg

1. In 3-quart saucepan, over medium-high heat, melt butter. Add pearl and red onion and dash pepper; sauté 5 minutes, or until tender. Stir in flour until blended; gradually add half-and-half, stirring until smooth. Bring to boiling, stirring; cook 1 minute.

2. Add peas, salt, pepper and nutmeg. Cook until heated through.

Makes 8 servings.

Herbed Wild Rice

(pictured, pages 212 and 213)

¼ cup butter
½ pound mushrooms, minced
½ cup sliced celery
¼ cup minced onion
¼ cup minced prosciutto
½ cup uncooked wild rice,
  rinsed
½ teaspoon dried sage leaves,
  crushed
½ teaspoon dried marjoram
  leaves, crushed
½ teaspoon dried thyme leaves,
  crushed
½ teaspoon dried rosemary
  leaves, crushed
½ teaspoon fennel seeds
⅛ teaspoon pepper
1 can (about 14 ounces)
  chicken broth
¼ cup uncooked long-grain
  rice

1. In heavy saucepan, over medium-high heat, melt butter. Add next 3 ingredients; sauté 8 minutes, until liquid has evaporated.

2. Add prosciutto; sauté 1 minute. Add wild rice, herbs and fennel seeds; sauté 1 minute. Stir in pepper and broth. Bring to boiling; simmer, covered, 30 minutes.

3. Stir in long-grain rice. Simmer, covered, 20 minutes, until liquid is absorbed.

Makes 3 cups.

Restuffed Sweet Potatoes

(pictured, pages 214 and 215)

6 medium sweet potatoes,
  scrubbed (3 pounds)
Salad oil
1 package (8 ounces)
  Neufchâtel cheese, softened
¼ cup firmly packed brown
  sugar
2 tablespoons butter or
  margarine
1 to 2 tablespoons cream
  sherry
¾ teaspoon salt
½ teaspoon pepper
⅓ cup coarsely chopped
  toasted pecans

1. Up to 2 days before serving: Preheat oven to 375°F. With fork, prick potatoes all over; lightly rub with oil. Place on jelly-roll pan; bake 1 hour, or until tender.

2. Cool potatoes slightly. With sharp knife, trim a lengthwise strip, about ¼-inch thick from one side of each potato. With spoon, scoop out cooked potatoes, leaving ¼-inch-thick shell (do not break skin); set shells aside.

3. Place cooked potato in large bowl of electric mixer. At medium speed, beat until smooth. Add cheese, sugar, butter, sherry, salt and pepper; beat until smooth. Spoon mixture into pastry bag fitted

with large star tip; pipe into reserved skins. Sprinkle potatoes with pecans, dividing evenly. If not baking potatoes right away, cover and refrigerate.

4. To bake: Preheat oven to 350°F. Place potatoes on large shallow baking pan. Bake 30 minutes, or until heated through.

Makes 6 servings.

Hot Chicken Puffs With Lemon-Dijon Sauce

1 cup water
½ cup butter or margarine
¼ teaspoon salt
1 cup unsifted all-purpose flour
4 large eggs
2 tablespoons minced green pepper
2 tablespoons minced red pepper
½ teaspoon poultry seasoning
2 cups chopped, cooked chicken
Salad oil
Lemon-Dijon Sauce (recipe follows)

1. In medium saucepan, bring water, butter and salt to boiling. Remove from heat; with wooden spoon, beat in flour. Cook, stirring, over low heat, 1 minute, or until mixture leaves sides of pan. Remove from heat; add eggs, one at a time, beating well after each until dough is shiny. Stir in peppers, poultry seasoning and chicken.

2. In deep-fat fryer or large saucepan, heat 2 inches oil to 375°F. Drop rounded tablespoonfuls of dough, 3 or 4 at a time, into hot oil. Fry 6 minutes, or until golden-brown. Drain on paper towels. Keep warm in low oven. Serve with Lemon-Dijon Sauce.

Makes 2½ dozen.

Lemon-Dijon Sauce

¼ cup butter or margarine
2 tablespoons all-purpose flour
¼ teaspoon salt
1½ cups milk
2 large egg yolks
3 tablespoons lemon juice
1 tablespoon Dijon-style mustard
Dash hot-red-pepper sauce

1. In medium saucepan, over medium-high heat, melt butter. Stir in flour and salt until smooth and bubbly. Gradually add milk, stirring until smooth. Bring to boiling, stirring constantly; boil 1 minute, or until slightly thickened.

2. In small bowl, combine egg yolks, lemon juice, mustard and red-pepper sauce; mix well. Stir some hot milk mixture into yolk mixture; return to saucepan. Cook, stirring constantly, until thickened.

Makes 2 cups.

Herbed Popovers

(pictured, page 214)

3 large eggs
1½ cups milk
1 tablespoon salad oil
½ teaspoon salt
1½ cups unsifted all-purpose flour
1 tablespoon minced thyme leaves
1 tablespoon minced chives
1 tablespoon minced parsley

1. Preheat oven to 425°F. Lightly grease 6 (4-ounce) popover-pan cups; set aside.

2. In blender, at high speed, combine eggs, milk, oil and salt. Add flour; at low speed, mix until smooth, scraping down the sides of the blender container as necessary. (Do not overblend.) Stir in thyme, chives and parsley.

3. Pour batter into prepared pans, dividing evenly. Bake 15 minutes. Reduce oven to 375°F. Bake 45 minutes longer. Serve warm.

Makes 6.

Leek and Carrot au Gratin

(pictured, page 214)

4 large leeks, split, rinsed and sliced crosswise in half
1 can (about 14 ounces) chicken broth
1 teaspoon salt
1 package (10 ounces) frozen whole baby carrots, thawed
5 tablespoons butter or margarine
3 tablespoons all-purpose flour
½ teaspoon dry mustard
⅛ teaspoon pepper
¾ cup milk
½ cup fine dry bread crumbs
¼ cup grated Parmesan cheese

1. In large saucepan, bring leeks, broth and ½ teaspoon salt to boiling. Simmer, covered, 5 minutes. Add carrots; cook 8 minutes, or until tender. Drain, reserving ¾ cup cooking liquid. Place vegetables in 13-by-9-inch broiler-safe baking pan; set aside.

2. In medium saucepan, over medium heat, melt butter. Pour 2 tablespoons into small bowl; set aside. To butter in pan, add flour, mustard, ½ teaspoon salt and the pepper; stir until blended. Gradually stir in reserved cooking liquid and the milk; bring to boiling, stirring constantly. Cook 1 minute, until mixture is thickened. Pour sauce over prepared vegetables.

3. To reserved melted butter, add bread crumbs and cheese; mix well. Sprinkle crumb mixture over vegetables. Broil, 4 inches from heat, 3 minutes, or until golden-brown.

Makes 8 servings.

Hazelnut-Cranberry-Cream Cake

(pictured, page 215)

Filling
3 cups cranberries
1⅓ cups sugar
2 tablespoons lemon juice
¾ cup butter
2 large eggs, beaten

Cake
2¼ cups cake flour
2¼ teaspoons baking powder
¼ teaspoon salt
9 large egg yolks
1½ cups sugar
¾ cup boiling water
1½ teaspoons vanilla extract

Frosting
1¼ cups heavy cream
⅓ cup sour cream
3 tablespoons sugar
½ teaspoon vanilla extract

1 cup hazelnuts, chopped

1. Make Filling: In heavy medium saucepan, combine cranberries, ⅔ cup sugar and the lemon juice. Over low heat, cook 15 minutes, until very soft. Place in food processor; puree. Pass puree through fine sieve; discard seeds and other solids. Place puree in same, clean saucepan; add butter and remaining ⅔ cup sugar. Bring to boiling. In medium bowl, beat eggs until well mixed; whisk in about one-third cup cranberry mixture. Pour egg mixture into cranberry mixture in saucepan; cook, stirring, until mixture starts to boil. Pour into medium bowl; cool. Cover mixture and refrigerate 4 hours, until firm.

2. Make Cake: Preheat oven to 375°F. Grease and flour three 9-inch square cake pans; set aside. On sheet of waxed paper, mix flour with baking powder and salt; set aside. In large bowl of electric mixer, at medium-high speed, beat egg yolks with sugar 5 minutes, until thick and light. At low speed, beat in boiling water until blended. Add vanilla and flour mixture; at low speed, beat just until moistened. Spoon batter into prepared pans, dividing evenly. Bake 18 minutes, or until cake tester comes out clean. Turn out onto wire rack; invert again so that cake layers cool top side up. Let layers cool completely.

3. Assemble Cake: Place one cake layer on serving plate. Spread with one-third cranberry mixture. Repeat with remaining cake layers and cranberry mixture. Cover; refrigerate at least 8 hours or up to 2 days.

4. Make Frosting: Place large bowl of electric mixer and beaters in freezer 10 minutes. When chilled, at high speed, beat heavy cream with sour cream until soft peaks form. Gradually beat in sugar. Add vanilla; beat until stiff peaks form. Set aside 1 cup whipped-cream mixture; place remainder in pastry bag fitted with star tip. With spatula, spread reserved cream over sides of cake. With hand, press hazelnuts into cream. Pipe remaining cream decoratively around top edges of cake. Cover; refrigerate at least 2 hours or up to 1 day. If desired, garnish with frosted cranberries and a mint sprig.

Makes 12 servings.

Red-Hot Wassail

(pictured, page 215)

3 small apples
1 tablespoon lemon juice
2 cups cinnamon schnapps, chilled
¼ cup superfine sugar
3 green candied cherries
3 bay leaves
3 (3-inch) cinnamon sticks
6 cans (12 ounces each) light beer, chilled

1. Preheat oven to 350°F. Core apples; pare top portion. Brush exposed apple flesh with lemon juice; place in baking dish. Bake apples 15 minutes, until heated through. Cool; freeze until firm.

2. At serving time, in chilled punch bowl, mix schnapps with sugar until sugar dissolves. Place a cherry, bay leaf and cinnamon-stick "stem" in top of each apple; place in punch bowl. Gently stir in beer.

Makes 10 cups.

Orange-Mincemeat Cheesecake

(pictured, page 212)

Crust
¾ cup unsifted all-purpose flour
3 tablespoons sugar
⅓ cup butter or margarine

Filling
2 cups prepared mincemeat
½ cup walnut pieces
2 teaspoons angostura bitters
2 packages (8 ounces each) cream cheese, softened
1¼ cups sour cream
3 large eggs
⅔ cup sugar
1 tablespoon grated orange peel
½ teaspoon grated lemon peel
¼ teaspoon ground nutmeg

Sweetened whipped cream
Sugared walnuts

1. Make Crust: Preheat oven to 350°F. In medium bowl, mix flour with sugar; with two knives or pastry blender, cut in butter until mixture resembles coarse crumbs. With fork, press mixture against bottom of 9-inch springform pan. Bake 20 minutes, until light brown. Cool on wire rack.

2. Make Filling: Increase oven to 450°F. In medium bowl, mix mincemeat with walnuts and bitters; spread over prepared crust. In food processor, blend cream cheese with sour cream, eggs, sugar, orange peel,

lemon peel and half the nutmeg until mixture is smooth, scraping sides of processor bowl once. Spoon over mincemeat; sprinkle with remaining nutmeg.

3. Bake cheesecake 10 minutes. Reduce oven temperature to 250°F. Bake 50 minutes longer, or until center is set. Cool completely on wire rack. Cover; refrigerate 6 hours, or until completely chilled. Garnish top of cake with whipped cream and sugared walnuts.

Makes 10 to 12 servings.

Sarah Bernhardt Cookies

1 can (8 ounces) almond paste
2 large eggs, separated
1¼ cups sugar
1 package (6 ounces) semisweet-chocolate pieces
¼ cup butter or margarine, softened
2 tablespoons instant coffee powder
2 tablespoons coffee-flavored liqueur
1 package (8 ounces) semisweet-chocolate squares
4 teaspoons shortening

1. Preheat oven to 325°F. Line 2 large baking sheets with aluminum foil; set aside. In small bowl, with electric mixer at low speed, beat almond paste with egg whites and sugar until smooth.

2. Place in pastry bag fitted with ½-inch star tip; pipe 1½-inch rosettes onto prepared baking sheets, or drop by rounded teaspoonfuls. Bake 15 minutes, or until golden. Cool until firm on pan on wire rack. With spatula, remove macaroons to wire rack; cool completely.

3. In top of double boiler, over hot, not boiling, water, melt chocolate pieces. Remove double-boiler top from pan. Whisk egg yolks, one at a time, into chocolate; whisk in

butter. In small cup, dissolve coffee in liqueur; whisk into chocolate mixture, mixing until butter is melted. Pour into medium bowl; set in large bowl of ice and water. Let cool, stirring occasionally, 20 minutes, or until the mixture thickens.

4. Spread 1 rounded teaspoonful chocolate mixture over bottom of each macaroon. Place chocolate side up on jelly-roll pan; refrigerate until chocolate sets.

5. Line another jelly-roll pan with aluminum foil; set aside. In top of double boiler, over hot, not boiling, water, melt chocolate squares and shortening, stirring until blended. Remove pan from heat, keeping chocolate mixture over hot water. Dip bottom and sides of macaroons in chocolate mixture. Place chocolate side down on prepared pan. Refrigerate until chocolate sets and ready to serve.

Makes 3 dozen.

Grape Sorbet

½ cup sugar
¼ cup water
2 pounds seedless red grapes, stems removed (see *Note*)
¼ cup blackberry brandy (see *Note*)
2 tablespoons lemon juice
1½ teaspoons grated lemon peel
1 cup chilled champagne (see *Note*)

1. In small saucepan, dissolve sugar in water. Bring to boiling, stirring; boil 1 minute. Cool to room temperature.

2. In food processor, puree grapes. Pass puree through food mill or strainer set over large bowl (there should be 3 cups puree). Stir in brandy, lemon juice, lemon peel and sugar syrup. Refrigerate mixture until very cold. Stir in champagne; pour into freezer container of ice cream maker. Freeze according to

manufacturer's instructions, until firm and slushy.

Makes 8 servings.

Note: For Grape Sorbet, three cups grape juice can be substituted for grapes. Blackberry soda can be substituted for brandy. Lemon-lime soft drink can be substituted for champagne.

Pecan-Pear Tart

½ package (15-ounce size) refrigerated all-ready piecrusts (1 crust)
⅔ cup sugar
¼ cup honey
½ cup water
2 cups chopped pecans
1 medium pear, pared, cored and chopped
½ cup heavy cream
3 tablespoons butter or margarine
½ teaspoon ground cinnamon
2 large egg yolks

1. Unfold piecrust; place in 9-inch tart pan with removable bottom. Trim edge; set aside.

2. Preheat oven to 375°F. In medium saucepan, bring sugar, honey and water to boiling. Cover; boil 3 minutes. Add pecans, pear, heavy cream, butter and cinnamon. Bring to boiling; simmer, uncovered, stirring, 15 minutes.

3. In small bowl, blend some of the hot pear mixture with egg yolks; stir into remaining pear mixture in pan. Cook, stirring, 5 minutes, or until mixture is very thick. Pour into prepared crust; bake 30 minutes. Cool tart in pan on wire rack. To serve, remove tart from pan. Serve warm or chilled.

Makes 8 servings.

■ Almonds take on greater flavor depth and richer aroma when roasted or toasted.

The Ultimate Christmas Cake

*Here's one present that's too nice to stay hidden under the tree.
It's just made to be the center of attention for the holiday
meal. Underneath the marzipan wrapping is your favorite cake,
brushed with brandy.*

Holiday Surprise-Package Cake

Fruitcake (see *Note*)
1 container (16 ounces) red, yellow and green-candied pineapple chunks
1 package (6 ounces) dried apple rings, coarsely chopped
1 package (8 ounces) dried apricots, coarsely chopped
1½ cups chopped pecans
1½ cups plus 2 tablespoons unsifted all-purpose flour
½ teaspoon baking powder
½ teaspoon salt
5 large eggs, separated, at room temperature
1 cup granulated sugar
2 cups butter or margarine, softened
¾ cup apricot brandy

Marzipan
1 can (8 ounces) almond paste
2 large egg whites
2 tablespoons apricot brandy
6 cups confectioners' sugar
Food paste colors: Christmas red, leaf green
¼ cup apricot preserves

Glaze
2 cups confectioners' sugar
3 tablespoons apricot brandy
¼ cup light corn syrup

1 large egg white, slightly beaten
Red and green edible glitter

1. Generously grease and flour two 9-inch cake pans. In large bowl, mix candied pineapple with dried apple rings and apricots, the pecans and 2 tablespoons flour; set aside. On sheet waxed paper, mix remaining flour with baking powder and salt; set aside.

2. Preheat oven to 325°F. In large bowl of electric mixer, at high speed, beat egg whites until soft peaks form. Beat in ½ cup sugar, 2 tablespoons at a time, until stiff. Transfer to medium bowl; set aside.

3. In same large bowl, with electric mixer at high speed, beat egg yolks with butter and ½ cup sugar until light and fluffy. At low speed, beat in ¼ cup brandy; beat in flour mixture. Beat until smooth; transfer to very large mixing bowl.

4. Stir one-fourth of egg-white mixture into flour mixture to lighten. Add fruit mixture; mix well. Gently fold in remaining egg-white mixture until no white streaks remain. Spoon batter into prepared pans, dividing evenly; smooth tops of batter. Bake 60 minutes, or until cake tester inserted in center of cakes comes out clean.

5. Cool cakes in pans on wire racks 10 minutes. Invert cakes onto racks; remove pans. Turn cakes top side up on wire racks; brush tops of cakes with ¼ cup brandy. When completely cool, brush with remaining brandy.

6. Make Marzipan: In food processor or with electric mixer, mix almond paste with egg whites, brandy and 3 cups confectioners' sugar until smooth. On surface dusted with confectioners' sugar, knead in the remaining 3 cups confectioners' sugar, ½ cup at a time. Divide dough in half; form one half into ball. Wrap; set aside. Divide remaining half dough in half. Tint one half with red food paste color; form into ball. Wrap in plastic wrap; set aside. Remove ¼ cup from remaining dough; tint with green food paste color. Leave remaining dough white. Form balls; wrap. Set aside.

7. Invert one cake layer onto wire rack placed over jelly-roll pan. Spread layer with apricot preserves. Set aside.

8. Lightly dampen counter. Place 10-inch square waxed paper on counter. Place small white marzipan ball on paper. With rolling pin, flatten in center; cover with waxed paper. Roll to 8½-inch square. Remove top sheet of paper. Lift marzipan by bottom sheet of paper; invert onto cake layer on rack. Remove paper; invert second cake layer onto marzipan-covered layer.

9. Make package: Lightly dampen counter; place 16-inch square waxed paper on counter (overlap 2 sheets to make square). Place large white marzipan ball on paper. Flatten in center; cover with waxed

paper. Roll to 14½-inch square. Remove top sheet of paper. Lift marzipan by bottom sheet; invert onto cake. Remove paper; press marzipan to sides of cake; trim off excess and press together cut edges.

10. Make Glaze: In medium bowl, combine glaze ingredients until smooth (mixture will be very stiff). Pour onto center of cake; with spatula, spread over top and sides of cake, allowing excess to drip into pan. Set aside.

11. Make ribbon: Lightly dampen counter; place another 16-inch square waxed paper on counter. Place red marzipan ball on paper. Flatten in center; cover with waxed paper. Roll to 14-by-11-inch rectangle. Remove top sheet paper; trim edges. Cut seven 1½-by-14-inch strips, cutting through waxed paper.

12. Lift one strip by bottom sheet of paper; gently invert and place

marzipan "ribbon" across cake "package." Repeat with second length of marzipan. Set cake aside.

13. Make bow: Cut one long red marzipan strip crosswise into one 6-inch strip and one 5-inch strip; cut out and remove a V-shape piece from one end of each. Remove waxed-paper backing; place on baking sheet. Cut off and discard 1 inch from one end of each of the remaining red marzipan strips. Cut strips crosswise in half; remove waxed-paper backing. Fold four strips into loops; pinch together ends. Place on baking sheet. Cut off and discard 1 inch from remaining red marzipan strips; fold into loops. Pinch together ends; place on baking sheet.

14. Make leaves: Roll green marzipan between sheets waxed paper to 3-by-5-inch strip. With sharp knife or holly-leaf-shape cookie cutter, cut out 6 leaves. With dull side

of knife, score "veins" in leaves. Place on baking sheet. Allow bow pieces and leaves to harden several hours or overnight.

15. Lightly brush beaten egg white over marzipan pieces. Sprinkle with edible glitter. Place cake on serving platter. Arrange 4 large bow loops on top of cake where ribbons intersect; tuck 4 smaller bow loops on top of large loops. Place the two ribbon ends at base of bow, placing forked ends out. Tuck holly leaves around bow.

Makes 18 servings.

Note: A square yellow or white cake may be substituted for the fruitcake. Prepare two (9-inch) square white or yellow cake layers. With fork, prick surfaces of cake layers; brush with ¼ cup brandy. At this point, omit first 5 steps in recipe and begin with step 6. Complete remaining steps.

Quick-as-a-Wink Holiday Cookies

Christmas and cookies naturally go together, like Santa and his elves. And our sweet treats are so easy to make, they're as much fun to create as they are to eat—well, almost!

Espresso Oatmeal Crisps

2 large eggs
1 cup sugar
2 cups uncooked rolled oats
2 tablespoons butter, melted
2 teaspoons instant espresso powder
2 teaspoons pumpkin-pie spice
1 tablespoon baking powder
½ teaspoon salt
Melted white or dark chocolate

1. Preheat oven to 350°F. Line 2 baking sheets with aluminum foil. In large bowl, with wire whisk, beat eggs with sugar until blended. Whisk in oats, butter, espresso powder, pumpkin-pie spice, baking powder and salt.

2. Drop by rounded teaspoonfuls 2 inches apart onto prepared baking sheets. Bake 15 minutes, or until edges are golden. Cool 5 minutes; remove from foil. Drizzle with melted chocolate.
Makes 2½ dozen.

Pages 224 and 225: A sleigh full of cookies—24 varieties in all. See page 227 for identification.

Shortbread Cutouts

1 cup butter or margarine, softened
¾ cup sugar
2 cups unsifted all-purpose flour
1 teaspoon vanilla extract
¼ teaspoon salt
4 rolls (.9 ounce each) assorted fruit-flavored roll candy

1. In food processor, process butter with sugar until creamy. Add flour, vanilla and salt; process until smooth. Gather dough into a ball; flatten into ½-inch-thick disk. Wrap in plastic wrap; chill 30 minutes.

2. Meanwhile, keeping colors separate, place candies in plastic bags. With hammer, crush candies into ¼-inch pieces.

3. Preheat oven to 350°F. Cover baking sheets with aluminum foil. On well-floured board or cloth, roll out dough to ⅛-inch thickness. With 3- or 4-inch cookie cutters, cut out cookies. Using smaller cookie cutters, cut out and remove dough from centers of cookies; reserve. Transfer cookies to prepared baking sheets. Gather dough scraps and dough from centers into a ball; reroll and cut out.

4. Spoon a small amount of crushed candy into cutout area in center of each cookie. Bake 10 minutes, or until golden around edges. Cool on baking sheet. With spatula, carefully remove from aluminum foil. If desired, make ornaments: Tie each desired length of ribbon in a loop. With frosting, attach a loop to the back of each cookie.
Makes 3½ dozen.

Gingerbread Cutouts

2 packages (14.5 ounces each) gingerbread cake-and-cookie mix
1 cup honey, heated to liquefy
Royal Frosting (page 229) or tubes (4½ ounces each) of colored decorating icing
Assorted candies for decoration

1. In large bowl of heavy-duty electric mixer, mix cake mix and honey until well blended (dough will be stiff). Gather dough into a ball; divide in half. Flatten each half into a ½-inch-thick disk; wrap in plastic wrap. Chill 30 minutes.

2. Preheat oven to 375°F. Line baking sheets with heavy-duty aluminum foil. With stockinette-covered rolling pin, roll out dough onto prepared baking sheets to ⅛-inch thickness. Using 5-inch or 8-inch cookie cutters placed ½ inch apart on dough, cut out cookies. Remove excess dough; reserve.

3. Bake cookies 8 to 12 minutes, or until firm and golden around edges. Cool in pans on wire racks 5 minutes. Carefully loosen cookies; cool completely. Repeat with remaining dough scraps. Decorate

with Royal Frosting and candies.

Makes 2½ dozen small or 1 dozen large cookies.

Easy Lemon-Curd Tarts

**1 package (15 ounces)
  refrigerated all-ready
  piecrusts (2 sheets)
2 large egg yolks
1 can (14 ounces) sweetened
  condensed milk
1 teaspoon grated lemon peel
½ cup lemon juice**

1. Preheat oven to 400°F. Unwrap and unfold piecrusts. Place on lightly floured board. Roll out each to 12-inch round. With 3-inch round cookie cutter, cut out 14 rounds pastry from each large round, rerolling scraps if necessary. Line 2½-inch shallow muffin cups or tartlet pans with small pastry rounds; place foil or paper muffin-cup liners over pastry in each. Bake 10 minutes, or until golden. Remove liners. Cool pastry completely.

2. In medium bowl, with wire whisk, mix egg yolks with milk, lemon peel and lemon juice until blended. Spoon 1 tablespoonful

mixture into each pastry shell. Place on tray; cover loosely with plastic wrap. Refrigerate several hours, or until filling is set.

Makes 28.

Walnut Spirals

**Dough
1 package (3 ounces) cream
  cheese, chilled
10 tablespoons butter, cut in
  1-inch pieces, chilled
1 cup unsifted all-purpose
  flour
1 teaspoon vanilla extract**

**Filling
1 tablespoon butter,
  melted
¼ cup sugar
2 teaspoons pumpkin-pie
  spice
¾ cup ground walnuts**

1. Make dough: In food processor, process cream cheese with butter, flour and vanilla until dough forms a ball. Shape into a ½-inch-thick disk; wrap in plastic wrap. Chill 30 minutes.

2. On well-floured board or cloth, roll out dough into 17-by-10-inch rectangle; brush with melted butter. In small bowl, mix sugar with spice; sprinkle over butter. Sprinkle walnuts over sugar, pressing gently into dough. With long side of dough facing you, roll up dough tightly, jelly-roll fashion. Wrap in plastic wrap; chill 1 hour.

3. Preheat oven to 350°F. Cut roll crosswise into ¼-inch-thick slices. Place on ungreased baking sheets. Bake 10 minutes, or until golden. Cool on wire rack.

Makes 3½ dozen.

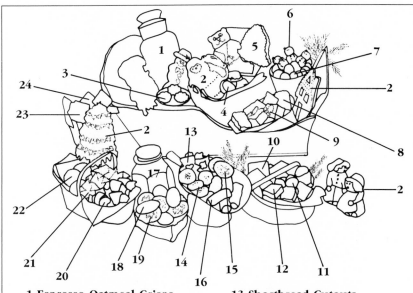

1 **Espresso Oatmeal Crisps**
2 **Gingerbread Cutouts**
3 **Easy Lemon-Curd Tarts**
4 **Orange Top Hats**
5 **Granola Bells**
6 **Meringue Snowmen**
7 **Walnut Spirals**
8 **Cranberry Crumb Bars**
9 **Kentucky Bourbon Bars**
10 **Black-and-White
  Cream-Cheese Brownies**
11 **White-Chocolate Coconut
  Clusters**
12 **Chewy Pecan-Pie Squares**
13 **Shortbread Cutouts**
14 **Peanut-Butter-and-Jelly
  Sandwiches**
15 **Chocolate Snowflakes**
16 **Sugar-Cookie Yule Logs**
17 **Hazelnut Puffs**
18 **Ginger Madeleines**
19 **Mint-Chocolate Wafers**
20 **Raspberry Rugelach**
21 **Poinsettia Cookies**
22 **Mini Mincemeat Pies**
23 **Cherry Linzer Bars**
24 **Crunchy Almond Triangles**
Photograph, pages 224-225

Quick-as-a-Wink Cookies

Cranberry Crumb Bars

**2¼ cups unsifted all-purpose
  flour**
1½ cups uncooked regular oats
1 cup sugar
1 cup butter, softened
**1 can (16 ounces) whole-berry
  cranberry sauce**
¾ cup orange marmalade
½ cup slivered almonds

1. Preheat oven to 350°F. Grease
13-by-9-by-2-inch baking pan.

2. In large bowl of electric mixer,
at low speed, mix 2 cups flour with
oats, sugar and butter until crumbly.
Reserve 1½ cups oat mixture; press
remaining mixture into bottom of
prepared pan. Bake 15 minutes.

3. In small bowl, mix cranberry
sauce with marmalade, almonds and
remaining ¼ cup flour; spoon mixture over oat mixture in pan. Sprinkle with reserved oat mixture. Bake
45 minutes, or until golden. Let cool
in pan on wire rack; cut into 2½-by-
1½-inch bars.
Makes 25.

Orange Top Hats

**1 package (16 ounces)
  pound-cake mix**
¼ cup butter, softened
1 large egg
**¼ cup orange-flavored liqueur
  or orange juice**
**1 tablespoon grated orange
  peel**
**2 tubes (4¼ ounces each)
  colored decorating icing, or
  Royal Frosting (page 229)**
Dragées or chopped gumdrops

1. Preheat oven to 350°F. Generously grease and flour inside all
cups and tops of three 1½-inch
muffin pans.

2. In large bowl of electric mixer,
at medium speed, combine pound-
cake mix, butter, egg, liqueur and
orange peel until smooth. Spoon

one level tablespoonful batter into
each muffin cup.

3. Bake 15 minutes, or until firm
and golden. (Cake will rise and bake
over edges of cups.) Cool 10 minutes. Gently loosen cakes and invert
pans onto wire racks; remove pans.

4. To decorate: Pipe icing "hat
band" around each cookie; pipe
icing "feathers" onto band. Decorate
with dragées or gumdrop pieces.
Makes 3 dozen.

Granola Bells

**1 package (10 ounces)
  marshmallows**
¼ cup butter or margarine
**½ package (16-ounce size)
  natural cereal with raisins
  and dates (6 cups)**
**Chocolate-covered chocolate
  candies**
Decorating icing
Dragées

1. Line 2 baking sheets with aluminum foil. With wooden pick,
using pattern on page 250, draw 4
bell shapes, about 5 by 5 inches, on
each sheet. Lightly grease foil.

2. In 5-quart saucepan, over low
heat, cook marshmallows with butter, stirring until melted and
smooth. Add cereal; stir until well
coated. Spoon about 1 cup warm
mixture onto foil outline of each
bell; with greased hands, pat to
shape. Cool completely. Decorate
with candies, icing and dragées as
desired.
Makes 8.

Meringue Snowmen

2 large egg whites
¼ teaspoon cream of tartar
½ cup sugar
**Semisweet-chocolate pieces and
  minipieces**
Dragées
Decorating icing

1. Preheat oven to 250°F. Line
baking sheet with aluminum foil. In
small bowl of electric mixer, at medium speed, beat egg whites with
cream of tartar until foamy. At high
speed, gradually beat in sugar; beat
until stiff, glossy peaks form. Spoon
meringue into pastry bag fitted with
⅜-inch plain tip.

2. Pipe 2-inch mound of meringue onto baking sheet to form
bottom of snowman. Pipe a smaller
mound onto baking sheet; attach to
the first to form torso. Pipe and attach a third small mound for head
next to second mound.

3. Repeat with remaining meringue, spacing snowmen 2 inches
apart. Bake 40 minutes, or until firm.
Turn off oven; cool completely.
Carefully peel cookies off foil. Decorate, attaching chocolate morsels
and dragées with icing.
Makes 15.

Kentucky Bourbon Bars

**1 package (16 ounces)
  pound-cake mix**
**1 tablespoon instant coffee
  powder**
¼ cup butter, softened
2 large eggs
**¼ cup bourbon whiskey or ¼
  cup milk**
½ cup chopped pecans
½ cup raisins
**½ cup semisweet-chocolate
  minipieces**
1 cup canned vanilla frosting
Candied cherries or gumdrops

1. Preheat oven to 350°F. Grease
9-inch square baking pan. Set aside
¼ cup pound-cake mix.

2. In large bowl of electric mixer,
at medium speed, beat remaining
cake mix and the coffee powder
with butter, eggs and bourbon until
smooth. In small bowl, toss reserved
cake mix with pecans, raisins and

chocolate pieces; stir into batter.

3. Spread batter in prepared pan. Bake 35 minutes, or until cake tester inserted in center comes clean. Cool in pan on wire rack. Spread top of cake with frosting; cut into 2-inch squares. Decorate with cherries or gumdrops.

Makes 16.

Peanut-Butter-and-Jelly Sandwiches

⅔ cup raspberry jam
60 round buttery crackers
1 package (12 ounces)
    peanut-butter-flavored
    morsels
3 tablespoons shortening
⅓ cup chopped peanuts

1. Spread 1 teaspoon jam on one side of cracker; top with another cracker. Chill 20 minutes.

2. In top of double boiler, over hot, not boiling water, melt morsels with shortening, stirring until smooth. Using fork, dip each sandwich into candy mixture; shake off excess.

3. Place sandwiches on waxed-paper-lined baking sheet; before coating hardens, sprinkle chopped nuts on top. Chill 10 minutes, until coating has set.

Makes 30.

Black-and-White Cream-Cheese Brownies

1 package (about 23 ounces)
    fudge-brownie mix
4 large eggs
1 package (8 ounces) cream
    cheese, softened
½ cup sugar
2 tablespoons all-purpose flour
1 teaspoon vanilla extract

1. Preheat oven to 350°F. Grease 13-by-9-by-2-inch baking pan. Prepare brownie mix as package label directs, using 2 eggs. Pour half of the batter into pan; reserve remainder.

2. In medium bowl, with electric mixer at medium-high speed, beat cream cheese with sugar, flour and vanilla until creamy. Beat in remaining eggs. Pour mixture over batter in pan. With spoon, drop dollops of remaining chocolate batter over cream-cheese layer. With table knife, swirl batters.

3. Bake 40 minutes, or until cake tester inserted in center comes out clean. Cool brownies in pan on wire rack; cut into 2-inch squares.

Makes 2 dozen.

White-Chocolate Coconut Clusters

⅔ cup flaked coconut
½ cup chopped macadamia
    nuts
¼ cup sweetened condensed
    milk
16 vanilla wafers
1 package (10 ounces)
    white-chocolate baking
    pieces (1½ cups)
3 tablespoons shortening
Edible glitter

1. In small bowl, combine coconut, nuts and milk. Spoon 1 rounded teaspoonful onto each wafer. Place on wire rack; chill thoroughly.

2. In top of double-boiler, over hot, not boiling water, melt chocolate with shortening; stir until smooth. Place rack with coconut clusters over sheet of waxed paper. Spoon about 1 tablespoonful chocolate mixture over each cluster, spreading with spatula to cover completely. Scrape off excess chocolate from waxed paper and remelt if necessary. Sprinkle glitter over clusters. Refrigerate until set.

Makes 16.

Crunchy Almond Triangles

1 package (about 18 ounces)
    yellow cake mix
⅓ cup butter, softened
3 large eggs
1 teaspoon almond extract
2 cups sliced almonds
3 tablespoons sugar

1. Preheat oven to 350°F. Grease 15½-by-10½-by-1-inch jelly-roll pan; set aside.

2. In large bowl of electric mixer, at low speed, combine cake mix, butter, 1 egg and ½ teaspoon almond extract until crumbly. Press mixture into bottom of prepared pan. Bake 15 minutes.

3. In small bowl, beat remaining eggs until well mixed. Add almonds and remaining almond extract; mix until blended. Pour over cake mixture in pan. Sprinkle with sugar. Bake 15 minutes longer, or until golden and set. Let cool in pan on wire rack.

4. Cut into fifteen 3-inch squares. Cut each square diagonally in half.

Makes 30.

Royal Frosting

1 pound confectioners' sugar
3 large egg whites, at room
    temperature
½ teaspoon cream of tartar
Food coloring

1. In large bowl of electric mixer, at medium speed, beat sugar with egg whites and cream of tartar until frothy. At high speed, beat 7 minutes, or until very thick.

2. In separate bowls, color frosting as desired. Keep frosting covered with plastic wrap or a damp cloth directly on icing surface when not in use. Spread or pipe frosting on cookies.

Makes about 3 cups.

Chewy Pecan-Pie Squares

1 package (18.25 ounces) yellow cake mix
5 large eggs
⅓ cup salad oil
1 cup dark corn syrup
1 cup sugar
¼ cup butter, melted
2 cups chopped pecans

1. Preheat oven to 350°F. Grease 13-by-9-by-2-inch baking pan. In large bowl, mix cake mix, 1 egg and oil until crumbly. Press into bottom of prepared pan; bake 20 minutes.

2. In large bowl of electric mixer, at medium-high speed, beat remaining eggs with corn syrup, sugar and butter until blended; stir in pecans. Pour on top of mixture in pan; bake 45 minutes, or until filling has set. Cool completely; cut into 2-inch squares.

Makes 2 dozen.

Sugar-Cookie Yule Logs

3 cups buttermilk baking mix
⅔ cup sugar
5 tablespoons butter, softened
1 large egg
2 teaspoons grated lemon peel
1½ cups prepared vanilla or chocolate frosting
Ground nutmeg or unsweetened cocoa powder

1. Preheat oven to 350°F. In large bowl of electric mixer, at low speed, combine baking mix with sugar, butter, egg and lemon peel until mixture resembles coarse crumbs. With hands, press dough together; divide into 24 pieces. Shape each into a 2½-inch log ½-inch thick.

2. Place cookies about 2 inches apart on ungreased baking sheets; bake 10 minutes, or until golden. (Cookies will flatten in baking.) While cookies are warm, reshape to form logs. Remove from pans; place on wire rack to cool.

3. Spread about 1 tablespoonful frosting on top of each cookie. With fork, score surface lengthwise to resemble bark. Sprinkle with nutmeg.

Makes 2 dozen.

Chocolate Snowflakes

1 package (20 ounces) refrigerated chocolate-chip or chocolate-chocolate-chip cookie dough
⅓ cup unsifted all-purpose flour
⅓ cup butter, softened

1. Freeze dough 1 hour. In small bowl, mix flour with butter until smooth; spoon into pastry bag fitted with ⅛-inch writing tip.

2. Preheat oven to 350°F. Cut dough crosswise into ¼-inch slices; place 2 inches apart on ungreased baking sheets. Pipe butter mixture in snowflake design onto each slice, dividing evenly. Bake 10 minutes, or until firm. Cool 1 minute; transfer to wire racks. Cool completely.

Makes 2 dozen.

Poinsettia Cookies

¾ cup butter, softened
1 cup sugar
1 large egg
1 teaspoon vanilla extract
2½ cups unsifted all-purpose flour
1 teaspoon baking powder
¼ teaspoon salt
Edible glitter

1. In food processor, mix butter with sugar until creamy. Add egg and vanilla; process just until blended. Add flour, baking powder and salt. Process until smooth. Remove dough; shape into a ball; flatten to ½-inch-thick disk. Wrap in plastic wrap; chill 1 hour.

2. Preheat oven to 400°F. On well-floured board or pastry cloth, roll out dough to ⅛-inch thickness. Cut into 2½-inch squares; place on ungreased baking sheets. With sharp knife, cut each square diagonally from each corner almost to the center. Fold every other corner to center to form pinwheel shape.

3. Sprinkle center of each with edible glitter. Bake 8 minutes, or until edges are golden. Cool 1 minute. With spatula, transfer to wire rack; cool completely.

Makes about 4 dozen.

Cherry Linzer Bars

1 package (8 ounces) cream cheese, softened
1 cup butter, softened
2 cups unsifted all-purpose flour
1 teaspoon almond extract
1 can (21 ounces) cherry pie filling
2 tablespoons sugar

1. In food processor, mix cream cheese with butter until blended. Add flour and almond extract; process until dough forms a ball. Wrap in plastic wrap; chill 30 minutes.

2. Preheat oven to 350°F. Divide dough in half. On well-floured board, roll out half of dough into a 15-by-10-inch rectangle; place dough rectangle in 15½-by-10½-by-1-inch jelly-roll pan. Coarsely chop cherries in pie filling; spoon pie filling and cherries over dough.

3. Roll out remaining dough into 15-by-10-inch rectangle; sprinkle with sugar. Using a fluted pastry wheel, cut lengthwise into ¾-inch strips. Arrange strips in crisscross pattern about 1 inch apart over filling, cutting strips to fit. Place remaining strips around edges of pan.

4. Bake 50 minutes, or until pastry is golden and filling is bubbly. Cool in pan on wire rack. Cut into 3-inch squares.

Makes 15.

Mint-Chocolate Wafers

1 cup butter, softened
¾ cup sugar
2 cups unsifted all-purpose flour
½ cup unsweetened cocoa powder
½ teaspoon mint extract
1 package (10 ounces) mint-flavored semisweet-chocolate pieces, melted
Green food color
4 ounces white chocolate, melted

1. In food processor, mix butter with sugar until blended. Add flour, cocoa powder and mint; process until dough forms a ball. Shape into a 9-by-3-inch log; wrap in plastic wrap. Chill 1 hour.

2. Preheat oven to 350°F. Cut dough crosswise into ¼-inch-thick slices; place 2 inches apart on ungreased baking sheets. Bake 10 minutes. Cool 1 minute; transfer to wire racks to cool completely.

3. Dip cookies halfway into semisweet chocolate; drain slightly. Place on waxed-paper-lined baking sheet. Chill until set. Stir food color into white chocolate to tint light green; drizzle over cookies.
Makes 3½ dozen.

Ginger Madeleines

1 package (14.5 ounces) gingerbread cake-and-cookie mix
1 large egg
½ cup honey, heated to liquefy
1 can (16 ounces) vanilla frosting
1 teaspoon grated lemon peel
Orange-peel strips

1. Preheat oven to 350°F. Generously grease and flour 3-by-2-inch-size madeleine pans.

2. In large bowl of electric mixer, at medium speed, beat mix with egg and honey until smooth. Spoon level

tablespoonfuls batter into molds; bake 12 minutes, or until firm. Cool 5 minutes; remove from pans. Cool on wire racks.

3. To glaze: In small saucepan, over low heat, heat frosting with lemon peel until thin. Place cookies on racks over waxed paper. Spoon about 1 tablespoonful glaze over each, using spatula to cover completely. Decorate with orange peel.
Makes 3 dozen.

Hazelnut Puffs

2 large egg whites
¼ teaspoon cream of tartar
1 tablespoon hazelnut- or almond-flavored liqueur or ½ teaspoon almond extract
½ cup sugar
1 cup (4 ounces) ground hazelnuts or almonds, toasted
Colored sugar

1. Preheat oven to 325°F. Line 2 baking sheets with aluminum foil.

2. In small bowl of electric mixer, at medium speed, beat egg whites with cream of tartar and liqueur until frothy. At high speed, gradually beat in sugar; beat until stiff, glossy peaks form. Fold in nuts. Spoon into pastry bag fitted with ½-inch star tip. Pipe 1½-inch-wide mounds, 1 inch apart, onto prepared baking sheets. Sprinkle with colored sugar. Bake 20 minutes, or until golden. Do not overbake. Cool on pan; carefully remove from foil.
Makes 2½ dozen.

Mini Mincemeat Pies

1 package (15 ounces) refrigerated all-ready pie pastry (2 sheets)
1 cup prepared mincemeat
½ cup chopped walnuts
1 large egg, lightly beaten
¼ cup cinnamon-sugar

1. Preheat oven to 400°F. Line baking sheet with aluminum foil. Place pastry on lightly floured board or cloth. Using a 2½-inch biscuit cutter, cut 14 rounds from each sheet. Reroll scraps; cut 12 rounds.

2. In small bowl, mix mincemeat with nuts. Spoon 1 level tablespoonful on half the pastry rounds; place on baking sheets. Brush edge of pastry with beaten egg. With tip of knife, score centers of remaining rounds; place on top of filled rounds.

3. With fork tines, press edges together. Brush tops with egg; sprinkle with cinnamon-sugar. Bake 12 minutes, or until golden. Cool 1 minute; transfer to rack. Cool.
Makes 20.

Raspberry Rugelach

Nonstick cooking spray
1 package (17 ounces) frozen puff pastry (2 sheets), thawed 20 minutes room temperature
1 cup raspberry jam
½ cup chopped almonds or walnuts
½ cup semisweet-chocolate minipieces
1 large egg, lightly beaten
2 tablespoons cinnamon-sugar

1. Preheat oven to 400°F. Line 2 baking sheets with foil; spray.

2. Unfold one pastry sheet. Place on lightly floured board or pastry cloth. Roll to 12-by-11-inches. Spread with half of jam; sprinkle with half of nuts and chocolate. Cut in half lengthwise; cut crosswise in thirds. Cut each rectangle diagonally in half. Roll up triangles, starting with short side.

3. Place triangles, point side down, onto prepared baking sheets. Brush with egg; sprinkle with cinnamon-sugar. Repeat with pastry and remaining ingredients. Bake 10 minutes, or until crisp and golden.
Makes 2 dozen.

No-Bake Cookie Houses

Country Christmas Cottage
(pictured, left)

HOUSE PATTERN PIECES
(pages 251, 252 and 253)
Front/back; roof; side; dormer-window front; dormer-window side; dormer-window roof; bench seat; bench back; bench leg; fence; shutter

TRIM PIECES
House roof; picture-window frame; dormer-window front; dormer-window roof; door

PROPS AND SUPPORT
X-acto knife; ruler; 48-by-32-inch foam-core board; marker; tracing paper; scissors; masking tape; waxed paper; 6 disposable pastry bags; glue; tall juice cans small brush; red marker; lollipop stick; packages; pastry tips: Nos. 3(3), 16, 352(2)

COOKIES, CRACKERS, CANDIES
4 packages (9 ounces each) large vanilla sugar wafers; 2 packages (9 ounces each) colored sugar wafers; 5 honey graham crackers; 5 cinnamon graham crackers; 6 packages (5 ounces each) lavash; silver dragées; 3 packages (8 ounces each) spearmint-leaf candies; pink and green jelly beans

4 recipes Royal Icing (page 243; make in separate batches)
Food paste colors: leaf green, yellow

1. With X-acto knife and ruler, cut 20-by-26-inch base and 6-inch round from foam-core; set aside. With marker and tracing paper, trace pattern pieces; enlarge to scale. Label pieces; cut with scissors. Set aside trim patterns; place remaining patterns on remaining foam core. Cut with X-acto knife.

2. Tape all trim pieces on work surface. Tape a sheet of waxed paper over each; with pastry bag fitted with number-3 tip and ½ cup icing, outline all trim pieces on the waxed paper. Let dry. Thin 1 cup icing to painting consistency; with brush, fill in the icing outline on all trim pieces. Let icing dry 24 hours.

3. Meanwhile, with spatula, cover one side of foam-core house front with icing. Starting at base of house, gently press wide surface of sugar wafers into icing, with long edge of wafers touching base; repeat to cover house front.

4. Make door: Spread icing on wide surface of six chocolate sugar wafers; place 3 wafers side by side, icing side down and short edge touching house base, onto center of house front. Place remaining wafers directly above first three, ends touching. Spread both sides of a whole honey graham cracker with icing; place over chocolate wafers. Top with another whole honey graham cracker; spread with icing. Top with another whole honey graham cracker. Spread with icing; top with 6 pink sugar wafers, arranged in same manner as chocolate wafers. With pastry bag fitted with number

(continued on page 234)

Houses designed and executed by Pat Darling.

16 tip and icing, cover seams where pink wafers join.

5. Make windows: With X-acto knife, cut 2 cinnamon graham crackers and 2 honey graham crackers into 3¾-by-2½-inch rectangles, scoring crackers several times for easier cutting. With icing, using photograph as a guide, attach one honey graham cracker rectangle onto each side of door of house front. With icing, attach a cinnamon graham cracker rectangle to each honey graham cracker rectangle, cinnamon side up; set aside. Place dormer-window pattern on whole cinnamon graham crackers; with X-acto knife, cut out three windows. With pastry bag fitted with number-3 tip and ½ cup white icing, pipe diagonal lines in a diamond pattern over cinnamon side of all windows. Set aside. Glue and tape together foam-core dormer-window roof pieces; tape to side pieces. Set aside.

6. Make house frame: Glue and tape house front to foam-core base, propping panels with tall juice cans. Glue and tape sides to front at right angles; glue and tape back to sides. With pastry bag fitted with number-16 tip and white icing, pipe a thick line of icing over seams of house on inside and outside. Dry overnight.

7. Next day: With pastry bag fitted with number-16 tip and white icing, pipe a thick line of icing over top edge of house frame. Attach foam-core roof pieces; let dry.

8. Place shutter panel pattern on pink sugar wafers; with X-acto knife, cut out 6 shutters. Cut out small heart shape in each shutter. Tint ½ cup icing green; place 2 tablespoons icing in pastry bag fitted with number-3 tip. Decorate shutters, using photograph as a guide. Set aside. Reserve remaining green icing.

9. With red marker, color lollipop stick; with X-acto knife, cut stick into three ½-inch lengths. Place on waxed paper. With yellow food color paste, tint 1 tablespoon icing yellow; place in pastry bag

fitted with number-3 tip. Pipe a dot of icing onto one end of each length lollipop stick, drawing tip up to make a candle flame. Let dry.

10. With X-acto knife, cut breadflats lengthwise in half, scoring breadflats several times for easier cutting. With spatula, evenly spread icing over one side of roof. Beginning at lower edge of roof, press breadflat halves, jagged side down, into icing. Arrange second row above first, overlapping slightly. Repeat with remainder of roof; with icing, attach breadflats to exposed underside of roof. If desired, break a few breadflat halves crosswise into pieces; in covering roof, alternate pieces with breadflat halves. Let dry 30 minutes.

11. Attach dormer windows: With pastry bag fitted with number-16 tip and white icing, attach dormer roof-and-side frames to roof, using photograph as a guide. Let dry. With icing, attach breadflats to dormer-window roof pieces. Pipe icing over front edges of window frame; gently press front in place. Attach shutters to windows. Pipe icing around seams to fill in any gaps. Let icing dry.

12. Attach trim and decorations: Carefully peel waxed paper from trim. With pastry bag fitted with number-16 tip and white icing, pipe a thick line of icing around frame of door. Attach door trim, holding gently in place until icing is set. Repeat with windows, roof of house and dormer-window roofs. Pipe icing around edges of roof. With pastry bag fitted with number-352 tip and white icing, pipe holly leaves along corners of house side; while icing is soft, using tweezers, attach dragées. With pastry bag fitted with number-3 tip and white icing, pipe icicles along roof edge.

13. With remaining green icing in pastry bag fitted with number-352 tip, pipe holly leaves over lower ledge of each window. While icing is soft, attach dragées. In dormer

windows, place candles.

14. Make tree: On 6-inch foam-core or cardboard round, with pastry bag fitted with number-16 tip and white icing, pipe 20 dots of icing in a ring. Place spearmint leaves over icing; layer icing and spearmint leaves to build a tree, decreasing number of leaves in a ring as tree increases in height. With pastry bag fitted with number-352 tip and white icing, decorate tree with holly leaves; while icing is still soft, decorate with dragées.

15. Make bench and fence: Place patterns for bench back and legs on chocolate sugar wafers; with X-acto knife, cut out two bench backs; cut hearts from each; cut bench legs. With icing, join together backs; for bench seat, attach short ends of 2 chocolate sugar wafers. Let dry. With icing, attach legs and bench back; let dry. Place pattern for fence on pink sugar wafers; with X-acto knife, cut out 8 shapes. With pastry bag fitted with number-3 tip and white icing, using photograph as a guide, decorate fence and bench.

16. To finish: Place house on large cloth-covered surface; arrange tree and bench around house. Pour sugar around scene in mounds; stick fence pieces in snow as desired. Scatter jelly beans in front of house for a path; arrange packages all around the bench.

Pages 232 and 233: Country Christmas Cottage is a festive creation built from ready-made cookies and candies.
Page 235: Mini-goldfish crackers lend a weathered look to our Colonial Saltbox.
Page 237: Santa's "Sweet Haus" is a tastefully decorated Swiss chalet.

No-Bake Cookie Houses

1. Make house frame: With marker and tracing paper, trace pattern pieces; enlarge to scale. Label all pieces; cut out with scissors. Place pattern pieces on cardboard; cut out with X-acto knife. Glue and tape sides to front, at right angles. Glue and tape one back section to the two sides; glue remaining back section to top of first to form the bottom half of the roof. Glue roof sections to frame. Center house frame on felt side of covered board; using some white icing, attach at base of frame.

2. With pastry bag fitted with number-8 tip and white icing, attach 4 cracked-grain crackers to house front and 4 cracked-grain crackers to each side for windows; attach remaining cracked-grain cracker to house front for door. With white icing, attach a pumpernickel cracker stick to top and bottom of each window and to right and left of door; attach a candle to center of each cracker stick on bottom of a window. Stack remaining cracker sticks to door front for steps, piping white icing between crackers to hold steps in place.

3. With small spatula, spread white icing over front on areas not covered by windows and door. Starting at house base, gently press cheese crackers into icing, overlapping rows; repeat with sides and back. Using white icing and pretzels, cover roof in similar fashion, starting at base of roof and overlapping rows. Let icing harden.

4. With white icing, attach chocolate side of biscuit wafer to house front, above door; attach butterfly-shape crackers, lower wings facing each other, on each side of window for shutters.

5. With white icing, join the long sides of crackers topped with sesame seeds at right angles to form chimney; let harden. Attach to center of roof with dollop of white icing. Spoon some white-icing snow

(continued on page 236)

Colonial Saltbox
(pictured, above)

HOUSE PATTERN PIECES
(page 254)
2 side; 1 front; 2 back; 2 roof

PROPS AND SUPPORT
Marker; tracing paper, scissors; 4 (15-inch) square sheets corrugated cardboard; X-acto knife; glue; masking tape; 20-inch square board, covered on one side with green felt; 2 disposable pastry bags; pastry tips: Nos. 8 and 66; 12 red birthday candles, cut to 1 inch; 1-inch red ribbon bow; small metal spatula; 4-inch piece blue felt, cut in kidney-shape pond

CRACKERS AND CANDIES
13 large, double crackers with cracked grain; 30 (2½-inch) pumpernickel cracker sticks; 3 bags (6 ounces each) tiny, fish-shape Cheddar-cheese crackers; 3 bags (15½ ounces each) tiny, fish-shape pretzels; 1 biscuit wafer topped with chocolate and pecans; 24 large, butterfly-shape, butter-flavored crackers; 4 rectangular crackers topped with sesame seeds; ¼ pound small toasted-marshmallow-flavored jelly beans

4 recipes Royal Icing (page 243; make in separate batches before using)
Food paste color: leaf green

No-Bake Cookie Houses

on top of chimney.

6. With leaf-green food color paste, tint 1½ cups icing green. With pastry bag fitted with leaf tip and green icing, pipe leaves at base of each candle. Pipe a garland of leaves over top of wafer above door; attach red bow in center. Pipe trees onto each corner of house.

7. With glue, attach felt pond in one front corner of yard; glue a few fish-shape crackers on pond.

8. Using white icing and jelly beans, build low wall around pond.

Santa's "Sweet Haus"
(pictured, right)

HOUSE PATTERN PIECES
(pages 256, 257 and 258)
Section A: #1-3, cupola; #4-6, dormer window; #7, roof; #8, front; #9, back; #10, sides; #11, tree. Section B: #1, roof; #2, front/back; #3, left side; #4, right side. Section C: #1, roof; #2-4, dormer window; #5, front; #6, side

PROPS AND SUPPORT
X-acto knife; ruler; 2 (48-by-32-inch) sheets, ¼-inch-thick, foam-core board; marker; tracing paper; scissors; metal spatula; small paintbrush; red marker; 2 lollipop sticks; waxed paper; 5 disposable pastry bags; pastry tips: Nos. 3 (two) 16 (two), 352; glue; masking tape; tall juice cans; 2-foot-long, ¼-inch-wide green ribbon

8 recipes Royal Icing (page 243; make in separate batches before using)

Food paste colors: leaf green, yellow

COOKIES, CRACKERS AND CANDIES
3 packages (1 pound each) graham crackers with cinnamon and sugar topping; 1 package (1 pound) red and green gumdrops; 3 packages (12 ounces each) vanilla-type wafers; 2 packages (1 pound each) Starlight mints; 12 candy canes; red cinnamon candies; granulated sugar

1. With X-acto knife and ruler, cut out 34-by-32-inch base from foam-core board; set aside. With marker and tracing paper, trace pattern pieces; enlarge to scale. Label all pieces; cut out with scissors. Set aside A #1, A #4, A #7, A #11, B #1, B #2, C #2, C #3, C #4. Place all remaining pattern pieces on remaining foam core. Cut out with X-acto knife.

2. With spatula, evenly cover one side of foam-core house front (A #8) with icing. Gently press whole graham crackers, cinnamon side out, into icing; repeat to cover house front. Repeat with foam-core pieces A #3, A #5, A #6, A #9, A #11, B #2, B #3, B #4, C #5, C #6. Let icing harden 30 minutes. Score crackers several times with X-acto knife; trim off excess.

3. Make house-front windows: With X-acto knife, trim a graham cracker to shape of A #2; reduce to window size, using photograph as a guide. With icing, attach to center of cracker side of A #2. With icing, attach 2 whole graham crackers side by side to center of cracker side of A #8, 2½ inches from base. With icing, attach 1 whole graham cracker to center of cracker side of C #5, long side down and 2 inches from base. With X-acto knife, score outline C #3 on graham cracker; cut out. With X-acto knife, cut ½ graham cracker lengthwise in half for shutters. Thin 1 cup white icing to painting consistency. With paintbrush, cover windows on A #2, A #8, C #5 and both sides of shutters.

Let dry 4 hours.

4. Make Christmas trees: With X-acto knife, score outline A #11 on each of 3 whole graham crackers; cut out. Thin ¼ cup green icing to painting consistency. With paintbrush, cover both sides of each tree. Let dry 4 hours.

5. With red marker, color lollipop sticks; with X-acto knife, cut sticks into ten ½-inch lengths. Place on waxed paper. With pastry bag fitted with number-3 tip and 1 tablespoon yellow icing, pipe a dot of icing onto one end of each length lollipop stick, drawing tip up to make candle flame. Let dry.

6. Make door: With small spatula, using photograph as a guide, evenly spread icing over an area in center and at base of B #2 large enough for 6-by-4 rows of gumdrops and including 3 gumdrops over all for an arch. Attach gumdrops; let dry.

7. With pastry bag fitted with number-3 tip and 2 tablespoons green icing, pipe diagonal lines in a diamond pattern over icing side of all windows. With pastry bag fitted with number-16 tip and white icing, using photograph as a guide, pipe a line of icing over window on front of section A; attach tree pieces. Pipe decorative trim around windows and door. Let dry.

8. Glue and tape house front to foam-core base, propping panel with tall juice cans. Glue and tape sides to front a right angles, propping as necessary; glue and tape back to sides. Glue and tape sections B and C to section A. With pastry bag fitted with number-16 tip and white icing, pipe a thick line of icing over seams of house on inside and outside. Let dry overnight.

9. Next day: With pastry bag fitted with number-16 tip and white icing, pipe a thick line of icing over top edge of house frame. Attach foam-core roof pieces; let dry. Attach dormer windows and cupola; let dry.

(continued on page 238)

10. With spatula, evenly spread icing over one side of house roof. Beginning at lower edge of roof, press wafers into icing. Arrange second row above first, overlapping slightly. Repeat with remainder of house roof; with icing, using photograph as a guide, attach wafers to front edge of roof on section A and back of section C. Using more icing and photograph as a guide, cover cupola roof with rows of Starlight mints and dormer roof on section A with gumdrops. With pastry bag fitted with number-16 tip and white icing, pipe a thick line of icing over seam of dormer roof; press a row of Starlight mints into icing. Let dry.

11. With pastry bag fitted with number-16 tip and white icing, using photograph as a guide, pipe around each wafer and house-frame seam; press Starlight mints and candy canes into icing on seams while icing is wet. Pipe icing around edges of tree; while icing is wet, press lollipop candles into icing. Let icing dry.

12. With pastry bag fitted with number-3 tip and 2 tablespoons green icing, using photograph as a guide, pipe dots of icing along house-frame seams. With pastry bag fitted with number-16 tip and ¼ cup green icing, pipe decorative trim around each shutter. With pastry bag fitted with number-352 tip and ½ cup green icing, using photograph as a guide, pipe holly leaves around windows and on candy canes, shutters and roof. While icing is wet, attach cinnamon candies for holly berries.

13. With pastry bag fitted with number-16 tip and white icing, make icicles on roof and over the windows.

14. Make fence: With X-acto knife, cut several candy canes to make ten 2-inch lengths. With icing, attach Starlight mint to one end of each length. With more icing, attach a cinnamon candy to center of top of each mint. Let dry.

15. To finish: Mound sugar in drifts around house. Arrange candy-cane fence posts in drifts; wrap a length of ribbon around each post to make fence. Arrange Starlight-mint path around house.

Boston Brownstone Town House
(pictured, right)

HOUSE PATTERN PIECES
(page 255)
2 front/back; 2 side; 4 narrow roof; 4 wide roof

PROPS AND SUPPORT
Marker; tracing paper; scissors; 3 (12-inch) square sheets corrugated cardboard; X-acto knife; glue; masking tape; 24-by-13-inch board, covered on one side with green felt; 2 disposable pastry bags; pastry tips: Nos. 8 and 66; 24 red birthday candles, cut to 2 inches; 6 (1-inch) red ribbon bows

4 recipes Royal Icing (page 243; make in separate batches before using)

CRACKERS AND CANDIES
38 rectangular crackers topped with sesame seeds; 60 (2½-inch) pumpernickel cracker sticks; 60 (2½-inch) plain cracker sticks; 2 pounds small strawberry-daiquiri-flavored jelly beans; 2 pounds small blueberry-flavored jelly beans; 52 rectangular crackers with wheat and honey flavor; ½ pound small toasted-marshmallow-flavored jelly beans; 1 biscuit wafer topped with chocolate and pecans

1. Make house frame: With marker and tracing paper, trace pattern pieces; enlarge to scale. Label all pieces; cut out with scissors. Place pattern pieces on cardboard; cut out with X-acto knife. Glue and tape sides to front, at right angles. Attach back section to the two sides. On front and back, with marker, draw a line down the center; designate one side as left house and the other as right house. On the front and on the back of left house, tape one narrow roof section. Tape a wide roof section to each side of house; tape to narrow roof pieces. Repeat with remaining roof pieces on right house. Center house frame on felt side of covered board; using some white icing, attach house frame at base.

2. With pastry bag fitted with number-8 tip and white icing, attach 8 rectangular crackers topped with sesame seeds onto house front, 8 rectangular crackers with sesame seeds onto house back, and 4 rectangular crackers with sesame seeds onto each side for windows. On left house and right house fronts, backs and sides, attach one rectangular cracker with sesame seeds about 1 inch higher than base of house for the doors.

3. For left house, with same pastry bag and white icing, attach a pumpernickel cracker stick at sides, top and bottom of each window, and at right, left and top of doors; attach a candle to center of each cracker stick on bottom of a window. Stack two pumpernickel cracker sticks at bottom of each door for steps, using same pastry bag and white icing to attach to house. Using plain cracker sticks, repeat on right house.

4. On left house, with small spatula, spread white icing over areas not covered by windows and door,
(continued on page 240)

Right: Our authentic Boston Brownstone Town House is built of multiflavored jellybean "bricks" and topped with cracker chimneys.

including front roof piece. Press strawberry-daiquiri-flavored jelly beans into icing for bricks. Using blueberry-flavored jelly beans, repeat on right house, except for roof. For all remaining roof sections, with small spatula, spread sections with white icing. Starting at roof base, gently press all but 6 rectangular crackers with wheat and honey flavor into icing, shorter end down, and in overlapping rows. Let icing harden.

5. With same pastry bag as above and white icing, attach chocolate side of biscuit wafer to jelly beans on left house front roof. With same pastry bag and white icing, join the long sides of four crackers topped with sesame seeds at right angles to form a chimney; repeat with remaining four rectangular crackers with sesame seeds; let icing harden. With dollop of white icing, attach one chimney to center of each roof.

6. Make front walk: Place 6 rectangular crackers with wheat and honey flavor on felt covering at house front, with long edges of crackers touching base of house. With white icing in same pastry bag, pipe around base of house and front walk. Press toasted-marshmallow-flavored jelly beans into icing. With remaining icing in bag, pipe snow on top of each chimney and on corners of rooftop.

7. Tint remaining icing green; place in pastry bag fitted with number-66 tip. Pipe leaves at the base of each candle. Pipe garland of greenery around each door; attach red bows over each door. Pipe trees onto corners of houses.

Victorian Dream House
(pictured, right)

HOUSE FRAME PIECES
(cut according to dimensions)
1 (16-by-16-inch) for base; 2 (12-by-7-inch) for front and back on first level; 1 (10½-by-7-inch) for left side on first level; 1 (10½-by-10¾-inch) for right side; 2 (5¹³⁄₁₆-by-4-inch) for doors; 3 (4-by-1³⁄₁₆-inch) for above doors; 1 (12-by-10½-inch) for roof on first level; 2 (5-by-2⅞-inch) for front and back on second level; 1 (9½-by-5½-inch) for left side on second level; 1 (9½-by-5½-inch) for roof on second level; 1 (4-by-1¼-inch), 1 (4-by-1½-inch) and 1 (4-by-1¾-inch) for stairs

HOUSE PATTERN PIECES
(pages 259, 260 and 261)
Right front room: section A; left side room; section B; widow's walk: section C #1,2,3,4,5; bay window: section D; sloped house roofs: left front, right side; trees; tree bases; door

PROPS AND SUPPORT
Marker; ruler; tracing paper; scissors; X-acto knife; 4 (40-by-30-inch) sheets, ³⁄₁₆-inch thick, foam-core board; 1½-by-1½-foot sheet pale orange cellophane; 1½-by-1½-foot sheet pale blue cellophane; glue; masking tape; 10 disposable pastry bags; pastry tips: Nos. 3 (two) and 17 (two); Nos. 4B, 5, 8, 17, 47, 66

Right: This charming Victorian cookie house is complete with a candy roof trimmed with peppermint candy and a traditional widow's walk made of tea biscuits and candy-cane columns.

COOKIES, CRACKERS AND CANDIES

12 honey graham crackers; 2 packages (10 ounces each) shortbread cookies; 14 pieces pink-and-white checkered peppermint-flavored bubble gum, cut crosswise in 4 pieces; 4 vanilla sandwich cookies; 1 package (11 ounces) tea cookies; red cinnamon candies; 6 rolls (.9 ounce each) cherry-flavored roll candy; 5 rolls (.9 ounce each) candy-cane-flavored roll candy; 8 fudge-covered graham cookies; 3 fudge-striped shortbread cookies; 4 (5-inch) peppermint sticks; silver dragées; 1 package (10 ounces) thin pretzel sticks (4 inches long); 12 sticks cherry-flavored striped stick bubble gum; 1 (.35 ounce) red fruit-flavored ring-shape lollipop; 2 small white oval mint candies; 3 large red gumdrops; granulated sugar

8 recipes Royal Icing (page 243; make in separate batches before using)

Food paste colors: Christmas red, leaf green

1. With marker, ruler and tracing paper, mark or trace all house frame and pattern pieces. (There are no patterns for frame; use marker and ruler to cut out pieces according to dimensions given.) Label; cut out with scissors. Place house frame pieces on foam-core board; cut out with X-acto knife. Cut out and reserve a 5-inch square from center of house base. With marker, outline windows, doors and section pattern pieces on foam core; cut out of frame pieces with X-acto knife. Outline door pattern pieces on 4 whole

(continued on page 242)

No-Bake Cookie Houses

honey graham crackers. With X-acto knife, cut out doors from crackers.

2. With scissors, cut out orange cellophane pieces to cover all windows except on section D and round window above door. Cut blue cellophane for windows on section D and round window above door. With glue or tape, attach cellophane in place on "inside" of respective house piece.

3. Make first level: Glue and tape front and back to sides of first level. Glue to foam-core base. Let dry. Meanwhile, with glue, sandwich together door pieces; sandwich together pieces for over front door. When dry, glue each in place on front of house as in photograph. With pastry bag fitted with number-3 tip and white icing, attach graham-cracker doors to foam-core doors.

4. Make second level: Glue flat roof onto first level. Glue and tape front and back pieces to side pieces of second level; when dry, glue to roof of first level. Glue and tape together section A pieces; when dry, attach to left side of second level. Glue and tape together section B; when dry, attach to right front of second level. Glue flat rooftop onto second level. Glue together sloped roof pieces as in photograph; glue to rooftop.

5. Make widow's-walk frame: Using photograph as a guide, alternately glue section C pieces #1 and #2 onto left side of roof to make

■ Making meringues for the holidays? We came up with this trick: Grind granulated sugar in the food processor, using on-and-off spurts for a few seconds. This sugar will dissolve very quickly in egg whites—and meringues won't have a gritty taste. (There's also another use for this handy trick: You can use this ground sugar in place of superfine sugar in beverages.)

octagonal shape. Alternately glue section C pieces #3 and #4 to section C piece #5. Set aside.

6. Make bay window frame: Glue together section D pieces as in photograph; let dry. Glue to right side of house as in photograph.

7. With pastry bag fitted with number-8 tip and white icing, using photograph as a guide, attach shortbread cookies to house, beginning with base of house front and cutting cookies with X-acto knife as necessary to fit.

8. With icing, using photograph as a guide, attach checkered bubble-gum pieces to side of house.

9. Split sandwich cookies; remove and discard creme filling. Set aside 4 cookie halves; with icing, using photograph as a guide, attach 2 cookies to each side corner of left front and right front on first level.

10. With X-acto knife, cut 25 tea cookies in half lengthwise; cut each half crosswise into three pieces; discard middle piece. With icing, using photograph as a guide, attach corner pieces of cookies to roofs of sections A, B and D, beginning at lower edge of each and overlapping rows. With icing, attach a whole tea cookie to each: top of roof of section A; bottom of section C; and underside of window of section D. Cut a tea cookie to fit above left side window on section B; attach with icing. With pastry bag fitted with number-17 tip and white icing, pipe along edge of top cookie on section A; while icing is wet, press cinnamon candies into icing at corners.

11. With small spatula, spread a thin layer of white icing over sloped roofs of house; let dry. With pastry bag fitted with number-5 tip and white icing, attach cherry-flavored and candy-cane-flavored roll candy in alternating rows to roofs, beginning at side edge and following angle, using photograph as a guide.

12. With pastry bag fitted with number-4B tip and white icing, attach fudge-covered grahams to the

rooftop, cutting grahams to fit. Pipe icing at edge of rooftop; attach checkered bubble-gum pieces, using photograph as a guide.

13. Make widow's walk: With X-acto knife, cut honey graham crackers to fit section C #3 and #4 foam-core pieces. With icing, attach crackers to foam-core pieces. Cut 2 fudge-striped shortbread cookies in half. With pastry bag fitted with number-4B tip and white icing, pipe a thick circle of icing around top edge of graham crackers. Gently press cookie halves, chocolate side down, into icing, arranging rounded edge of cookie halves to follow curved edge of roof. With white icing, attach whole fudge-striped shortbread cookie in center of arrangement of cookie halves. With white icing, using photograph as a guide, attach peppermint sticks to section C on roof; set aside to dry. Meanwhile, with pastry bag fitted with number-3 tip and white icing, decorate graham crackers on roof sides. With pastry bag fitted with number-4B tip and white icing, pipe rosettes on corners of roof sides, in between halves of fudge-striped cookies, and one rosette in center of cookie on rooftop. Place a cinnamon candy into rosettes on roof sides, a dragée into rosettes on cookie halves and a round peppermint candy into rosette on rooftop. With white icing, attach decorated roof to peppermint sticks. With pastry bag fitted with number-17 tip and white icing, pipe border of stars around lower roof edge.

14. Make parquetry roof: With X-acto knife, cut about 110 pretzels in 1-inch lengths. With small spatula, spread a thin layer of white icing over roof on first level. Using photograph as a guide, with pastry bag fitted with number-8 tip and white icing, pipe a grid of 1-inch squares. Shorten rows where necessary to cover roof. In every other square, pipe horizontal icing rows; in remaining squares, pipe vertical icing

rows. Over each icing row in each square, place a pretzel length.

15. Decorate windows and doors: With X-acto knife, cut each of 8 sticks of striped gum lengthwise into 3 strips. With pastry bag fitted with number-8 tip and white icing, attach gum strips to window edges on sections B and D, between other windows, around doors and around side edges of bay window. With pastry bag fitted with number-17 tip and white icing, and pastry bag fitted with number-4B tip and white icing, pipe icing around windows, door and edges of house and roof, using photograph as a guide; while icing is soft, decorate with dragées and cinnamon candies. With pastry bag fitted with number-47 tip and white icing, cover any exposed foam core. Pipe edges around door and window above door; while icing is soft, press a round peppermint candy into icing on each side of window. With pastry bag fitted with number-4B tip, pipe across top of panel above door; press remaining checkered gum into icing.

16. Make shutters: Split remaining sandwich cookies; remove and discard creme filling. Set cookie halves aside. In small bowl, mix 1 cup white icing with leaf-green color paste; in another small bowl, mix ½ cup white icing with Christmas-red color paste. With half of green icing in a pastry bag fitted with number-3 tip and half of red icing in another pastry bag fitted with number-3 tip, pipe dots of icing, alternating colors, around edge of top side of each cookie half. With pastry bag fitted with number-4B tip and white icing, attach sandwich-cookie shutters to windows on second level.

17. With pastry bag fitted with number-17 tip and remaining green icing, using photograph as a guide, pipe a bough over windows on first level. When dry, with pastry bag fitted with number-3 tip and red icing, pipe berries onto boughs.

18. With X-acto knife, cut stick off lollipop. With dollop of white icing, attach candy to roof of section A. To make wreath, decorate candy with green icing in pastry bag fitted with number-17 tip and dot with red-icing berries. With pastry bag fitted with number-66 tip and remaining red icing, pipe bows on doors. With pastry bag fitted with number-3 tip and green icing, using photograph as a guide, decorate bows; attach oval peppermint candies to doors for handles; decorate handles.

19. Make trees and bushes: With pastry bag fitted with number-17 tip and green icing, outline trees and cover center of trees with icing rosettes. With pastry bag fitted with number-3 tip and red icing, decorate trees with red-icing balls. If desired, attach small colored beads or star to trees. To make bushes, cover gumdrops with green-icing rosettes and red-icing balls. Arrange trees and bushes around house; place one tree in widow's walk and one inside house at front window.

20. Finish house: With glue, sandwich together foam-core stair pieces, stacking with the largest piece on the bottom and narrowest on top. With X-acto knife, cut all but 1 piece remaining striped gum pieces to cover stairs. With pastry bag fitted with number-17 tip and white icing, attach gum to foam core; attach stairs to base in front of doors. Pipe icing along edges of stairs. Pipe two icing rosettes onto narrow end of each step; place end of whole pretzel stick into center of each rosette. Let dry. Cut remaining piece of gum lengthwise in half; bend one end of each piece slightly. With a rosette of white icing on tip of each pretzel stick, attach gum railing, bent end at front. Heap sugar snow around house. If desired, embellish setting with mirror pond, miniature fence, pine branches, other Christmas decorations and a light inside the house.

Royal Icing

3 large egg whites, at room temperature
1 package (16 ounces) confectioners' sugar (sift if lumpy)
½ teaspoon cream of tartar
1 teaspoon peppermint extract (optional)

1. In small bowl of electric mixer, combine all ingredients. Beat at high speed until icing is stiff enough to hold its shape. (Add more sugar if necessary.)

2. Cover with a damp cloth or moist paper towel, or place plastic wrap directly on icing surface. If you have filled pastry bags with icing, cover tips with plastic wrap. Store excess icing in sealed container in refrigerator.

Makes about 2 cups.

Notes: When icing is used as mortar, the stiffer it is, the faster it will dry. To match icing color with gingerbread, add cocoa by tablespoonfuls while beating.

To prepare icing for decoration, use wooden picks to add dots of paste colors to icing until color is achieved. If painting with icing, place a small amount of icing in a custard cup; color; thin with drops of water until icing is spreadable with a paintbrush. If too thin, add more icing.

■ Planning a Christmas party? Here's one of our favorite holiday appetizers. It's delicious and, best of all, it's created in a jiffy. Simply combine equal parts brown sugar and pecans or walnuts, and sprinkle over a partially heated round of Brie. Heat at 350°F until sugar is melted and cheese is warm. Serve spread on very thin slices of toasted French bread. It's sure to be a hit with holiday guests.

Lite Eating:
Stuffed-Turkey-Breast Dinner

VEGETABLE-STUFFED
TURKEY BREAST
ORANGE RICE PILAF
CRANBERRY SHERBET MOLD

Vegetable-Stuffed Turkey Breast

1 tablespoon salad oil
1 medium onion, chopped
2 large cloves garlic, crushed
1 package (10 ounces) frozen leaf spinach, thawed
1 can (about 14 ounces) chicken broth
½ teaspoon poultry seasoning
½ teaspoon salt
⅛ teaspoon pepper
5-pound boned turkey breast
1 small red pepper, julienned
1 small yellow pepper, julienned
½ cup reduced-calorie Italian salad dressing
2 tablespoons cornstarch
¼ cup water

1. In large skillet, heat oil over medium heat. Add onion and garlic; sauté 3 minutes, until onion is just tender. Add spinach, ½ cup broth, the poultry seasoning, salt and pepper. Cook, uncovered, 2 minutes, or until liquid has evaporated.

2. Preheat oven to 325°F. Place turkey, skin side down, on work surface. With knife, butterfly breast, making horizontal cuts in thickest part. Spread spinach mixture over breast to within 1 inch of edge. Arrange pepper strips down center.

Bring long edges together and form a roll. With kitchen string, tie securely at 1-inch intervals. Place turkey roll on rack in roasting pan; brush with dressing.

3. Roast 1 hour; pour remaining broth over turkey. Roast 1¼ hours longer, or until meat thermometer registers 170°F. Place on carving board; for easier slicing, let stand 10 minutes.

4. Place cornstarch in small bowl; blend in water, and set aside. Place roasting pan on range; over high heat, stir to loosen brown bits. Strain into saucepan; spoon off fat. Stir in cornstarch mixture. Bring to boiling; cook, stirring, 1 minute, until thickened. Serve with turkey.

Makes 12 servings; 245 calories each serving.

Orange Rice Pilaf

1 tablespoon butter or margarine
2 cups uncooked long-grain rice
4 ounces uncooked spaghetti, broken into 1-inch pieces
2 cans (about 14 ounces each) chicken broth
1½ cups orange juice
¼ cup chopped green onions
2 teaspoons grated orange peel

In medium saucepan, over medium-high heat, melt butter; add rice and spaghetti, and sauté 3 minutes, or until golden. Add broth and

orange juice; bring to boiling. Simmer, covered, 20 minutes, or until rice is tender. Stir in green onions and orange peel.

Makes 12 servings; 108 calories each serving.

Cranberry Sherbet Mold

1 envelope unflavored gelatine
1 cup orange juice
2 cups cranberries
¾ cup sugar
1 cup water
2 large egg whites

1. In small bowl, sprinkle gelatine over orange juice; let stand 5 minutes to soften. In medium saucepan, combine cranberries, sugar and water; bring to boiling, stirring. Simmer 5 minutes.

2. Pour into food processor; puree. Return to saucepan; stir in soaked gelatine. Heat 1 minute, until gelatine dissolves. Place in 13-by-9-by-2-inch pan; freeze 1½ hours, or until slightly firm.

3. In small bowl of electric mixer, at high speed, beat egg whites until stiff; set aside. In processor, puree cranberry mixture; transfer to large bowl. With rubber spatula, fold in egg whites; spoon into 6-cup mold.

4. Freeze overnight, or until firm. To unmold: Dip mold in hot water; invert onto serving platter. If desired, garnish with orange slices and mint leaves.

Makes 12 servings; 71 calories each serving.

Quick & Easy: Gala Beef-Stroganoff Dinner

BEEF STROGANOFF
GARLIC GREEN BEANS
ANGEL-FOOD CAKE
WITH STRAWBERRY SAUCE

Beef Stroganoff

1 pound fillet of beef, 1 inch thick
¼ teaspoon freshly ground pepper
3 tablespoons salad oil
1 cup chopped onion
½ pound mushrooms, sliced
1 cup beef broth
2 tablespoons tomato paste
½ cup sour cream
1 tablespoon finely chopped parsley
Hot cooked orzo

1. Cut beef across grain into ¼-inch slices; cut slices to make 2-by-1-inch pieces. Sprinkle with pepper.
2. In large nonstick skillet heat 2 tablespoons oil over medium-high heat; add beef and sear, half at a time, until browned. With slotted spoon, remove beef to medium bowl; set aside.
3. Reduce heat to medium; heat remaining 1 tablespoon oil. Add onion and sauté until tender. Add mushrooms; continue cooking 10 minutes, or until tender. Add broth and tomato paste; stir until smooth. Blend in sour cream. Add beef, with juices in bowl, and parsley. Bring to a simmer; cook 5 minutes, or until heated through and sauce thickens slightly. Serve with orzo.
Makes 4 servings.

Garlic Green Beans

1 package (16 ounces) frozen whole green beans
1 tablespoon butter or margarine
1 large clove garlic, crushed
1 tablespoon lemon juice
Dash salt and pepper

1. In medium saucepan, cook green beans as package label directs. Meanwhile, in small skillet, over medium-high heat, melt butter. Add garlic; sauté 1 minute, or until golden. Add lemon juice.
2. Drain beans; place in serving dish. Pour garlic-lemon butter over beans; toss to coat. Sprinkle with salt and pepper.
Makes 4 servings.

Angel-Food Cake With Strawberry Sauce

Strawberry Sauce
1 container (1 pint) strawberries
1 jar (12 ounces) strawberry preserves
¼ cup orange juice
1 tablespoon orange peel, cut in thin strips

9-inch prepared angel-food cake
Fresh mint leaves

1. Wash berries; cut 8 in fans for garnish. Hull and slice remaining berries; set aside.
2. In small pan, combine preserves, orange juice and peel; heat until preserves melt. Remove from heat; stir in sliced berries. Decorate cake with berry fans and mint sprigs; serve with strawberry sauce.
Makes 12 to 16 servings.

4-in-1 Cookies

Basic Cookie Mix

2¼ cups unsifted all-purpose
    flour
¾ cup firmly packed
    light-brown sugar
½ cup granulated sugar
1 teaspoon baking soda
½ teaspoon salt
½ cup butter or margarine

In large bowl, combine flour, sugars, baking soda and salt. Using pastry blender or two knives, cut in butter until mixture resembles coarse crumbs. Cover and refrigerate mix up to one week.

Granola-Raisin Circles

2 large eggs
2 tablespoons water
1 teaspoon vanilla extract
Basic Cookie Mix
1 cup granola
½ cup raisins

Preheat oven to 350°F. Mix eggs with water and vanilla. Stir into cookie mix. Stir in granola and raisins. Drop batter by rounded teaspoonfuls, 2 inches apart, onto lightly greased baking sheets. Bake 10 minutes, or until golden. Remove to wire racks; cool.
Makes about 4½ dozen.

Candied Cookies

2 large eggs
2 tablespoons water
1 teaspoon vanilla extract
Basic Cookie Mix
1¼ cups candy-coated
    chocolate candies
½ cup chopped walnuts

Preheat oven to 350°F. Mix eggs with water and vanilla. Stir into cookie mix. Stir in candies and walnuts. Drop batter by rounded teaspoonfuls, 2 inches apart, onto lightly greased baking sheets. Bake 10 minutes, or until golden. Remove to wire racks; cool.
Makes about 4½ dozen.

Mint-Chip Coconut Rounds

2 large eggs
2 tablespoons water
1 teaspoon vanilla extract
Basic Cookie Mix
1 cup mint-flavored
    semisweet-chocolate pieces
½ cup flaked coconut

Left: (From top) Candied Cookies, Cream-Cheese-Frosted Bars.

Preheat oven to 350°F. Mix eggs with water and vanilla. Stir into cookie mix. Stir in chocolate pieces and coconut. Drop batter by rounded teaspoonfuls, 2 inches apart, onto lightly greased baking sheets. Bake 10 minutes, or until golden. Remove to wire racks; cool.
Makes about 4½ dozen.

Cream-Cheese-Frosted Bars

2 large eggs
2 tablespoons water
1 teaspoon vanilla extract
Basic Cookie Mix
Cream-Cheese Frosting (recipe
    follows)

Preheat oven to 350°F. Mix eggs with water and vanilla. Stir into cookie mix. Press into greased 9-inch square pan. Bake until cake tester inserted in center comes out clean—25 minutes. Cool in pan on wire rack 15 minutes; cut into 24 bars. Remove; cool completely on rack. Spread tops with frosting.
Makes 2 dozen.

Cream-Cheese Frosting

1 package (3 ounces) cream
    cheese, softened
½ cup confectioners' sugar
1 to 1½ teaspoons lemon juice

In small bowl mix all ingredients until smooth.

Micro-Way: Gifts from Your Kitchen

Creamy Lemon Curd

¾ cup butter or margarine
1½ cups sugar
2 teaspoons grated lemon peel
½ cup fresh lemon juice
6 large eggs

1. In large glass bowl, combine butter, sugar, lemon peel and lemon juice. Cover with plastic wrap, turning back one corner to vent. Cook on HIGH 6 minutes, stirring occasionally, until sugar dissolves and mixture is bubbly.

2. In medium bowl, with whisk, slightly beat eggs. Whisk in a little of the hot lemon mixture; return all to large bowl. Cook, uncovered, on HIGH 2 minutes; whisk to blend. Cook on HIGH 2 minutes longer; whisk until blended and smooth. Set aside to cool. Spoon into 2 sterilized ½-pint jars. Serve with berries or pound cake or use as filling for cake or tart shells.

Makes 2 cups.

Layered Truffle Bars

8 ounces semisweet chocolate
12 tablespoons unsalted butter or margarine, softened
½ cup orange marmalade
8 ounces white chocolate
¼ cup heavy cream
8 ounces milk chocolate
1 large egg yolk
2 tablespoons coffee-flavored liqueur
3 to 4 tablespoons unsweetened cocoa powder
12 ounces semisweet chocolate, melted or 12 ounces white chocolate, melted

1. Line 13-by-9-by-2-inch pan with foil, extending foil up long sides by 1 inch. In glass bowl, melt 8 ounces semisweet chocolate on MEDIUM 2 minutes, stirring occasionally. Whisk in 8 tablespoons butter; stir in marmalade. Pour into pan; refrigerate until firm—1 to 3 hours.

2. In glass bowl, melt 8 ounces white chocolate on MEDIUM 2 minutes, stirring occasionally. Beat in 2 tablespoons butter and the cream; spread over marmalade mixture. Refrigerate until firm.

3. In glass bowl, melt milk chocolate on MEDIUM 2 minutes, stirring occasionally. Beat in remaining butter, the egg yolk and liqueur. Spread over white chocolate; refrigerate until firm. Using foil, lift candy from pan. Cut into 1-by-½-inch bars.

4. To decorate, sift cocoa over truffles, or dip half the bars, one at a time, into 12 ounces melted semisweet chocolate; transfer to waxed-paper-lined baking sheet. Dip remaining bars into melted white chocolate. Store in refrigerator.

Makes 64.

Spirited Pear-Pecan Conserve

2 pounds Bartlett pears, pared, cored and coarsely chopped
2 Granny Smith apples, pared, cored and coarsely chopped
1 cup golden raisins
¾ cup dried currants
½ cup firmly packed light-brown sugar
1 teaspoon grated lemon peel
2 tablespoons lemon juice
1 teaspoon ground cinnamon
½ teaspoon ground nutmeg
¼ teaspoon ground ginger
1 cup coarsely chopped pecans
¼ cup B&B liqueur

1. In large glass bowl, combine pears, apples, raisins, currants, brown sugar, lemon peel, lemon juice, cinnamon, nutmeg and ginger; mix well. Cover with plastic wrap, turning back one corner to vent. Cook on HIGH 20 minutes, stirring occasionally.

2. Add pecans and liqueur; cook on HIGH 5 minutes more. Spoon mixture into five ½-pint sterilized

jars; seal with lids. Refrigerate. Serve conserve with pork or chicken or on ice cream.

Makes 5 cups.

Red-Onion Marmalade

2½ pounds red onions, cut in ¼-inch wedges
3 tablespoons salad oil
½ cup white wine
¼ cup red-wine vinegar
½ cup sugar
1 tablespoon grenadine
½ teaspoon salt
½ teaspoon pepper

1. In large glass bowl, combine onion wedges with oil. Cook, uncovered, on HIGH 8 to 10 minutes, stirring mixture occasionally. Drain and discard any liquid.

2. Add wine, vinegar, sugar, grenadine, salt and pepper; mix well. Cook, uncovered, on HIGH 15 minutes, stirring occasionally. Spoon into five ½-pint sterilized jars; seal with lids. Refrigerate. Serve marmalade with meat or pâté.

Makes 4½ cups.

■ Store a super-size salad for a holiday buffet in your crisper drawer—it can hold gallons of greens!

Cake and Cookie Patterns

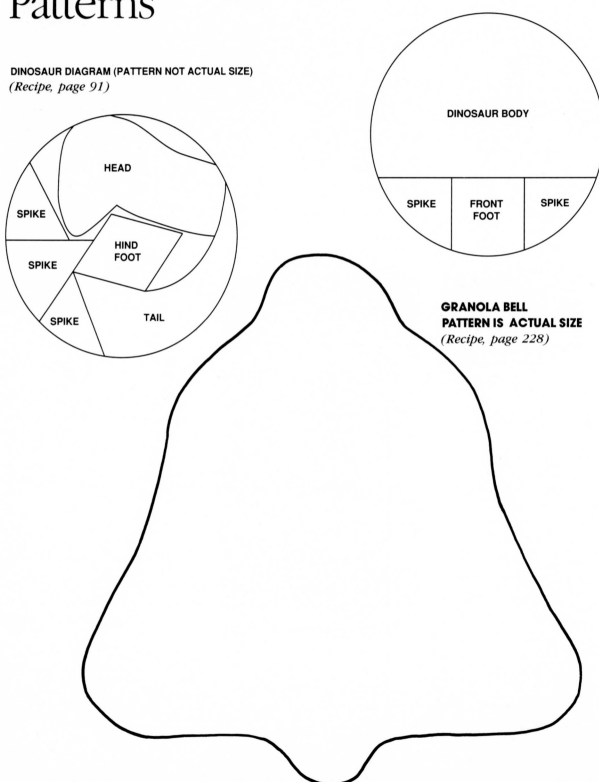

DINOSAUR DIAGRAM (PATTERN NOT ACTUAL SIZE)
(Recipe, page 91)

HEAD

SPIKE

SPIKE

HIND
FOOT

SPIKE

TAIL

DINOSAUR BODY

SPIKE

FRONT
FOOT

SPIKE

**GRANOLA BELL
PATTERN IS ACTUAL SIZE**
(Recipe, page 228)

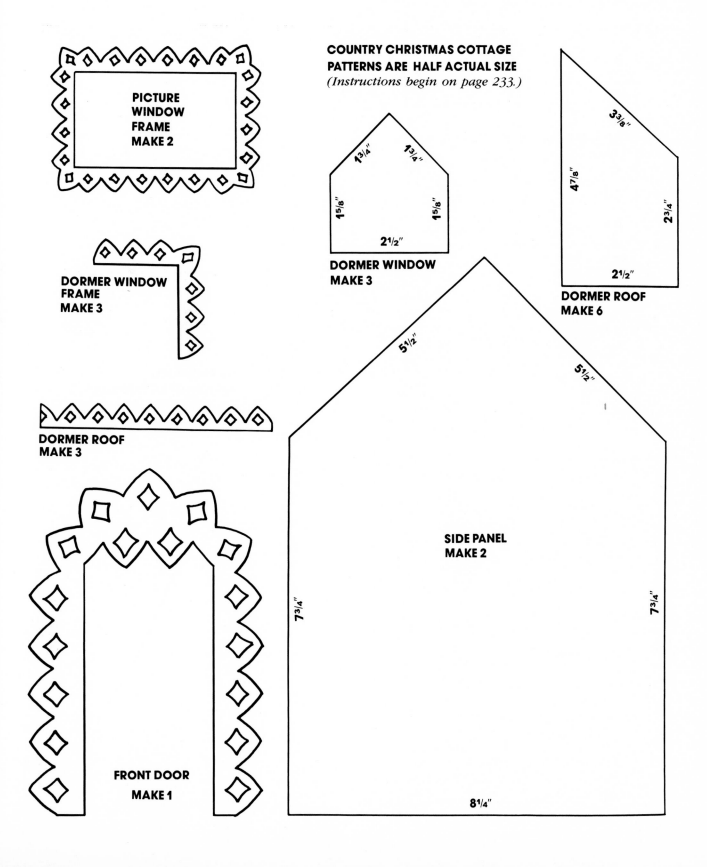

PICTURE
WINDOW
FRAME
MAKE 2

DORMER WINDOW
FRAME
MAKE 3

DORMER ROOF
MAKE 3

FRONT DOOR
MAKE 1

COUNTRY CHRISTMAS COTTAGE
PATTERNS ARE HALF ACTUAL SIZE
(Instructions begin on page 233.)

1³/₄" 1³/₄"

1⁵/₈" 1⁵/₈"

2¹/₂"

DORMER WINDOW
MAKE 3

3³/₈"

4⁷/₈" 2³/₄"

2¹/₂"

DORMER ROOF
MAKE 6

5¹/₂" 5¹/₂"

SIDE PANEL
MAKE 2

7³/₄" 7³/₄"

8¹/₄"

COUNTRY CHRISTMAS COTTAGE

ACTUAL SIZE

BENCH SEAT
MAKE 2

1"

2¼"

BENCH BACK
MAKE 2

1"

2¼"

FENCE
MAKE 8

1"

2¼"

1¼"

BENCH LEG
MAKE 8

1"

1"

SHUTTER
MAKE 6

1¾"

HOUSE FRONT AND BACK
MAKE 2

7⅛"

16⅝"

MAIN ROOF
MAKE 1

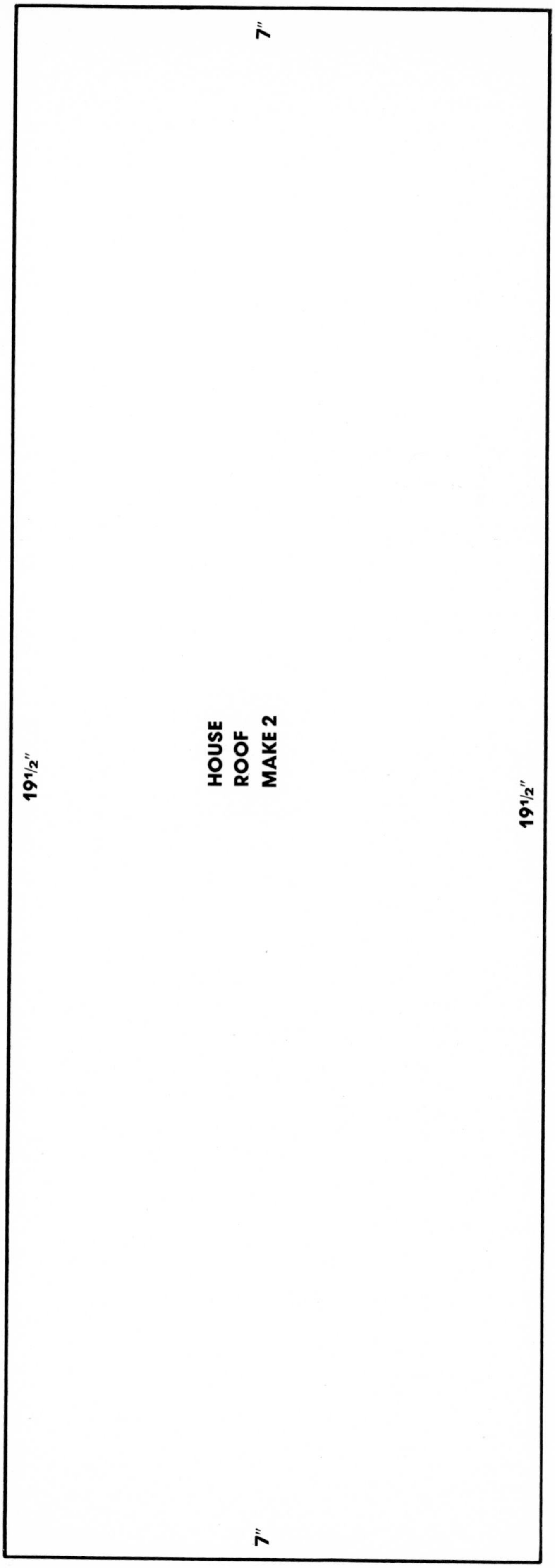

7"

19½"

HOUSE
ROOF
MAKE 2

19½"

7"

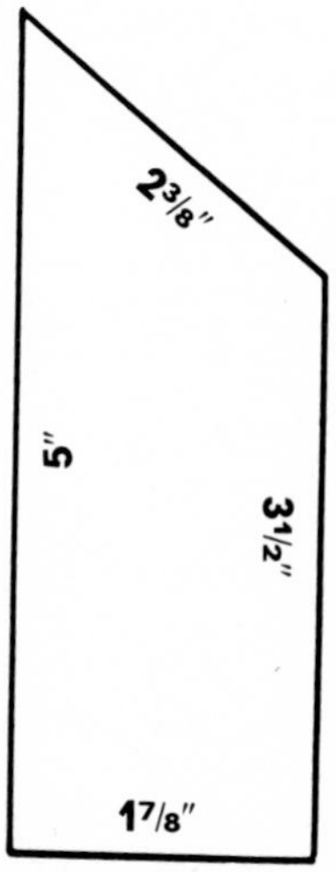

2³⁄₈"

5"

3½"

1⁷⁄₈"

DORMER-WINDOW SIDE
MAKE 2

COLONIAL SALTBOX
PATTERNS ARE ONE-FOURTH ACTUAL SIZE
(Instructions begin on page 235.)

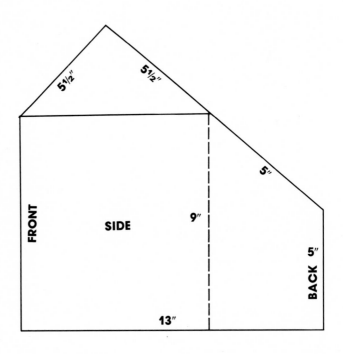

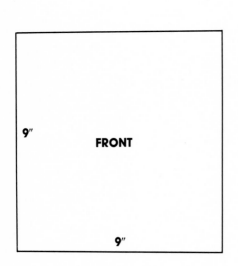

BOSTON BROWNSTONE TOWN HOUSE
PATTERNS ARE ONE-FOURTH ACTUAL SIZE
(Instructions begin on page 238.)

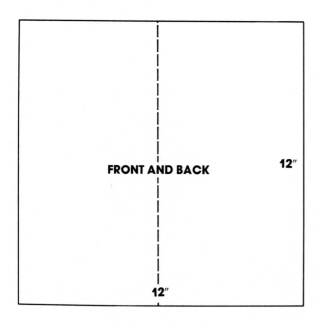

FRONT AND BACK   12″

12″

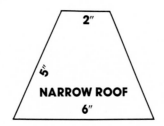

2″

5″

NARROW ROOF

6″

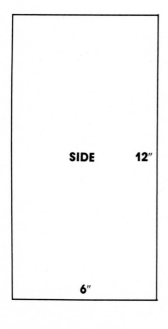

SIDE   12″

6″

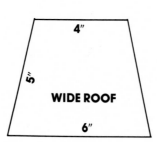

4″

5″

WIDE ROOF

6″

SANTA'S "SWEET HAUS"
ONE-FOURTH ACTUAL SIZE
(Instructions begin on page 236.)

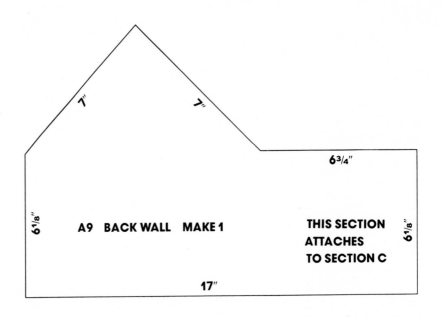

7″ 7″ 6³⁄₄″ 6¹⁄₈″ 6¹⁄₈″

A9 BACK WALL MAKE 1

THIS SECTION
ATTACHES
TO SECTION C

17″

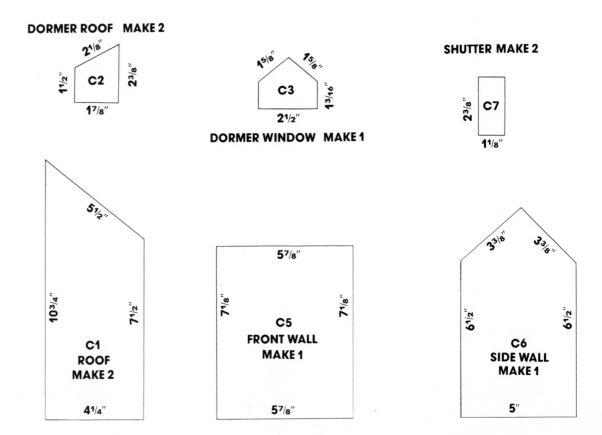

DORMER ROOF MAKE 2

2¹⁄₈″ 1¹⁄₂″ C2 2³⁄₈″ 1⁷⁄₈″

1⁵⁄₈″ 1⁵⁄₈″ C3 1³⁄₁₆″ 2¹⁄₂″

DORMER WINDOW MAKE 1

SHUTTER MAKE 2

2³⁄₈″ C7 1¹⁄₈″

5¹⁄₂″ 10³⁄₄″ 7¹⁄₂″

C1
ROOF
MAKE 2

4¹⁄₄″

5⁷⁄₈″ 7¹⁄₈″ 7¹⁄₈″

C5
FRONT WALL
MAKE 1

5⁷⁄₈″

3³⁄₈″ 3³⁄₈″ 6¹⁄₂″ 6¹⁄₂″

C6
SIDE WALL
MAKE 1

5″

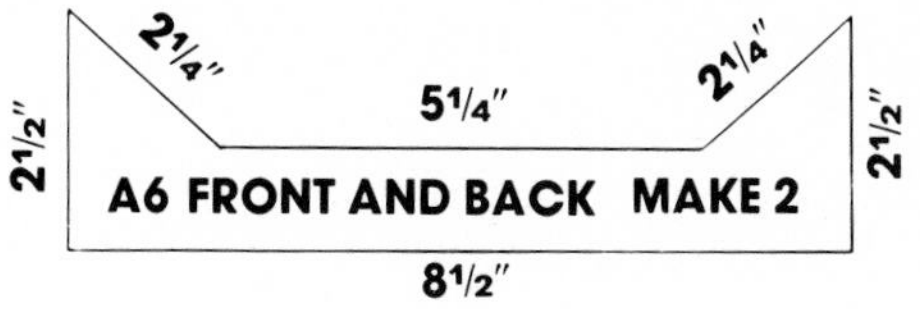
2 1/4"
5 1/4"
2 1/4"
2 1/2"
A6 FRONT AND BACK MAKE 2
2 1/2"
8 1/2"

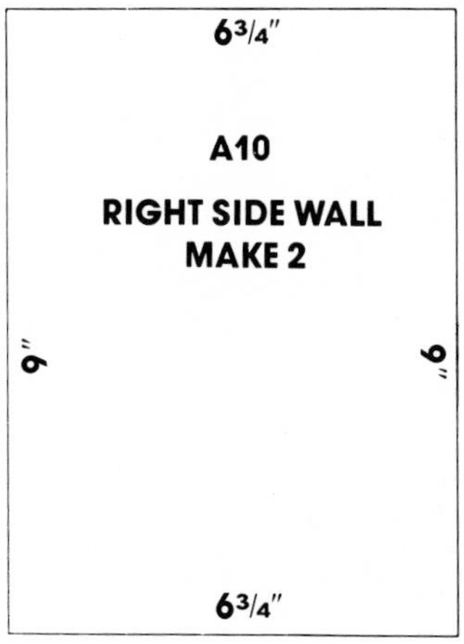
6 3/4"
A10
RIGHT SIDE WALL
MAKE 2
9"
9"
6 3/4"

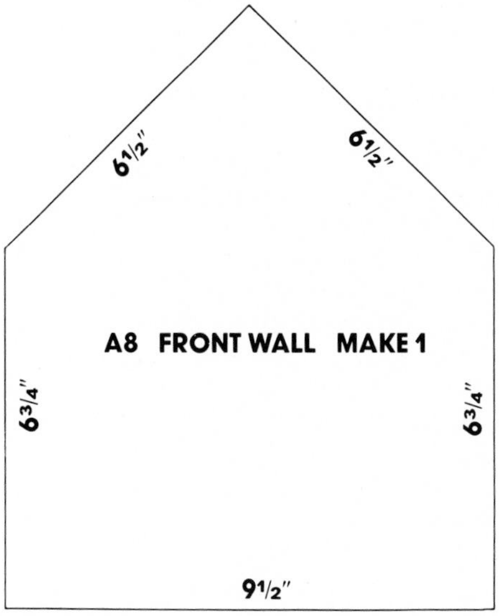
6 1/2"
6 1/2"
A8 FRONT WALL MAKE 1
6 3/4"
6 3/4"
9 1/2"

RIGHT SIDE—DO NOT FACE
WITH CRACKERS;
THIS IS AN INNER WALL

LEFT SIDE ONLY FACE FROM FRONT
EDGE IN 5" WITH CRACKERS

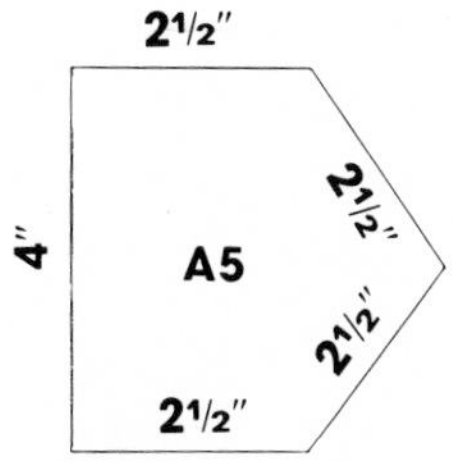
2 1/2"
4"
A5
2 1/2"
2 1/2"
2 1/2"

SIDE
MAKE 2

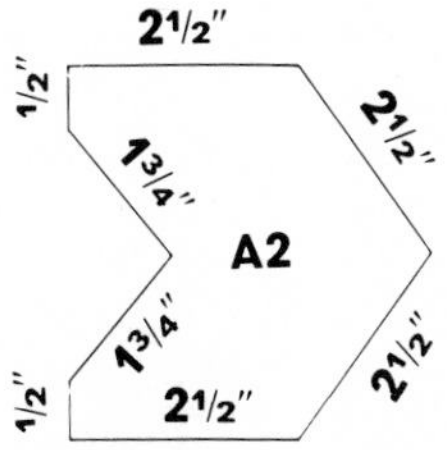
2 1/2"
1/2"
1 3/4"
2 1/2"
A2
1 3/4"
2 1/2"
1/2"
2 1/2"

CUPOLA
FRONT AND BACK
MAKE 2

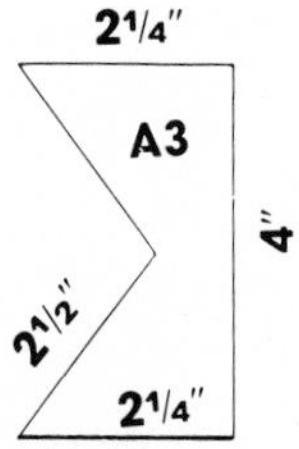
2 1/4"
A3
4"
2 1/2"
2 1/4"

CUPOLA
SIDE
MAKE 2

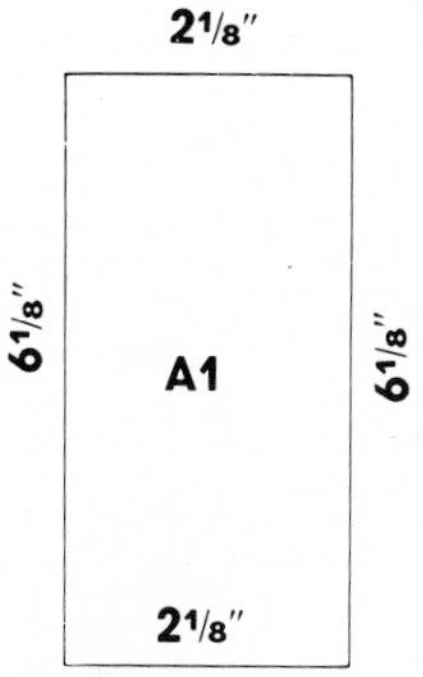
2 1/8"
6 1/8"
A1
6 1/8"
2 1/8"

CUPOLA
ROOF
MAKE 2

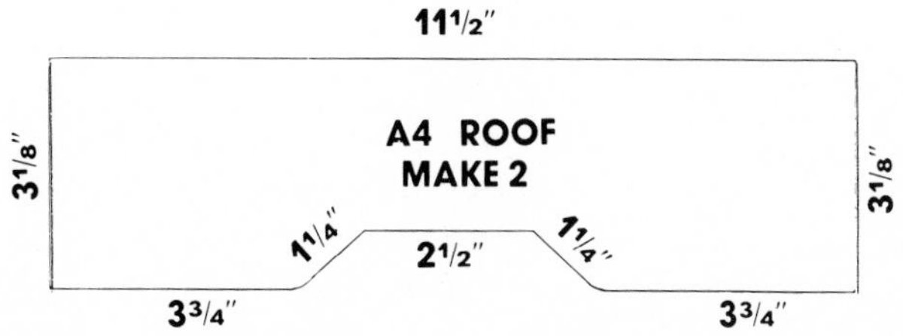
11 1/2"
A4 ROOF
MAKE 2
3 1/8"
3 1/8"
1 1/4"
2 1/2"
1 1/4"
3 3/4"
3 3/4"

Cake and Cookie Patterns

SANTA'S "SWEET HAUS"
ONE-FOURTH ACTUAL SIZE

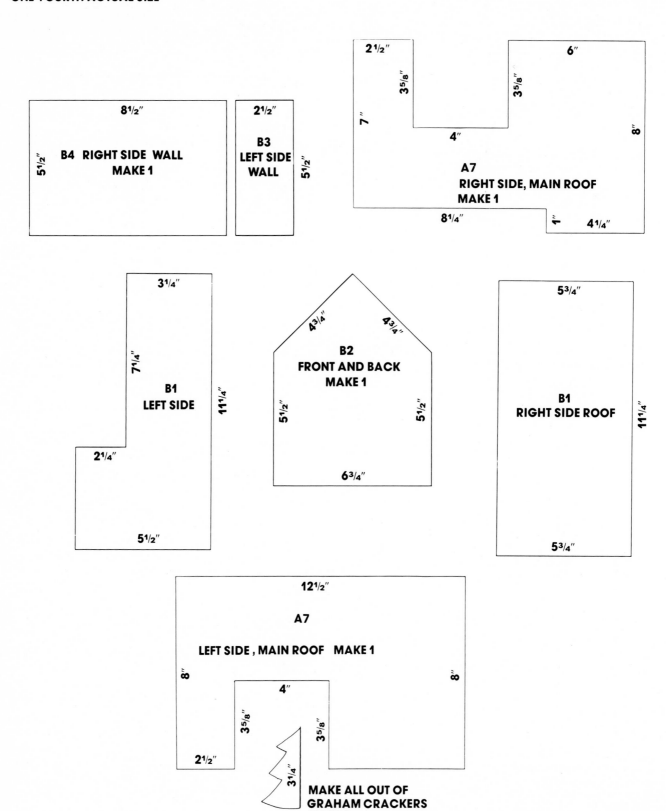

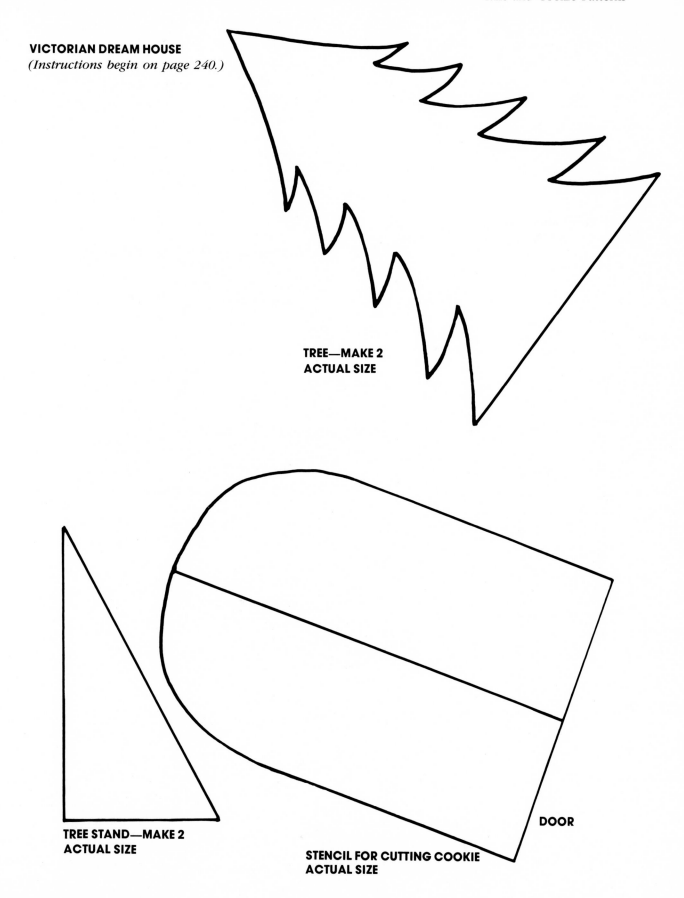

VICTORIAN DREAM HOUSE
(Instructions begin on page 240.)

**TREE—MAKE 2
ACTUAL SIZE**

**TREE STAND—MAKE 2
ACTUAL SIZE**

**STENCIL FOR CUTTING COOKIE
ACTUAL SIZE**

DOOR

**VICTORIAN DREAM HOUSE
PATTERN IS HALF ACTUAL SIZE**

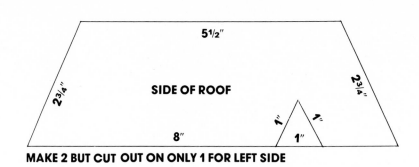

SIDE OF ROOF

5½"

2¾"

2¾"

8"

1" 1"

1"

MAKE 2 BUT CUT OUT ON ONLY 1 FOR LEFT SIDE

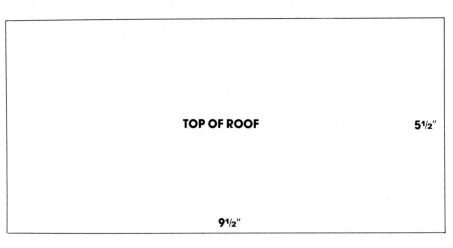

TOP OF ROOF

5½"

9½"

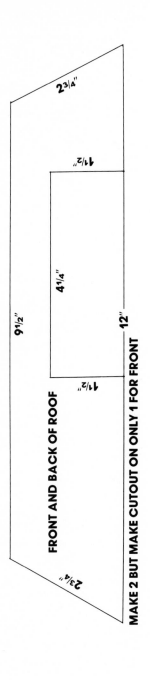

2¾"

1½"

4¼"

9½"

12"

1½"

2¾"

FRONT AND BACK OF ROOF

MAKE 2 BUT MAKE CUTOUT ON ONLY 1 FOR FRONT

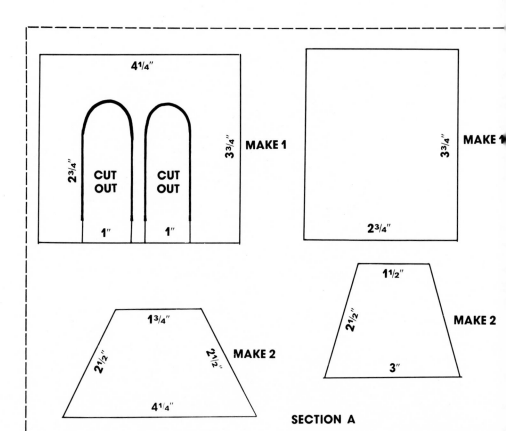

4¼"

2¾"

CUT OUT

CUT OUT

3¾"

MAKE 1

1"

1"

3¾"

MAKE 1

2¾"

1½"

1¾"

2½"

2½"

2½"

MAKE 2

4¼"

3"

MAKE 2

SECTION A

SECTION B

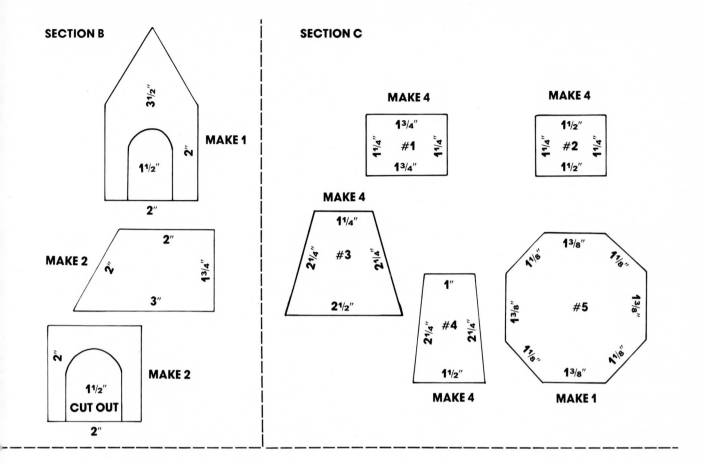

MAKE 1

MAKE 2

MAKE 2

CUT OUT

SECTION C

MAKE 4
#1

MAKE 4
#2

MAKE 4
#3

MAKE 4
#4

MAKE 1
#5

SECTION D   RIGHT SIDE BAY WINDOW

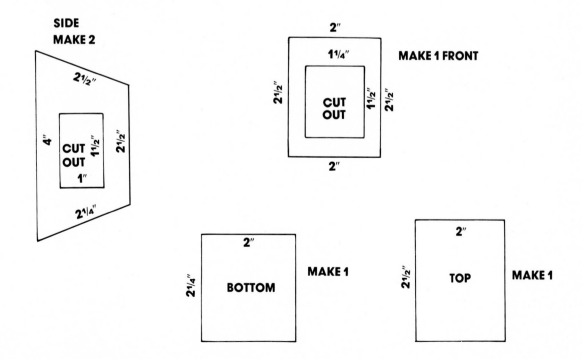

SIDE
MAKE 2

CUT OUT

MAKE 1 FRONT

CUT OUT

BOTTOM   MAKE 1

TOP   MAKE 1

General Recipe Index

General Recipe Index

General Recipe Index

Recipe Title Index